NEITHER CARPETBAGGERS NOR SCALAWAGS:

Black Officeholders during the Reconstruction of Alabama,

1867-1878

by
Richard Bailey
Montgomery, Ala.

First Edition

Designed and
published by   Richard Bailey Publishers
                  P. O. Box 1264
                  Montgomery, AL 36102-1264
                  ISBN 0-9627-218-0-8

PRINTED IN THE UNITED STATES OF AMERICA

ii

To

Judy C., Judy T., Valerie, Lottie,
and the late Raymond, Sr.

iii

CONTENTS

PART 2 THAT SUN ALSO SETS

ILLUSTRATIONS

FOREWORD

It is with great pleasure that I write a brief statement for Richard Bailey. The pleasure comes in part from my sharing in the satisfaction of a long and difficult project now brought to completion. This project, which began many years ago under different circumstances, has involved the considerable talents and energies of Dr Bailey for a number of years. For many historians projects of this sort take on a life of their own, and we sometime wonder if we can ever let them go and to seek their own place in the world of letters and scholarship. We also fear that a project of this scope and importance may not see the light of day. Thus the pleasure is double: The project is at an end, and it has been published.

As I said, I am pleased to add my small part to the completion of *Neither Carpetbaggers Nor Scalawags*, but, having said a few words in the beginning, I wish to stand aside and point with pride to Dr Bailey's accomplishments. His commitment to his subject is complete. When he defended an earlier version of this work as a doctoral dissertation, the committee was so impressed with the quality of his defense that they voted him a "pass with distinction," a category that did not exist officially until Richard Bailey created it by dint of his superior performance. That that early work would some day find its way into print surprises none of us who were on that committee. Dr Bailey's indefatigable efforts on its behalf have guaranteed it.

While there is no shortage of work on Reconstruction or even on Reconstruction in Alabama, there is no comparable work on black leadership (and specifically black officeholders) in Alabama during Reconstruction. Thus his work is important because it fills a gap in the historical record. But its importance transcends the simple matter of gap filling. For too long historians have viewed the Reconstruction era through a lens that focused only on white participants, whether Southern or Northern. Since African Americans were significant in the process of Reconstruction, it is important to view this process from a biracial perspective. To the extent that African Americans are made a part of the Reconstruction record, their role has been consistently distorted. Either they are the villains of the drama, or, in an equally demeaning way, they are depicted as passive recipients of historical actions not of their own making. Both portrayals are false and racially insensitive.

Now comes Richard Bailey to set at least part of that record straight. In *Neither Carpetbaggers Nor Scalawags*, Bailey shows us how African Americans sought to become full citizens and take part in the political processes, including office holding. The growth and development of leadership among American blacks is a subject that has long needed adequate historical treatment. This study, long aborning, will help to correct the record and thereby begin the process of dealing fairly and accurately with the history of Reconstruction and the history of race relations in the United States.

Joseph M. Hawes
Memphis, Tennessee
November 1990

Acknowledgments

Work on this project began during the latter part of 1980 as part of a dissertation requirement at Kansas State University. Along the way, many persons provided the assistance and inspiration needed to bring this work to fruition.

I am deeply indebted to the entire staff of the State Department of Archives and History, in Montgomery, for considering my work as their own. Staffs at the Library of Congress, National Archives, and Howard University (all located in Washington, D.C.) went of their way to help. Dr Joseph M. Hawes continued to serve as a reader and mentor even after I had completed my dissertation. His assistance was invaluable, and his questions caused me to reconsider many of my assumptions. Alfred B. Hill, Daniel H. McCalib, and Bessie E. Varner read the manuscript several times and posed many "What if?" questions. Other persons provided copies of photographs: The Tyus family for the photograph of Samuel J. Patterson; Dr Zelia S. Evans for persmission to use a photograph of the Dexter Avenue Baptist Church; and Thomas L. French, Jr., for the photographs of Horace King. Dr Reva White Allman, a mentor since my undergraduate days, provided consistent encouragement. The Albert W. Mitchell family and Robert (Bobby) Jackson went beyond the call of duty.

Despite the gracious efforts of these and other persons, I alone accept responsibility for the shortcomings of this study.

PART 1

THE SUN THAT RISES

INTRODUCTION

The chief proponent of the scarcely challenged Dunning school of
historical interpretation in Alabama has been Walter Lynwood
Fleming. The son of William LeRoy and Mary Love Edwards Fleming,
young Fleming was born near Brundidge in Pike County on 4 April
1874. He grew up hearing strongly personalized stories about the
Confederacy from his father--a man who had fought in the war as a
cavalryman. His experiences no doubt colored the stories he told
his son. In any event, in her 1978 introduction to *Civil War and
Reconstruction in Alabama*, Sarah Woolfolk Wiggins justifies
Fleming's sweeping views on Reconstruction by noting that he "was
not the son of a planter ruined by the war" as other historians
have concluded.[1]

Fleming received the bachelor of science and master of science
degrees in 1896 and 1897, respectively, from the Alabama
Polytechnic Institute in Auburn. He later worked there as an
instructor of history, English, and mathematics, and he also served
as assistant librarian. Continuing his study of history at
Columbia University, Fleming graduated with both a master of arts
degree and a doctor of philosophy degree--the former in 1901 and

the latter in 1904. Whatever else one argues about Fleming, we must agree his dominant views on Reconstruction were shaped first by his father, second by Professor George Petrie of Auburn University, and third by Dr William Archibald Dunning of Columbia University.[2]

Like Dunning on the national level, Fleming shaped the views of a generation of Alabama historians through the pages of his carefully researched but sectionally and racially biased *Civil War and Reconstruction in Alabama*. He found what were to him good reasons for heaping much blame on the North and absolving the South of responsibility for the coming of the war and its tumultuous aftermath, Reconstruction. Fleming goes on to suggest that if the Radicals had allowed the South to run its own postwar political affairs, little chaos would have occurred during Reconstruction. More specifically, although Fleming was especially critical of the Freedmen's Bureau, Union League agents, and carpetbaggers, he saved his most critical remarks for black lawmakers. Thus, he constantly referred to Reconstruction as an era of "Negro rule," one filled with "Negro domination." Paradoxically, neither Fleming nor any of the other Dunningites conducted a single study of the actual black lawmakers of the Southern states.[3]

Not surprisingly, one result has been that the findings of their less-than-balanced studies have gone unquestioned for more than three-quarters of a century. This study, then, since it attempts to shed new and more even light on the men who served as

2

officeholders in Alabama between 1867 and 1878, is long overdue. These pages bring to light for the first time both their public utterances and some of their private deeds. It is my hope that, after reading these pages, the unbiased reader will find that the Dunningites' chief thesis--and many, if not most, of their findings--will crumble forever. Let a more firmly grounded, if less polemic, view of these stark times replace those findings. This study also contrasts events in Alabama with other Southern states. In all modesty, despite the truly new insights this study offers with which to analyze Alabama's black officeholders during these turbulent years, it does not provide a definitive evaluation. That remains to be written. Still, the evidence gathered here should withstand vigorous scrutiny and supply the firm but new steps toward such an evaluation.

CHAPTER 1

Political democracy descended upon Alabama initially during
Reconstruction. The unprecedented participation of African
Americans in the state's political arena was one manifestation of
that new democracy. Other arenas in which democracy appeared
during those years included public education and transportation,
land reform, and social equality. Yet, whether these changes
occurred at all, and whether they endured, depended upon the
ability of the National Republican party and its new Alabama
affiliate to articulate its objectives successfully to the state's
citizenry and thereby remain in power. Meanwhile, Alabamians were
confronted with a formidable task--how to reshape a devastated
society and a woefully depleted economy--before they could give
full meaning to new democratic tendencies that began to surface.

Results of the War

The Civil War ended in Alabama on 8 May 1865 when Confederate
General Richard Taylor--ironically, both the son of former
President Zachary Taylor and the brother-in-law of Confederate
States of America President Jefferson Davis, by his first marriage-

-surrendered to United States General Edward R. S. Canby. Taylor's surrender came at Citronelle, 40 miles north of Mobile. Paradoxically, the last cargo of African slaves disembarked from the *Clotile* in 1860, near the town of Plateau, only miles from Citronelle.[1]

With the cessation of hostilities, nearly 439,000 Alabama slaves received their freedom. They learned of their new freedom either from elements of the invading Federal army or from their former owners.[2]

Newly freed African Americans reacted to freedom in a variety of ways. Unfortunately, few of these reactions to freedom contributed to social stability. Some African Americans remained on the plantation, where they had been slaves, but refused to work. Poorly informed and inadequately educated, they expected to receive a division of the property of their former owners. Other African Americans remained on plantations where they had worked as slave laborers. These people--with much justice, as events later confirmed--believed they could not sustain themselves in a different environment. Other African Americans remained on plantations because they feared physical reprisals for leaving--a fear which later, for some, proved surprisingly real.[3]

African Americans who were willing to challenge the unknown frequently traveled to other parts of the state. They moved from Selma, Eufaula, and Opelika to larger towns such as Mobile and Montgomery, the capital city. Most of them traveled by foot, and those who were able to pay to use the state's war-impaired railroad system often encountered whites who forced them to occupy the worst sections of the train. This happened despite their having paid the same fare the white passengers had paid. For example, on an Opelika-to-Montgomery train, African Americans objected to having to huddle around a box and stove to keep warm. The quick, angry, and illogical response to their complaint was, "You're free ain't you? Good as white folks? Then pay the same fare and keep your mouth shut."[4]

The state population census of 1866 shows that the lure of towns continued to fascinate blacks. Like their brethren in Louisiana, Alabama's African Americans moved in large numbers to neighboring cities with their few worldly possessions. Foremost in their minds was an expectation of better economic opportunities and greater legal protection.[5] It was to address these and other needs of African Americans that Congress had established the Freedmen's Bureau in the War Department on 3 March 1865. It charged the Bureau with supervision and management of abandoned land and of matters pertaining to African Americans in the South. Union General Oliver Otis Howard became the Bureau's first and only commissioner.[6]

As one might have expected, the confusion and the hardships borne of sudden emancipation increased relentlessly as African Americans moved steadily into the cities. Once there, and owning only the clothes on their backs, they found housing difficult, if not impossible, to obtain. Therefore, they often assembled in

EMANCIPATION AND THE PROMISED LAND

"deserted and ruined houses, in huts built with their hands with refuse lumber, under sheds and under bridges over creeks, ravines, and gutters and in caves in the back of rivers and ravines."[7] Some African Americans had only the "sky for a roof and the ground in a fence corner for a bed."[8] At one housing settlement called "Hard Times," Montgomery's African Americans "lived on the old fair grounds in shelters erected out of pine poles."[9] The Montgomery *Daily Advertiser* found thousands of the city's African Americans "living in shanties, old furnaces, boilers, and at the ruins of the arsenals' foundries, and under shelters on the banks of the river and other such places as they can squat upon and remain undisturbed. The manner in which they are living is calculated to arouse the sympathies of everyone."[10]

African Americans living in Columbus, Georgia, and Opelika, Alabama, experienced similar housing difficulties. There, police officials moved in and demolished more than 30 shanties at local depots after asking homeless African American families to remove themselves.[11] Exorbitant rents, which few African Americans had the means to pay, were an unholy and ill-conceived alternative that only exacerbated an already deplorable housing condition. Consider the barn without a fireplace, which sometimes might cost as much as $20 each month. It was not surprising, then, that for African Americans who were unable to construct housing or to pay rent, death by freezing during the extremely cold winter of 1865-66 was a distinct possibility.[12] Looking immediately ahead, the Mobile

7

NEITHER CARPETBAGGERS NOR SCALAWAGS

Tribune predicted a famine for the winter and urged citizens "to call meetings and memorialize the legislature on the subject, urging them to...dispatch agents to the West to purchase corn, forthwith. There is not sufficient provender in the country to winter the horses and mules for the next crop. Something must be done, and that quickly."[13]

Sadly, something was not done quickly, despite the appeal of Alabama's Provisional Governor Lewis E. Parsons and General Wager Swayne, assistant commissioner of the Alabama Freedmen's Bureau. These men even sought help on Wall Street in New York City and, later, in Boston. With the onset of winter, food became scarce for blacks and whites alike--so much so that an estimated 200,000 Alabamians stood in danger of dying from starvation.[14]

Reports circulated of circumstances that forced whites and blacks to resort to stealing hogs, chickens, and stray animals. Freedmen's Bureau agents issued rations to more than 70,000 destitute persons in November 1865 alone; yet, they incorrectly-- and over-optimistically--assumed economic conditions would improve during the following year. As a result, poor crops during the summer of 1865 caused Bureau agents to issue 792,349 rations during the early months of 1866. Between November 1865 and September 1866, Bureau agents issued 3,789,788 rations to about 166,589 white and 72,115 African American indigents. Imagine the near-famine conditions a typical ration installment--cornmeal, salt pork or

8

fatback, flour, and sugar--sought to relieve for one week at a time.[15]

Assessing at least a large part of the desperation of the times, though unfortunately not of African Americans in Alabama, the Montgomery *Daily Advertiser* sympathized with the destitution of north Alabama whites. Reasoned the *Daily Advertiser*, "This region supplied the army with men, even though there was little slave labor to replace them; their money was consumed by the Confederate army; their crops were destroyed by drought; they owned no cotton, stores of food, stocks of cattle nor flocks of sheep, no herds of swine. They are starving but they are not paupers."[16] North Alabama whites were among the large number of destitute caucasians. Except for whites living in Choctaw, Clarke, Dale, Fayette, Greene, Marion, Perry, Sumter, and Tuscaloosa counties, some 12,530 destitute white families, numbering 52,921 persons, lived in Alabama. One source estimated the expenditures required for the support of these persons at $181,997 monthly or $2,183,964 annually.[17]

The Freedmen's Bureau

To meet the medical needs of the sick, indigent, disabled, and aged of both races, the Freedmen's Bureau established regional medical facilities in Mobile, Selma, Garland, Montgomery, Demopolis, Huntsville, and Talladega. Beginning on 1 September 1865 the Bureau operated its own medical department in Mobile with

9

hospitals and colonies that cooperated with civil authorities in campaigns against smallpox, cholera, and yellow fever. Table 1 shows the operation of one Bureau hospital from January to October 1866.

TABLE 1
OPERATIONS OF AN ALABAMA BUREAU HOSPITAL

	Admitted	Discharged	Died	Remaining
Adult Males	93	81	6	6
Adult Females	124	112	2	10
Male Children	50	45	1	4
Female Children	38	30	3	5
Total	305	268	12	25

Source: Bureau of Refugees, Freedmen, and Abandoned Lands, NA.

Rightly or wrongly, civil authorities usually interpreted Bureau cooperation to mean they (civil authorities) were to provide assistance to the state's white population, while the Bureau was to meet the medical needs of Alabama's African American populace. State authorities considered African Americans as wards of the national government and, as such, outside the realm of state responsibility. Despite this, Bureau agents offered assistance for the sick and indigent of both races.[18]

Such intense acrimony surfaced between Bureau agents and Montgomery city officials that it seriously hampered operation of the city's hospital. Despite a city ordinance that could have forced both black and white paupers out of the city, Montgomery city officials sought to construct adequate housing for the city's large number of smallpox victims. Mayor Walter L. Coleman introduced a resolution in the city council to have suitable homes constructed for smallpox cases. The council then authorized the Committee on Public Works to have the homes built. In spite of this relative success, the smallpox victims would have received greater care had municipal and Bureau officials not quarrelled so often over the control of the city's hospital.[19]

In other parts of the state, matters were worse. County commissioners opposed the establishment of any structures for the relief of the poor or diseased.[20] Despite the feelings of many white Alabamians, Charles J. Lipp, the Bureau's optimistic surgeon in chief, reported to Wager Swayne, "All of these hospitals...are now in charge of efficient medical officers and supplied with everything necessary for the comfort of the patient."[21] His report listed the number of surgeons, stewards, attendants, and beds at hospitals in Selma, Montgomery, Demopolis, Huntsville, Home Colony, and Talladega. Just two surgeons were in residence in Selma and Montgomery; the other hospitals operated with fewer surgeons. Moreover, the Talladega hospital ended operations in July 1866.[22] Closings were particularly devastating for African Americans.

Labor and Economic Justice

Besides housing and health care, the need for a new system of labor reciprocation was the most pressing problem confronting

11

blacks and whites in Alabama. African American workers, freed for the first time, had to adjust to a wage labor system; for their part white planters, also for the first time, had to regard blacks as free laborers and wage earners. Remarked the *Daily Advertiser*, "You have been accustomed to direct[ing] their labor by your sovereign mandate; now you can command it only by contract. The black man is dazzled, if not intoxicated, with the idea of freedom suddenly thrust upon him."[23] Bureau District Inspector Charles Buckley voiced a similar concern when he said, "Many of the colored people must of necessity be grossly ignorant of their true position and at a loss to know what is for their best interest."[24]

The transition was a difficult and critical one for both groups but for significantly different reasons. Most of all, African Americans refused to sign long-term contracts. Until January 1866 most former slaves assumed the Bureau would divide plantation properties among them; thus, only a small number wanted to contract for a year. Faced with this situation, General Swayne cautioned them to "hope for nothing, but go to work and behave yourselves."[25] Hearing these words from Swayne, disconcerted African Americans were uncertain whether he was their friend.[26]

To compound an already difficult situation, some planters formed illegal combinations against African American workers. In these instances, planters agreed among themselves whether to hire African Americans and at what wages. Yet, contrary to the widely popular notion, many African Americans truly wanted to work. The *Daily*

Advertiser confirmed this by noting that African Americans seemed anxious to work; their only interest was in finding men who would be kind and humane to them. The same newsorgan also cautioned African Americans against their inclination to leave their old places of employment to seek new ones.[27]

The situation was not helped when many planters strongly opposed African Americans observing the first postwar anniversary of the Emancipation Proclamation. They noted that African Americans had not signed contracts for the coming year and that, if they did not do so soon, white laborers would get the good contracts.[28] Also, through advertisements by (B. O.) Hardaway and (E. H.) Harris, among others, African Americans began to realize the importance of their services. This Montgomery employment agency kept a register of farm hands and "mechanics," such as blacksmiths, carpenters, wheelwrights, shoemakers, draymen, ostlers, male cooks, washers, ironers, and house servants, and they promised to bring together employers and employees. Wager Swayne endorsed this agency.[29]

The Freedmen's Bureau also helped African American workers to make contracts. Swayne and his agents were as intensely interested as former plantations owners were in inducing African Americans to contract. Since the former owners needed a source of labor, the Bureau agents often negotiated contracts that benefitted both employers and workers. Therefore, Swayne directed his agents to request that employers write contracts for services done for more than 30 days and to explain verbally to African Americans contracts

13

of shorter duration.[30] Bureau officials publicly authorized no single form of contract; instead, they accepted any agreement assented to by both parties.[31] Still, contracts usually required employers to recognize the legal rights of African Americans. Bureau officials expected employers to provide for "food, quarters, and medical attendance for the entire family and such other compensation as should be agreed upon; in addition, such contracts should be a lien upon the crop, not more than one-half of which could be removed until final payment was made and the contract should be released by the Bureau official."[32]

Former slave Jo Acre agreed to one such contract; it read:

State of Alabama, Clarke County Jan. 1st 1866. This shows that Jo Acre [freedman] for himself and his wife Ellen and children, namely Willis, Ann, Alek, Charlotte, Yancey, and Laura agrees to do all reasonably work or service required of them on, or for the farm, or interest, or benefit of Mary Josephine Rivers and family during this year respectively obeying hers or her agent's orders and not to leave the premises without permit; for and in consideration of two hundred and sixteen dollars to be paid by M. J. Rivers at the end of said term of service, to said Jo Acre, and Eight dollars per month for Willis. And quarters, and food, and cotton, and cards, wheels, loom, and leather to be furnished for their two suits of clothes and shoes during this year: And their Doctors bill, which with all other things furnished them not afore mentioned is to be deducted from their pay. All lost time for sickness or otherwise to be deducted from their pay. Therefrom also shall be duducted all burial expense.[33]

For their part, whites did little to placate blacks' fear of long-term contracts and of possible reenslavement. The phrases in Jo Acres' contract concerning leaving "the premises without permit," "doctors bill(s)," and "lost time for sickness," all tended to support this pervasive African American fear. Other

14

whites even predicted the African American's extinction because of his refusal to marry. These whites, showing their ignorance of the radically changed societal position of African Americans, assumed because slavery had prohibited marriage, African Americans would not marry once slavery had ended. Acting equally out of ignorance-- mixed with a fear of the unknown, carried-over prejudice, and arrogance--whites often maintained that blacks and whites could not coexist, except as masters and slaves.

As the situation continued to unfold, there was often little distinction between the attitudes of poor whites and former slaveowners. Thus, poor whites, struggling to secure for themselves a safe position in the new society, changed their public posture. Poor whites who had associated with blacks earlier now took pains to separate themselves from them and to make certain African Americans realized the planter's will would prevail.[34]

Whites' reaction to emancipation was evidenced in Union Springs, where United States military authorities charged that former Confederate William C. Jordan violated his parole when he refused to emancipate his slaves.[35] Elsewhere, according to Bureau agent Charles Buckley, other planters willfully misled former slaves by urging them to return to work, alleging the government had revoked the Emancipation Proclamation.[36] This is hardly a small matter of passing importance. If former slaves had accepted this ruse, especially in large numbers, the chances were great they would have returned to the plantations and worked on as they had done during

15

slavery. The attitude of some white United States Army officers was little better. Arriving in Opelika on 27 January 1866, en route to Girard, Brvt Col C. Cadle, Jr., was alarmed to learn that C. J. Lewis--who was probably in charge of a local militia--and his officers were speaking of African Americans "using seditious or insurrectionary language." Lewis even ordered his "men to proceed forthwith with the collection of arms and ammunition found in the hands of freedmen." In contrast, as far as Cadle was concerned, the peaceful conduct of freedmen during the previous six weeks had already earned the praise of "every right-minded man."[37]

Ironically, but scarcely surprisingly, the new postbellum labor system closely resembled slavery. The compensation for field hands ranged from $10 to $12 a month for men and from $6 to $10 a month for women. The salary for domestic work was usually higher. African Americans received only a partial payment through the working year, on either 1 August or 1 October, and did not get the remainder due them until 1 January of the following year. Employers deducted from wages a charge for food, lodging, and medical expenses; they also subtracted from wages any expenses incurred by nonlaboring members of the family. Also, employers deducted from wages all time lost for illnesses, refusal to work, breakage of tools, and abuse of stock.[38] This arrangement became increasingly apparent as time passed, and it helped mightily to destroy the economic potential of African American laborers. Although they initially worked for wages, African Americans in increasing numbers began to accept portions of the crop as partial payment in lieu of wages. They also often purchased goods on credit, hoping to redeem their debts at the end of the year.[39]

Employers arranged a certificate system on some plantations. This was a procedure with some theoretical merits, but it proved ineffective for African American laborers. The certificate system permitted African American laborers to purchase goods on credit in anticipation of paying for them at harvest time. Humane and reasonable on the surface, this system--in practice--was fatally flawed. Events showed that by the end of the year, these debts usually exceeded earnings, especially when the crop failed. Thus, the system became one of virtual peonage and resulted in planter paternalism. The harsh reality was that sharecropping came to tie the African American laborer to the land as tightly as slavery had bound them legally.[40]

Matters worsened when some planters came to rely on the absence of a uniform labor code to avoid their legal and moral obligations to their African American employees. Some even drove their African American workers off the land to avoid paying them. African Americans also suffered economic and social abuses under the sharecrop and credit system because of their inability to read and to comprehend contractual stipulations. Yet, when many African Americans sought assistance from civil authorities, they found the courts slow and inadequate. In addition, African Americans often lacked sufficient financial resources to initiate litigation.[41]

17

NEITHER CARPETBAGGERS NOR SCALAWAGS

What were the underlying reasons for the mounting difficulties African Americans met under the contract system? Three that stand out include the reluctance of the planter to trust the innovative free labor system, the inability of the African American employee to understand the agreements, and the lack of Bureau enforcement of labor contracts.[42]

Still, contrary to the objections of the Freedmen's Bureau, both planters and African Americans preferred the sharecrop system. Most planters believed that Alabama blacks shared their appreciation of the sharecrop system, but their reasons for doing so were different. African Americans recognized the sharp contrast between the individual freedom it permitted in their living arrangements and the featureless coldness of the collective huts in which they had lived during their previous years of slavery. They also disliked intensely the regimented work of the slave gang. Besides, the sharecrop system also promised something tangible they could look forward to; something they could claim as their own--a portion of the crop. Finally, African Americans preferred the wage system most because it allowed them both to work and concurrently to imagine themselves as truly "free" men.[43]

On the other hand, the planters liked the sharecrop system for very different reasons. A major one was the scarcity of currency. An unusual one was that it allowed some planters to turn their stock and the farming facilities over to their African American laborers to avoid regular contact with them. Yet, whether it was

18

the sharecrop system, the crop lien system, or the certificate system, planters usually emerged as the long-term beneficiaries; African American laborers emerged as the unfortunate losers because they did not comprehend contracts, Bureau enforcement of the law was deficient, and they often didn't press charges to redress unfair treatment.[44]

African Americans suffered tremendously under Alabama's new labor system because 1)many of the state's civil authorities--as former Confederates of the same mind despite having lost the war-- were unjust in their dispensation of justice, 2)their orphans were apprenticed by justices of the peace to former slaveowners, and 3)vagrancy and stay laws made leaving the land or suing for payments impossible. Thus, despite the repeal of the stay law on 7 December 1866 and of the vagrancy law on 12 February 1867, those civil authorities who wanted to discriminate found ways of doing so. By way of comparison, African Americans in Louisiana, for example, also found sharecropping disappointing.[45]

The Bureau and Education

It must be said then, either the Bureau did not adequately seek economic justice for African Americans or it badly handled the assignment. Its work in education was only slightly better. The Bureau wanted African Americans to learn the rudiments of reading and writing so they could become good citizens and make contracts. This Bureau position reflected the personal position of

Commissioner Oliver Otis Howard who, like most other nineteenth-century Americans, held that a proper education, once acquired, enabled anyone to conduct himself as an American citizen. More specifically, the Bureau held that educational training would protect African Americans once Bureau agents and the United States military had departed the South. It was largely because of the interest and direction of Commissioner Howard that the Bureau made giant strides in education, establishing--as it did--the earliest schools in the South for former slaves.[46]

The Bureau established its first Alabama school for African Americans in Mobile and its second in Montgomery. John Alvord, the Freedmen's Bureau General Superintendent of Education, wrote that in Mobile 15 teachers instructed 817 pupils. Opening in May 1865, the Mobile school classes, according to Alvord, were well graded; its teachers were thorough; and its discipline was excellent. The progress made by most of the Mobile students surprised even Alvord. Although the monthly tuition ranged from just $.25 to $1.25 per pupil, the school had received $7,845.18 in tuition by 10 October 1867. The Montgomery school, "with 325 pupils who pay in the aggregate $118 per month tuition," also was very good. The Bureau operated 11 other schools in Huntsville, Athens, and Stevenson. Alvord also issued a report on Bureau-operated schools in 14 other states.[47]

Several Northern aid societies shared Howard's interest in African American education in Alabama. One of these, the

20

Pittsburgh Freedmen's Aid Society of the Methodist Episcopal church, established schools in the Tennessee Valley towns of Huntsville, Athens, and Stevenson. Other benevolent societies followed the movements of Federal occupational forces southward to other parts of Alabama. For example, the National Freedmen's Relief Association provided food and clothing; the Southern Famine Relief Committee alleviated some of the food shortage; and the American Union Commission assisted indigent African Americans. Congress enhanced the efforts of these aid societies when it passed a bill on 16 July 1866, thereby extending the Bureau for another two years and increasing its appropriations. This congressional funding gave the Bureau the impetus and the security it needed to continue its work, and near the close of 1865, the Alabama Bureau boasted of "175 day and evening schools, serving close to ten thousand students."[48]

Bureau agents carefully instructed African Americans to support their education. Consequently, from meager resources, freedmen paid a monthly tuition of up to $1.25 per student. Thus, with the avid support of Northern teachers, aid societies, and the Bureau, African American education became a reality in Alabama. Beginning in 1865 most Southern whites accepted African American education. Although not employed by the Bureau, Jabez L.(amar) M.(onroe) Curry and Porter King, among other Southern whites, helped to garner financial support and incorporation for African American schools in Marion and in other parts of the state.[49]

21

NEITHER CARPETBAGGERS NOR SCALAWAGS

By late 1867 white opposition had surfaced. The Constitutional Convention of 1867 may have been a symptom, if not a catalyst, but the growing political influence of African Americans and the Republican party was the overriding cause. Southern white opposition charged that African Americans spent too much of their earnings on political campaigns and that Northern teachers, appealing to societal and racial fears and prejudice, taught social and political equality with whites among blacks.[50]

Thus, the rising adverse attitude of whites toward African American education became tied directly to the presence of Northern teachers. For example, after 1870, when many of these teachers returned to the North, Southern opposition to African American education subsided. Since the number and influence of Northerners remained strong, Southern whites burned school houses and refused to rent buildings for educational purposes or to board teachers. In defense of their actions, many Alabama whites denied opposition to the idea of African American education. Instead, they claimed to disagree with how Northern teachers spread hatred of Southerners among African Americans and taught them a classical education that made them unfit for the Southern way of living.[51] In Louisiana whites also opposed African American education.[52]

As time passed, however, whites in Alabama and Mississippi became more supportive of African American education. This change became especially revealing after 1870, when many Northern teachers had departed Alabama. Governor Robert M. Patton bluntly

22

articulated the concern of Southern whites in an address to the state legislature in which he stated, "They [African Americans] should be especially taught the utter absurdity of expecting or aspiring to a condition of social equality with the white race."[53] Bureau State Superintendent of Education Reverend Charles Buckley voiced a similar position in his address before the Alabama Association in late 1866, saying, "The only question is: Who shall educate these people? I say to you as a mere question of interest, it is ruinous to permit others to educate them."[54]

Bureau-operated schools floundered in Alabama for several reasons. For one thing, the crop failure of 1867 hurt them. Then, too, the lack of financial and political support did little to enhance their success. Elizabeth Bethel writes that extremely cold weather and the ravages of the cotton worm vitiated an efficient system of justice and good race relations. Already in strong disagreement with the presence of Northern teachers, Alabama whites also found a poor crop another reason to keep African Americans on the land and away from the schoolhouse door. Funding and internal Bureau flaws provided two other reasons. Frequent changes in leadership were of foremost importance especially when the Bureau reassigned the affable Swayne in January 1868 and the fair-minded Buckley resigned less than 24 hours later. When Henry M. Bush, a former Army captain and a native of Illinois, replaced Buckley, he learned the Bureau had routinely not paid rent or teachers' salaries and had not provided for their transportation. Given

23

these self-destructive handicaps, as well as internal confusion over school enrollment, the repair of buildings, staff turnovers, and bureaucratic red tape, it is hardly surprising that the Bureau failed in Alabama. It would have done so even in the absence of white opposition.[55]

African Americans' zeal for learning continued. "Too much cannot be said of the desire to learn among this people," Swayne remarked of Alabama's African Americans. Other accounts attested to the marked enthusiasm of freedmen for an education and their capacity for absorbing knowledge. One Bureau teacher commented, "So far as I have had the opportunity to observe, their progress is about the average of white children under far more favorable circumstances."[56] John Alvord offered an explanation for the African American's thirst for learning. He wrote that the African American "had seen power and influence among white people always coupled with learning--it is the sign of that elevation to which they now aspire."[57] Still, enthusiasm alone was not enough to overcome the insurmountable obstacles that confronted African American education--which were compounded by insufficient funding, the burning of facilities, and atrocities leveled against teachers.

Restoration of Civil Government

As the state grappled with the education of African Americans, it also sought to restore civil government. To this end, a constitutional convention convened in Montgomery on 12 September 1865.

The state had gone 50 days without a civil government, and to help restore Alabama to its prewar position in the Union, President Andrew Johnson had appointed Lewis E. Parsons as provisional governor on 21 June 1865.[58]

Parsons moved to Alabama from New York in 1840 and set up a law practice in the Piedmont town of Talladega. A Whig and later a Douglas Democrat in 1860, he opposed secession, but as matters deteriorated, he aided the Confederacy, although still adamantly opposed to it in spirit. Johnson's plan for reconstruction was clear: Parsons was to establish rules for calling a constitutional convention to amend the state constitution. Presidential Reconstruction also required that Alabama, as other Southern states, repudiate its ordinance of secession and war debts and abolish slavery.[59]

The conciliatory tone of Presidential Reconstruction did little to abate the volatile political climate in Alabama. When the Constitutional Convention of 1865 assembled in Montgomery, no African American had voted in the 31 August election in which delegates had been chosen. Thus, the twin issues of suffrage and representation hovered over the convention.[60]

Invoking the old, controversial three-fourths rule, the antebellum legislature had used the slave population to decide legislative representation. In the state's earliest postbellum assembly, with 36 delegates from north Alabama and 63 from southern and central Alabama, delegates from the northern section, sometimes

25

derisively called "Unionists," sought the "white basis" for representation. This plan considered only the state's white population, a certain advantage for the northern section of the state. On the other hand, delegates from the southern and central sections, the areas with large concentrations of slaves during the antebellum period, wanted to include the African American, since slavery had ended, but only for reapportionment. The conventioneers finally passed an ordinance providing for apportionment on a "white basis" and made no provisions for African American suffrage, despite the pleas of the state's First Freedmen's Convention requesting them to do so.[61]

The suffrage position of the convention delegates mirrored the attitudes of most of the state's white population and clearly showed that, although the long war had ended slavery and the delegates had abolished it, the stultifying impact of racial prejudice lingered on. One white observer noted that "no sort of legislation would make a good servant or citizen out of the negro because of his weak character," and suggested that colonization offered the only solution. The Huntsville *Advocate* hedged and asked its patrons to recognize what the war has done for African Americans. But, "legal rights and political privileges are essentially different. He has been granted the former—not the latter."[62] Governor Robert M. Patton was much more candid when he stated, "We shall extend to the Negro all their legitimate rights...but shall throw around them such effectual safeguards as

26

will secure them in their full and complete enjoyment. It must be understood that politically and socially ours is a white man's government."[63] At least politically, like white North Carolinians, Alabama whites were willing to accept reunion and emancipation but nothing more.[64]

The convention did not address the issue of legal rights for African Americans, despite the urging of General Swayne. However, within Article IV, Section 36, of its proceedings, the delegates did request the legislature to pass laws to protect Alabama's African Americans in the "full enjoyment of their rights, person, and property and guard them and the state from all evil that might arise from their sudden emancipation."[65] Also, before the adjournment of the convention, the delegates legalized all African American marriages made by a minister during the prewar period and African American marriages consummated since then. Yet, they remained adamant in their opposition to mixed marriages. In addition, whether by inadvertence or design, they did not give voters the opportunity to approve the constitution by referendum, choosing instead to ratify the proceedings themselves. This was the same procedure the loyal faction had objected to at the secessionist convention of 1861.[66]

The conventioneers set the state's first postbellum election for 30 October 1865. Then voters were to elect a governor, state legislators, and congressmen. State legislators chose lesser state officials. The choice of candidates for governor reflected the determination of the Unionists to control state politics. The three candidates—Michael J. Bulger of Tallapoosa County, William Russell Smith of Tuscaloosa, and Robert M. Patton of Lauderdale County—lived in north Alabama and adhered to the Whig political tradition. Bulger, a captain in the 47th Alabama infantry, had participated in the battles of Cedar Run and Gettysburg, where he was wounded but later cared for by Federal troops. Smith had raised the 6th Alabama Regiment and had served in the Confederate House of Representatives throughout the war. Unionists applauded the victory of Patton, who received nearly the combined votes of his two opponents. Like Parsons, his predecessor, Patton had opposed secession in 1861, but unlike Parsons, he had served briefly in the Confederacy. Patton declared, "The Negro must be made to realize that freedom does not mean idleness and vagrancy."[67]

The election of congressmen did not give north Alabamians a similar opportunity to celebrate. Five of the six new congressmen had opposed secession, and several of them had served with the Confederate army or held Confederate civil offices. Joseph C. Bradley, a Huntsville Unionist, challenged the election of these men in a written complaint to President Andrew Johnson. He charged that the amnesty oath had been circumvented in Alabama and that those who had done so had proceeded to elect other men to office who had compromised their loyalty to the Union by serving the Confederacy. He asked the president to reappoint Parsons as

28

provisional governor and to initiate Presidential Reconstruction a second time.[68]

However, despite the objections of Bradley and other Unionists, the Patton administration proceeded with the mandates of Presidential Reconstruction and began its work on 20 November 1865. Most of the initial work of the state's first postwar legislature focused on the status of African Americans. Lawmakers quickly passed the Thirteenth Amendment and continued to legislate the future of African Americans by proposing laws to control labor in reaction to rumors that African Americans refused to make contracts because they expected to receive portions of the properties of former owners.[69]

The earliest of these proposals was a contract bill, which forced African Americans to make contract. Neither General Swayne nor Governor Patton agreed to this bill. Swayne believed the bill was a revival of slavery, and Patton feared Northern reaction. A second bill extended to African Americans the criminal laws applicable to Alabama's antebellum small free African American population. This code had permitted the testimony of free African Americans in cases involving African American parties and decreed the death penalty for persons found guilty of rape or the attempted rape of a white woman. When the legislators returned from a month-long recess on 15 January 1866, they discovered the holiday period had passed without any insurrection and African Americans had settled down and made contracts. Consequently, Governor Patton

29

vetoed all previous bills pertaining to African Americans, excluding the Thirteenth Amendment. The legislature made no serious effort to override his veto.[70]

Other measures passed by the legislature did not advance African Americans beyond emancipation. Instead, the legislators imposed a set of laws generically known as the "Black Code of Alabama." The final version of this code outlined provisions for vagrancy, apprenticeship, labor, weapons, and other proscriptions that, on the surface, did not appear discriminatory. Both Patton and Swayne considered the code as an obstacle to the readmission of Alabama. White Southerners relied on vagrancy laws to control African American labor, whether such was the intent of the legislature or not. The loose definition of a vagrant as "any runaway, stubborn servant, or child, a common drunkard, or any person who habitually neglects his employment" allowed state officials to hire out the vagrant for not more than six months or until someone honored the fine of $50.00.[71]

A second bill, an apprentice law, governed the relation of master and apprentice; yet, the results paralleled the vagrancy law since this bill placed minors without parental support in the hands of the court of their respective counties until the male minors reached the age of 18 and female minors reached the age of 21. The former owner was to provide for the minor and to inflict the punishment a father or guardian inflicted upon a child if the minor had been a slave. If the apprentice ran away, state law then classified him as a vagrant.[72]

Patton and Swayne objected to the Black Code, and Swayne saw to the strict enforcement of a provision requiring the former owner to be a suitable person. A third law placed a $2 tax on all pistols owned by private individuals and made it practically impossible for African Americans to arm themselves.[73]

The legislature likewise granted few civil rights. African Americans could sue and be sued, and could testify only in cases in which both parties were African Americans. Whether in resignation, overoptimism, misinterpretation, or foolish acceptance of the legislature's good will, once the legislature granted these rights to African Americans, all Bureau courts ceased to hear cases involving African American plaintiffs. Still, Bureau officials renewed their efforts to see to it the magistrates trying these cases remained judicious. As events turned out, the caprice of the magistrates determined the severity of the Black Code. As time passed, Bureau agents discovered to their dismay that many magistrates had served in the Confederate government and showed extreme hostility toward African Americans. Inevitably, they began to fill many jails in Alabama. Initially, persons jailed for offenses committed during the latter stages of the war received a pardon from Governor Patton, but many African Americans crowded the jails because of crimes committed after the commencement of Presidential Reconstruction.[74]

NEITHER CARPETBAGGERS NOR SCALAWAGS

Especially harsh were city ordinances. As one example, a Mobile city ordinance prescribed that African American offenders receive double the time of white offenders. The actual jailing resulted from comparatively trivial offenses, such as one half-naked Montgomery African American who was sentenced to hard labor for stealing a coat. Additionally, in another case--that of an African American Selma laundress--the inequities of the state's tax laws became clear, as she was taxed at a rate of $5 a year, although a white Selma lawyer was taxed $10 for the same year. The penalty of a jail sentence for failure to pay taxes underscored the gravity of the inequity.[75]

The harshness of the Alabama Black Code, harsher in its application than the codes of other Southern states, severely neutralized the efficacy of the Thirteenth Amendment. As a result, many observers criticized Presidential Reconstruction for being too lenient with local and state officials. General Swayne called Alabama's legislators "anything but fair and just." He explained to Bureau Commissioner Howard that "it would be difficult to tell the wickedness to which they have been and are still instrumental."[76] Yet, not all white Alabamians considered the Black Code to be fair. Some laid the blame at the doorsteps of the Bureau and charged that it had set the precedent by approving laws to coerce African Americans to work. One observer noted, however, the harmful effects of the Alabama Black Code resulted from its implementation and not its theoretical framework.[77]

32

During the early months of 1866 most Blackbelt legislators had come to accept African American suffrage as essential to their dominance of state politics. State Representative Nathan L. Brooks, of Blackbelt Lowndes County, introduced a bill calling for a qualified African American suffrage based on education and property ownership. The passage of this legislation would wrest control of Alabama politics from the hands of Unionist forces and return Blackbelt legislators to the dominance they had enjoyed during prewar days. Paradoxically, Blackbelt politicians advanced a qualified African American suffrage because they hoped to control African Americans, many of whom were their former slaves. On the other hand, whites in north Alabama, where slaves were fewest, disagreed most vehemently with the notion of African American suffrage. Governor Patton, a resident of the region, echoed the sentiments of his fellow north Alabamians when he said, "This is a white man's government."[78] In the end, the legislature defeated the suffrage resolution of Brooks. Still, his resolution had served notice to north Alabama that Blackbelt lawmakers would enfranchise African Americans--if necessary--to return to power.[79]

The United States Congress held an interest in the civil rights and economic welfare of African Americans in Alabama. The civil rights bill of 1866 defined citizenship and provided for its enforcement in Federal courts. It was introduced in the Senate with the intent to nullify the Alabama Black Code and similar codes implemented in other Southern states by prescribing the same rights and penalties for blacks and whites alike. President Johnson vetoed the measure on 27 March 1866, but Congress overrode his veto on 9 April. White Alabamians did not give serious consideration to the Civil Rights Act, because they realized enforcement relied on the whims of magistrates, although Congress authorized the Freedmen's Bureau to initiate proceedings against violators of the act. The Bureau no longer could suspend civil officers, since the Alabama legislature now permitted the testimony of African Americans in court. Their testimony seemed a mixed blessing, for now they were without the protection of the Bureau. Alabama laws were at variance with the Civil Rights Act of 1866 by providing dissimilar penalties for a black and a white defendant in a rape case. General Swayne influenced Governor Patton to commute the sentence of an African American defendant or to give the same penalty specified for a white defendant. Since there were many African American defendants in Alabama, the governor found it impractical to commute all sentences; thus, Swayne sought to arraign magistrates who levied discriminatory sentences or to force them to resign. Despite the efforts and intentions of Swayne, Governor Patton, and the United States Congress, the Civil Rights Act of 1866 remained ineffective. The reason was that enforcement remained in the hands of the legislature and civil magistrates, who continued to levy discriminatory sentences.[80]

Although congressional radicals continued to seek ways to nullify the Black Code, Governor Patton, recipient of a good press, turned his attention to economic matters. In a state devastated by war, he carefully pushed railroad subsidies, using the state's credit to provide for the sale of bonds to finance this expansion. Providing aid in the construction of railroads was one of the most controversial issues during Reconstruction. Few Alabama governors had been successful in handling this economic matter. Patton was no exception.[81]

Even during antebellum times men of vision in Alabama had recognized the need for linking the northern part of the state with its Southern section, particularly Mobile. A committee of the legislature had sought an endorsement of $2 million in 1851. Governor John A. Winston's reluctance to approve state aid was attributed to the failure of state banks during the Jacksonian period. Winston vetoed 33 railroad bond bills during his tenure. Since public sympathy was so large for the enactment of railroad bonds, the legislature overrode Winston's veto and passed a bill awarding $900,000 to the Alabama and Tennessee Rivers Railroad, the Memphis and Charleston, and the Mobile and Ohio. Although the war caused a cessation in railroad construction, the Confederate government rendered assistance whenever possible. Such was the public sentiment and the reaction of the legislature in 1865-66; Northern Republicans continued the policy already in existence.[82]

Governor Patton received the authorization to endorse a railroad's first-mortgage bond for $12,000 per mile on 19 February 1867. This was done under the act of 1867 that authorized Patton to

35

issue a first-mortgage bond when 20 continuous miles at one or both ends of a road had been "finished, completed, or equipped."[83] This authorization applied to both interstate and intrastate railroad construction and served as the foundation for all state aid laws passed during the period. The act also mandated the completion of the first 70 miles within three years or by 1 November 1870. Meeting the following year, the legislature amended the act to allow endorsement in five-mile blocks after the completion of the first 20 miles of a road. The legislature also increased the rate of its endorsements from $12,000 to $16,000 per mile. They hoped this increase in endorsement would help to attract capital from Europe and the North. If realized, this plan would give Alabama in a few years a railroad system to rival Pennsylvania's rail system.[84]

State aid or some variation of public aid was crucial to the development of a Southern railway network because the region's railway companies lacked both the credit and the cash to complete their operations. During the latter part of the Patton administration, the Northeast and Southwest defaulted on the $300,000 loan owed the State of Alabama. Patton reluctantly put the company up for sale. With the progression of time, Patton realized he was not without a friend who had capital. This friend was railroad magnate James W. Sloss, who, like Patton, was also a resident of north Alabama. Sloss merged three north Alabama railroads into the Nashville and Decatur railroad. He also wanted to link Montgomery with the Nashville area by way of important cities of north Alabama. With Patton as governor, the state's inclination to finance railroad construction, and Sloss' desire to make north Alabama an industrial empire, the north Alabama delegation, receiving credit for Patton's success, seemed destined to control state affairs for the immediate future.[85] Such a scenario was likely if the Alabama legislature had not rejected the Fourteenth Amendment. Incensed at the leniency of Presidential Reconstruction, Congress passed the Reconstruction Act of 2 March 1867 over the veto of President Johnson, thus initiating Congressional Reconstruction, the third phase of Reconstruction in Alabama. Under this act, Congress divided the South into five military districts, each headed by a general, and stipulated that a constitutional convention, comprised of male delegates, chosen by all citizens 21 years of age and older, except persons disfranchised for their participation in the rebellion or for crime, should frame a new constitution. The act also specified that when the electorate had ratified a provision calling for African American suffrage and the legislature had adopted the Fourteenth Amendment and had made it part of the state's constitution, then the senators and representatives who had been disallowed admission since 1865 would be readmitted to Congress. Congress amended the initial act with two supplementary acts, one dated 23 March and the other dated 19 July. The act of 23 March directed the commanding general in each district to register all male citizens who were qualified to vote and provided that, at the

37

time of election for delegates, the voters also could decide the desirability of holding a convention. The state would assemble a convention if most of the voters favored such and if the total vote on the question represented most of those registered. The act of 19 July gave the commanding generals the power to remove state officers and to appoint others, who were required to take the iron-clad oath, in their places.[86]

Passage of the Reconstruction Acts caused Alabama Unionists to change directions. No longer would they and former Confederates debate the feasibility of African American suffrage; the enfranchisement of former slaves had arrived, and neither side could claim responsibility for its success. The issue for both groups was the control of the new voters, most of whom lived in the Blackbelt. The organization of the Republican party of Alabama coincided with the passage of the Reconstruction Acts and the reorganization of Unionist forces in Alabama. Unionists began their reorganization in early 1867 and held their initial meeting on 4 March, two days after passage of the initial Reconstruction Act. They also called, after a meeting at Decatur in April, for a state convention to assemble in Montgomery in June to structure the new Alabama Republican party. The Unionists sought to woo the African American vote by pledging their (Unionists) allegiance to the new state Republican party and by controlling the new African American members whom they planned to entice to join them. For Unionists, getting Alabama's African Americans to join the

Republican party posed no major problem. After all, the Republican party was the party of Lincoln, had issued the Emancipation Proclamation, and had fought a war to end slavery. Controlling former slaves did not occur immediately for Unionists, because in passing the Reconstruction Acts, Congress, through the Fourteenth Amendment, simultaneously disfranchised many Unionists who had held office in the Confederate government to escape conscription.[87]

Alabama African Americans held ambitions of their own. They and their peers in the other Southern states had begun to hold political rallies and meetings as early as November 1865. The freedmen's convention of 1865, like other freedmen's conventions held in 1865 and in 1866, stressed moderation. The First Freedmen's Convention assembled in Mobile on 28 November 1865. With Methodist minister E. S. Winn presiding and J. S. Holmes serving as secretary, the 56 delegates did not advance any resolutions they considered objectionable to whites. They instead urged a policy of "peace, friendship, and goodwill toward our white fellow-citizens among whom our lot is cast." The delegates proposed to "perform faithful labor for every man who will pay us just wages" and promised not to take a man's "property without giving him a just equivalent." They issued the latter resolution to negate rumors that African Americans expected to receive a division of the property of former plantation owners.[88]

The minister-delegates clearly set the tone for the convention. Besides its moderate tone, the conventioneers revealed a reliance on divine guidance and invoked the name of God in three of their nine resolutions. They mentioned no grievances. Instead, their resolutions expressed a profound willingness to love and to work within the framework of the American political system. Their resolutions revealed a preoccupation with image and offered no hint that former slaves drafted the resolutions.[89] To be sure, Alabama delegates were not alone in drafting conciliatory resolutions. African American delegates in Georgia and South Carolina drafted resolutions with similar moderate tones. They also seemed preoccupied with image.[90]

Alabama whites did not consider the resolutions of the state's First Freedmen's Convention as moderate, particularly the memorial asking for the extension of suffrage. General Swayne of the Freedmen's Bureau delivered the resolutions to the Alabama legislature, and the legislature, in turn, unanimously agreed to table the resolution. Although the legislative body warmly discussed the rights and new status of African Americans, as they tabled legislation of benefit to African Americans and approved legislation that did not improve their status, it became obvious that what was best for former slaves and what they wanted were of little importance to the legislators.[91]

Alabama's Black Code, passed by the legislature, exemplified its sentiments and molded the attitudes of Alabama's white citizenry. Most white Alabamians agreed with one Unionist who stated, "I want the negro to have his legal or political rights and nothing more.

He is not fit for enfranchisement--as a race the blacks are not capable of appreciating the ballot box or a free government. If they were qualified and could appreciate the right of suffrage, I would feel differently."[92] With greater candor, the Huntsville *Advocate* exclaimed, "This is a white man's government and a white man's state. We are opposed to any changes in the government except such as are necessary to get the state into the Union again."[93]

The Union League and Party Formation

The notions of the Freedmen's Bureau and the Union League conflicted with the goals of both Unionist and Blackbelt legislators. When it became apparent Alabama would give African Americans their legal rights only with reluctance, the Bureau and later the Union League sought to enhance the African American's possibilities for securing the suffrage. The Union League was organized in Philadelphia in the fall of 1862, when it appeared the North would lose the war. Once Congress passed the Reconstruction Acts, the Union League realized that through indoctrination African Americans could become members of the Republican party and, concurrently, the Republican party could easily dominate Alabama political affairs, with or without the cooperation of the Unionist and Blackbelt factions.[94]

Appearing in Alabama in 1863 as Federal troops occupied the Tennessee Valley towns of Huntsville, Athens, and Florence, the

League initially attracted area Unionists. In 1865 and 1866, when 40 percent of the white population of north Alabama held League membership, whites began to leave the League because its agents lobbied in the halls of Congress in support of radical measures, including African American suffrage; this was particularly true in 1866. The League was one of the earliest organizations to call for African American suffrage. Thus, when Congress passed the initial Reconstruction Acts, Union League officials, who often worked with the Bureau, had begun their formation of a Republican party in Alabama and their efforts to recruit African American members.[95]

Unionists and Union Leaguers perceived that African American enfranchisement was forthcoming and sought to control it. Both groups hoped to control not only a possible African American vote but also the political affairs of the state. They considered the organization of the state's Republican party as the best means to accomplish these feats. Unionists called for an assembly at the Tennessee Valley town of Moulton for 8-9 January 1867. They then decided to reassemble in Huntsville on 4 March. No African Americans attended either of these meetings, but Unionists from across the state did attend. From Huntsville came William Bibb Figures, editor of the Huntsville *Advocate*, and attorneys Joseph C. Bradley and Nicholas Davis.[96]

Then sectional lines began to crumble as Unionists united to control state affairs. The Huntsville meeting attracted such Freedmen's Bureau officials as Wager Swayne, John B. Callis of

Wisconsin, and John C. Keffer, Pennsylvania native and president of the Alabama Union League. The Saffold brothers, Milton J. and Benjamin F., represented Blackbelt Dallas County. Former Confederate Adam C. Felder of Montgomery considered the urgency of forming the Republican party and joined the convention. The conventioneers wanted Alabama to take its proper relation within the Federal Union. They ended their meeting by pledging to reassemble in Montgomery in June.[97]

The Alabama Union League met in Decatur in April 1867. The unprecedented assembly witnessed the first political meeting African Americans attended and, more important, the earliest meeting in which African Americans and whites sat as equals. With Aaron Boysam presiding and Lewis Stribling serving as secretary, the delegates of the Colored Union League resolved to "thank Almighty God and the loyal people of the United States for sharing the right to choose their rulers." They also pledged "to vote for none other for office than those who have been the tried and true friends of our race and government." These delegates also endorsed the Reconstruction Acts, helped to organize the Republican party of Alabama, and called for a meeting in Montgomery in June to continue the effort to organize the party.[98] All across the state Union League officials boasted of African Americans who flocked to join. One official in the Piedmont town of Talladega wrote that he had taken in 500 hundred at a rate of 100 a week. Another official, stationed in Huntsville, reported that "we have a perfect

43

organization in this city and can carry this county almost to a man (col'd)."[99]

The League transformed Alabama's political climate. The meeting of the state's Second Freedmen's Convention revealed the extent of this transformation. Meeting on 1 May 1867 and again in Mobile, this convention included many veteran African American delegates. Also present were some newcomers to the political arena, such as D. M. Hill of Bullock County and Greene Shadrack Washington Lewis and John Dozier, both of Perry County. The Second Freedmen's Convention delegates were disappointed with the state government but showed a strong faith in the national government. Delegates claimed that "our confidence in the government of the United States has been strong but our people are still subjected to so many wrongs, not only by our former owners but also by the soldiers of the United States; we have not received redress or protection from the government."[100]

The conventioneers asked each delegate to report on the condition of affairs in his region. The concluding resolutions evidenced a new spirit of radicalism, as delegates claimed the "same rights, privileges, and immunities as enjoyed by white men." No longer interested in placating the fears of their white neighbors, they exclaimed that "it is our undeniable right to hold office, sit on juries, to ride on all public conveyances, to sit at public tables and in public places of amusement."[101]

44

African Americans grew more vocal. In Mobile the editor of the *Nationalist*, the city's earliest black newspaper, wrote that the city's African Americans disagreed with a circular requesting that Mayor John Withers and John Forsyth, the editor of the Mobile *Advertiser and Register*, address the "colored citizens of Mobile on their rights and duties, etc." The editor suggested that "their appearance as speakers would be comparatively harmless, were it not that the letter is drawn so as to disparage those who have all along struggled to secure for the colored people their rights." The editor concluded that "when such men have abandoned their old doctrines, and joined the Republican party, it would be time enough to trust them." Besides, the editor reminded his readers of a similar meeting held at Columbia, South Carolina, when Wade Hampton, Confederate cavalry commander and later governor and US senator of the state, addressed a meeting of African Americans. Other noted rebels and two African American men, who were unaware of their freedom, also addressed the meeting. The editor warned that the conservative Montgomery *Advertiser* would view the event as evidence that African Americans would vote for their old masters and would telegraph accounts of the events to every other conservative newspaper in the country. The editor asked, "While Wade Hampton is our Forsyth, but who is our [William Beverly] Nash?" and warned its readers to be "careful of allowing old rebels to speak to the black populace."[102]

45

NEITHER CARPETBAGGERS NOR SCALAWAGS

Alabamians of varying political persuasions awaited the assemblage of the state's first Republican meeting. The convening of a Republican body was unprecedented in Alabama, and the list of invitees--African Americans and Northern and Southern whites--was unparalleled. The nation also watched as the 4 June date came even closer. They, with members of Congress, wanted to learn whether the Alabama Republican party would enhance the state's chances for readmission.

Summary

The Civil War produced many changes in Alabama. It ruined the state's economic and political systems and forced Alabama officials to treat African Americans as free people. Slavery had provided no model for the new relationship of African Americans and whites. After the war, African Americans wanted to test their freedom by leaving their antebellum residences and getting an education, and former slaveowners tried to maintain the status quo.

The National Republican party attempted to guide postwar affairs and decided that enfranchisement provided a practicable means of maintaining power in Alabama. Reconstruction in Alabama then was a chronicle of a three-way struggle--involving Southern whites, Northern whites, and African Americans--for control of political affairs.

Regions of Alabama

Alabama Department of Archives and History, Montgomery.

CHAPTER 2

REPUBLICAN COALITION AND DEMOCRATIC CHALLENGE

The end to the Civil War produced many changes in Alabama, and African Americans were the focal point of most of these changes. Both Northern and Southern whites sought to lead Alabama's newly freed African Americans. They no doubt considered the number involved and realized whoever controlled the African American vote controlled political affairs in Alabama. Of course, most African Americans assumed allegiance to the Republican party because of the role of Abraham Lincoln in issuing the Emancipation Proclamation. Therefore, many organizations ventured into Alabama after the war to entice African Americans into the Republican party and to control their votes. In contrast, Democrats maintained an ambivalent attitude toward African Americans, challenging the African American vote when they could not control it. Thus, Alabama Reconstruction emerged as a chronicle of the two dominant parties who battled for control of the African American vote and of

African Americans themselves as they tried to carve out a political legacy.

Black Suffrage and Economic Reprisals

First, the Reconstruction Act of 2 March 1867 enfranchised freedmen; second, by a supplementary act of 23 March, Congress authorized military commanders to enroll voters and to supervise an election for a constitutional convention for the following November. Throughout this time, the Union League of Alabama stood ready to help freedmen register and vote. That the League sought to make certain freedmen became loyal members of the Republican party was significant. In fact, the League played a leading role in the steadily increasing political activities of freedmen and the advancement of the Alabama Republican party.[1]

Early in its involvement in Alabama, the Union League began to influence Alabama's African Americans. As one of the earliest organizations to petition for African American suffrage and the disfranchisement of former Confederates, it came to Alabama in 1863 with the operation of the Freedmen's Bureau in north Alabama. Within a few months after the end of the war, its influence had spread rapidly to other parts of the state. Some Union League officials enticed freedmen into their fold by promising them a portion of the property of former slaveholders. League officials also relied on the attraction of their secret and mysterious rituals to persuade African Americans to join them. This way, the League's initiation process, during which League officials conducted rituals at night, was especially influential. League officials appealed to the patriotic sentiments of African Americans by stating that the purpose of the organization was to "preserve liberty, perpetuate the union [Federal Union], maintain the laws and the constitution, to secure the ascendancy of American institutions, to protect, defend, and strengthen all loyal men and members of the Union League of America in all rights of person and property, to demand the elevation of labor, to aid in the education of laboring men, and to teach the duties of American citizenship."[2]

The League easily molded many new African American union leagues. Building on various religious structures the antebellum South allowed and African American preachers perpetuated after the war, the League steadily and adroitly converted these informal gatherings into lodges or councils. For their part, as they joined, African Americans pledged "to defend and perpetuate freedom and the Union." Each took the solemn oath: "I pledge my life, my fortune, and my sacred honor. So help me God."[3] Among others, Mobile freemen rejoiced at the opportunity to affiliate with the League. They envisioned the organization as an agent for fair and equal wages and for justice when authorities charged them with petty offenses.[4]

Nevertheless, the enthusiasm of African American Union Leaguers in Perote, Alabama, caused much consternation in the Bullock County area. This was especially true of their assumption of civil authority and their later arrest of the African American sheriff and his deputy and innocent whites en masse. Some African American Union Leaguers went on to list crimes and punishments for the area and claimed to have the endorsement of General Swayne. African Americans who refused to join the League suffered physical reprisals from other African Americans. In some instances, African American women refused to perform domestic duties when their spouses declined to join the League.[5]

In sharp contrast, whites frequently used economic retaliation against African American League members. One white landlord in Henry County demanded that two of his African American laborers sign a statement pledging not to attach themselves to the Loyal League and not to attend any of its meetings without his consent. Whites who opposed the League made a mistake when, assuming African American laborers would deny affiliation, they issued a circular exclaiming they would not be deceived by a "nigger excuse" in which an African American laborer might charge that someone--undoubtedly a Northern white of Republican persuasion--had forced him to join the League. Such Whites considered the fact of League affiliation, when proven, as enough reason in itself, to "seek him out of [to remove the culprit from] your employment."[6]

Continued efforts by planters to control the Union League extended beyond economic reprisals against African Americans. These planters stereotyped all freedmen as League members or at least as persons under its influence. Many planters, if not most, also incorrectly assumed freedmen had to be under the League's influence whenever they appeared assertive. Naturally, then, such whites considered their authority threatened whenever and wherever African Americans either belonged to the League or became involved with politics.[7]

The fear of the Union League was vividly portrayed as military commanders began their selection of registrars. The congressional mandate divided Alabama into 45 registration districts and ordered military commanders to seek two white registrars and one African American registrar in each district. The result was that, since the Reconstruction Acts required each registrar to take an "iron-clad oath," in which as a man of good faith, he declared his intention to "support, protect, and defend the Constitution of the United States," more Northern whites than Southern whites came to serve as registrars.[8]

Across the state, Alabama freedmen quickly responded to the opportunities to become registrars by organizing themselves, calling meetings, and drafting resolutions. First, in Florence future constitutional convention delegate James Thomas Rapier assembled more than 150 freedmen at the Florence African Methodist Episcopal Church and helped to draft his foster father, John H. Rapier, Sr., to represent Lauderdale County as a registrar. The younger Rapier cautioned his audience to "proceed with calmness, moderation, and intelligence."[9]   Second, Lafayette Robinson, another convention delegate, led the movement to organize freedmen in Huntsville.   Third, future legislator William V. Turner led the efforts to organize freedmen in Wetumpka, Elmore County.   Fourth, James K. Greene, future Hale County lawmaker, urged fellow African Americans to register and to vote.   Fifth, in Mobile, African American minister Lawrence Berry told a crowd, "We are here tonight to tell the world that after being enfranchised, we are wise enough to know our rights, and we are going to claim those rights."[10] Sixth, at the same meeting, John Carraway, another future convention delegate and one of the state's most influential African American lawmakers, set the tone for future African American-white relations.   He exclaimed, "We can be good friends with white conservatives, but they have no right to control our political future."[11]

A paradox of the early stage of Congressional Reconstruction in Alabama became painfully clear when Unionists opposed the appointment of African American registrars with a vehemence equal to that of their peers from south Alabama.   Thus, Huntsville Unionist Joseph C. Bradley complained that the selection of African American registrars would impede the growth of the Republican party in areas of the state populated mainly by poor whites. Accordingly, he advocated the selection of only white registrars in north Alabama counties.   Bradley's position advanced the typecasting of the Union League as the controller of African American politics. The stereotype also suggested that the control of African Americans was outside the realm of Southern control. It became abundantly clear neither Unionists nor former Confederates cared for the idea of African American enfranchisement or for African American politicians. Yet, both groups considered it paramount that if African American enfranchisement became a reality, they should control its development.[12]

The search for registrars began in April 1867, when Major General John Pope assumed command of the Third Military District. These registrars were to enroll a new electorate who would then decide the desirability of convening a constitutional convention in November. Pope selected future Alabama governor William Hugh Smith as general supervisor of registration.[13]

Both the strong objection of whites in the area involved and the small African American population of some Alabama counties made it very difficult for Smith to find African Americans to appoint as registrars in these areas. To resolve this dilemma, Smith decided to appoint African Americans from more populated regions, such as Montgomery, to enroll voters in other areas with small concentrations of African Americans.[14]

Other problems, such as African Americans' fear of economic and physical reprisals, compounded Smith's selection of African American registrars. In addition, the quarrels between Republican factions, represented by Union League officials and Unionists,

54

added yet a third dimension to an already difficult task. For example, Huntsville Unionist Joseph C. Bradley advised John C. Keffer, Pennsylvania native and state president of the Union League, against the appointment of African American registrars, charging that white sentiment made such appointments impractical. Yet, on the same day, John B. Callis, subassistant commissioner of the Freedmen's Bureau in Huntsville and future congressman, appointed Henderson Hill as the African American registrar of Madison County.[15]

In response to the audacity of Callis for making such an unprecedented gesture, Bradley came up with his African American appointee, the Reverend Alfred Barnett, an elderly Methodist minister who Bradley claimed represented the wishes of African Americans from Madison County. One can argue that Callis accepted the selection of Hill because African Americans had chosen him by convention votes. Still, Hill's appointment made Republican factionalism widen even further, and it caused far more harm for the moment than Democratic opposition.[16]

Whites in the Tuscaloosa area found particularly distasteful the appointment of African American registrar George W. Cox, whom Smith had chosen to represent the county. Cox, who later represented Montgomery County in the legislature, advised Tuscaloosa's African American residents to register and then to vote for the convening of a constitutional convention. He warned them to be aware of false friends such as the Democrats. In opposition to the Cox appointment, one of the county's two white registrars resigned, and R. Blair, of the Tuscaloosa Office of Registration, wrote to Smith that "the appointment of Cox has done more to injure the 'cause of the Union' than any other in that county."[17]

Cox, too, was unhappy with his role in Tuscaloosa, especially with the passivity of Tuscaloosa's African Americans. Although he was a Tuscaloosa native, Cox, an antebellum blacksmith, wanted to return to his new home in Montgomery.[18] So Smith apparently sought to appease Tuscaloosa whites by replacing Cox with Albert Smith, only to be informed by Blair four days later that "Albert Smith cannot serve for want of funds to pay his expenses."[19]

The appointment of Alexander Webb, however, showed that white opposition to African American registrars could--and in some cases would--proceed beyond vocal opposition. Smith had appointed Webb as registrar for Blackbelt Hale and Sumter counties. Then, on 13 June, John C. Orrick, a Hale County store owner, shot and killed Webb after a heated argument on the streets of Greensboro. With a pistol still in his hand, Orrick walked up the street, where observers heard him say he would allow "no damn nigger to call him a liar."[20]

It was obvious that Orrick murdered Webb, yet local whites blandly denied Webb's political role was connected to his murder. Thus, when this murder was coupled with the Kelley "riot," the postelection disturbance that Congressman William D. "Pig Iron"

Kelley caused in Mobile, it seemed doubtful that African American political participation would become a reality. However, heartened by the assistance of the Union League and the Freedmen's Bureau, African Americans began to participate in the political affairs of the state over the bitterest opposition of some whites.[21]

As the state's earliest group of black public officials, African American registrars--one chosen for every two white registrars--helped to enroll 160,991 voters--72,748 whites and 88,243 African Americans--between 1 July and 20 August 1867. When the board of registrars met as a group and deleted the names of 405 African Americans they considered ineligible to vote, the African American majority of 15,495 decreased to 15,090, a slightly smaller majority; but, the board also added the names of 1,702 other whites to the list. General Pope then scheduled an election for 13 October 1867, when Alabama voters would pick delegates to the convention and, simultaneously, decide the desirability of holding a convention.[22]

Democrats Woo the Black Vote

In contrast to North Carolina, where Democrats did not seek African American voters, both parties in Alabama campaigned for the black vote in 1867. Joseph Hodgson, editor of the Montgomery *Mail*, John Forsyth, of the Mobile *Register*, and James Holt Clanton led the Democratic effort to woo the African American electorate. Both a lawyer and a former state legislator, Clanton was a veteran of both the Mexican and Civil wars. It was an ironic twist for former Confederates, such as Clanton, to court African American voters. Tragically, when these efforts failed, most Democrats turned on African Americans and claimed they were innately inferior. Hodgson contrived a more elaborate scheme: a plan to urge whites to register but not to vote. He suspected the convention would fail, because most voters would not have endorsed it.[23]

In any event, the election results were never in doubt as 90,283 voters--71,730 blacks and 18,853 whites--voted to hold the convention. Only a few whites--5,583--voted against holding the convention, since most of them listened to the urging of Democrats such as Clanton and boycotted the election. There is no account of the reason 18,620 African Americans refused to participate in the election. Perhaps a fear of economic or of physical reprisal accounted for their absence. However, because of the election results, 100 delegates--18 black and 79 white Republicans and three white Democrats--assembled in Montgomery on 5 November 1867.[24]

The Democrats, or Conservatives, who were largely a fragmented party as early as August 1866 but reorganized by July 1867, charged that Republicans had ruined state government as they sought to deny the "rightful" leaders of Alabama a place in government. Democrats also emphasized that Republicans insisted on African American enfranchisement when it was clear freedmen were unfit for such a role. Also, many Democrats charged that Republicans were attempting to divide the races by controlling the African American vote. In addition, most Democrats held Northerners responsible for the increase in the state's debt. The Unionists, noted the Democrats, only sought the spoils of war; they lacked concern for the welfare of their native state. Democrats in both Alabama and North Carolina claimed not only that the vast majority of African Americans were illiterate and poor, but they voted only as Union League officials and Freedmen's Bureau agents dictated. Democrats maintained that African Americans, Unionists, and Northern whites had caused state affairs to reach a low point.[25]

The Constitutional Convention of 1867

The gathering of delegates to the Constitutional Convention of 1867 in Montgomery was the first time Democrats and Republicans had assembled in Alabama. But more importantly, it was also the first meeting of African Americans and whites--Democrats or Republicans-- at the legislative table.

Background of African American Delegates

African American delegates assembled in Montgomery for the Constitutional Convention of 1867 comprised the state's earliest group of African American lawmakers. Yet, few of them were a part of the group that had assembled at the First Freedmen's Convention of 1865. That delegation was comprised largely of persons belonging to the ministry, one of the few professions whites entrusted to African Americans in the antebellum South. Thus, of the 56 delegates who had attended the First Freedmen's Convention, only Holland Thompson and William V. Turner continued to participate in the political arena. Surprisingly, most of the convention delegates also had not attended the Second Freedmen's Convention of 1867. Instead, most of the convention's black delegates were new to the political arena, and 11 of them enjoyed subsequent political careers as legislators or congressmen.

Nevertheless, an astoundingly large number of these delegates saw their careers end abruptly after they had served only one term in the House of Representatives. Three of the African American delegates enjoyed long political careers after they left the convention, but death ended the careers of four other delegates who might have survived politically had they lived longer. Astonishingly, of the 18 African American delegates, only Thomas Diggs of Barbour County served three terms in the House. Similarly, James K. Greene of Hale County was the only African American delegate who served for the duration of the period and one of just three African Americans to serve in both state houses. Then there was Bullock County's Benjamin F. Royal, who managed to serve three successive terms in the senate. Yet, Diggs, Greene, and Royal were the only African American delegates to serve after 1870. Also James Thomas Rapier of Lauderdale County was the only member of the body elected to Congress. Sadly, Benjamin Inge of Sumter County,

60

Columbus Jones of Madison County, Perry County's Thomas Lee, and Ovide Gregory of Mobile all died in 1869, before they could take their seats in the upcoming legislature, and though John Carraway of Mobile was elected to the House in 1868, he no longer participated in political affairs after 1870.[26]

The absence of an experienced core of lawmakers had a devastating impact on the effectiveness of the state's African American lawmakers, and this lack of experience helps to dismiss the accusation by Democrats of a "negro-dominated government."[27] The untimely deaths of experienced lawmakers, coupled with the inability of other African American delegates to win seats in the legislature, kept African Americans from developing a basic and experienced cadre of representatives during the 1870s.

Although most of the 18 delegates came from slave backgrounds, three of the 18 delegates had been emancipated before the war, and another three had been born free. James Thomas Rapier, of Florence in Lauderdale County, was one of two free-born African American delegates. He was the best educated of the African American delegates and had received a much better education than most of the white ones. Rapier had received his education in Canada, but he became a planter when he returned to Florence after the war.[28] Ovide Gregory, another free-born delegate, represented Mobile County. He spoke fluent French and Spanish and was the most cosmopolitan of the African American delegates, having traveled

61

widely in the United States and Latin America prior to the Civil War.[29] Peyton Finley of Montgomery, who already had served as doorkeeper at the House of Representatives, may have been free before the war.[30]

Three, or one-sixth, of the 18 African American delegates, had attained freedom before the dawn of the Civil War. One of these, John Carraway, was the son of a wealthy white planter and a slave mother. He received his freedom upon the death of his white father, traveled to the North, and became a tailor in New York. After the war, he journeyed to Alabama in search of his mother. He found her in Mobile and then decided to make the port city his home.[31] Perhaps two other delegates--Lafayette Robinson of Huntsville and J. Wright McLeod of Marengo County--had been freed before the war.[32] Although little is known about the antebellum years of McLeod, it is known that the legislature of 1830 authorized Lafayette Robinson's mulatto father to free him, his mother, and his sister. After the Constitutional Convention of 1867, Robinson left the political arena and returned to his position as cashier of the state's earliest Freedmen's Saving Bank in Huntsville. He had held this position since the establishment of the bank in December 1865.[33] Whatever the reason, of the six freed delegates at the convention, only three--mulattoes Gregory, Rapier, and Carraway-- spoke frequently.[34]

Although several of Alabama's African American delegates had enjoyed special privileges as slaves, few of them experienced significant economic advantages. Of these, Hale County delegate James K. Greene had served as a family coachman.[35] Another, Thomas Lee of Perry County, had worked as a carpenter on the Henry C. Lee plantation.[36] These occupations, especially carpentry, were the only sources of education, though vocational, for many slaves in the South. The reason was that plantation owners had obeyed Southern proscriptions against the formal education of slaves. Therefore, many slaves relied on these privileged occupations as sources of survival in postbellum Alabama, especially since antebellum society had prohibited compensatory manumission.[37] Despite the head start provided by such vocational efforts during slavery, most of Alabama's African American convention delegates did not enjoy any significant economic advantages in postbellum society, such as African Americans enjoyed in South Carolina.[38]

As contemporary observers may expect, most of the African American convention delegation came from the western Blackbelt counties and served for single terms in the House. For example, Benjamin Alexander of Eutaw represented Greene County.[39] Also, Simeon Brunson of Pickens County[40] and Thomas Lee of Perry County later served single terms in the legislature. Still, for reasons of their own, some delegates, such as Jordan Hatcher[41] and Henry Stokes,[42] both of Dallas County, and Washington Johnson[43] of Russell County, chose not to participate in political affairs after the close of the convention. Benjamin Inge,[44] Columbus Jones,[45] Ovide

63

Gregory, and Thomas Lee won seats in the first post-Civil War legislature, but all died before completing their terms. Lee County's Samuel Blandon served in the legislature of 1868 only.[46] Of the 18 convention delegates, former slaves James K. Greene, Thomas Diggs,[47] and Benjamin F. Royal[48] served for more than one term in the legislature. Royal was the state's first African American senator. Only Mississippi chose an African American United States senator during Reconstruction.[49]

Again, like their peers in South Carolina, most of the convention's African American delegates had been slaves before the war. But, some fundamental differences existed between the backgrounds of the African American lawmakers of South Carolina and Alabama. For one thing, the leadership cadre in South Carolina had been drawn largely from an antebellum African American middle class that included tradesmen, merchants, teachers, ministers, and small farmers. In comparison, Alabama's postbellum middle class had been drawn from a small and inconspicuous group; less than 1 percent of Alabama's African Americans had been free before the war. Thus, if the distance between rich and poor delegates was great in South Carolina, the distance in Alabama was even greater, for despite the proscriptions of slavery, some slaves in South Carolina had enjoyed greater opportunities than most slaves had known Alabama. The Brown Fellowship Society of South Carolina, for one example, had helped some slaves to purchase their freedom. Similar to the role of the Brown Fellowship Society, but to a considerably smaller degree, the Catholic Church in Louisiana and a metropolitan atmosphere, such as that provided by the City of New Orleans, helped to shield African Americans from the negative impact of slavery. In contrast, however, African Americans in Alabama could not rely on these advantages.[50]

Background of Unionist Delegates

Unionists comprised the second part of the Republican coalition at the convention. Mostly representative of north Alabama and divided into a moderate, an extremist, and a vacillating faction, the Unionists--later derogatorily called "scalawags"--could have controlled the convention had not factionalism developed within their ranks.[51] Prominent among the scalawags were Elisha Woolsey Peck, Arthur Bingham, Benjamin F. Saffold, Gustavus Horton, Henry Churchill Semple, and Joseph H. Speed. The latter two were among the 15 moderate Unionists present. The delegates chose Peck, an attorney, as their president. A native of Syracuse, New York, he had practiced law in Alabama since his arrival in 1824, first at Elyton for 14 years, and later at Tuscaloosa, a town of some importance during the antebellum years. Peck was a Whig who had opposed secession and later had ignored the Confederacy. A delegate to the Constitutional Convention of 1865, he was 68 years old when the delegates chose him president of the convention.[52]

65

NEITHER CARPETBAGGERS NOR SCALAWAGS

The convention was also the first meeting of Unionists and
Democrats.

Background of Northern Delegates

The Northern delegates, like their African American and Unionist
peers, represented diverse backgrounds and held different motives
for their affiliation with the Republican party. Prominent among
the Northerners at the convention were Charles Buckley, his brother
William M., and Andrew Applegate, all natives of New York; Charles
A. Miller, of Maine; Datus E. Coon, of Iowa; and Pennsylvanian John
C. Keffer, Union League state president and Peck's opponent for
the presidency of the convention. Several Northerners had served
with the Freedmen's Bureau. Of these, Samuel S. Gardner served as
chaplain of an African American regiment, and Charles Buckley
worked as superintendent of education for the Bureau in Montgomery.
Also, John Silsby, Benjamin Yordy, N. D. Stanwood, W. T. Blackford,
Pierce Burton, M. D. Brainard, Charles A. Miller, and Benjamin W.
Norris worked with the Bureau, thus laying the basis for the
assertion by Democrats that Bureau agents controlled the Republican
party.[53]

One Northerner whose profile countered the carpetbagger
stereotype was Samuel S. Gardner, Maine native and Bowdoin College
graduate. Gardner, rightly or wrongly, regarded the Republican
party as a vehicle for political and social change in the South.
Though he was idealistic and paternalistic, Gardner still embraced

66

the notion of African American enfranchisement.   Therefore, his views were at odds with most members of his party.[54]

Convention's Proceedings

As president of the convention, Peck appointed 16 committees: (1) preamble and bill of rights, (2) the legislative department, (3) the executive department, (4) the judicial department, (5) the elective franchise, (6) representation, (7) elections, (8) corporations, (9) county and (10) municipal organization, (11) the public debt, (12) education and (13) the school fund, (14) public state institutions, (15) the militia, and (16) the constitution. Geographically, Northerners received the chairmanships of nine of these committees--more than likely an attempt by Peck to placate the fears of his Northern friends.   Peck also named Southerners to the chairmanship of six committees, and although he selected no African American delegate as a committee chairman, Peck recognized African Americans by naming them to all but three of the committees.   He also appointed many African Americans to several positions of lesser importance, such as door keepers, secretaries, pages, and messengers.[55]

So, even before the convention began, it was abundantly clear the power of African Americans would be disproportionate to their numbers.[56]   The committee assignments and lesser positions notwithstanding, the largest question confronting these delegates was, how workable was the new Republican coalition of African Americans, Unionists, and Northerners? Would their diverse backgrounds and interests divide them? or would they subordinate personal interests and work for Republican unity? Seeking the answers, Alabama, the first of the Southern states to assemble a constitutional convention under the guidelines of Congressional Reconstruction, could not rely on precedent for instructions.

Thus, the state's historic second postwar constitutional convention began without any indication of trouble. There was the usual roll call and, likely, many political newcomers maneuvered about the convention chamber to acquaint themselves with their peers and to express routine amenities. So the congenial tone continued until the committee on the elective franchise offered its report. A committee of great importance, the franchise committee was composed of three Northerners, three Southern whites, and a lone African American. Committee members divided their report into three sections. The beginning section encouraged immigration and declared that every male citizen, 21 years of age or over, might become an enfranchised Alabama citizen by expressing his intention to become a citizen and by adhering to a residence requirement of only six months--reduced from the old one-year residence requirement. The second section invited dissent by disenfranchising many persons who had belonged to the Confederacy. It declared that officers in the Confederate government or those who had been convicted of treason, malfeasance in office, or crime, and any registered voter who refused to vote on the question of the ratification of the constitution when it was submitted, lost all voting privileges. The final section evoked great grumbling across the state. As expected, it required citizens to swear they never would oppose African American suffrage, they would accept the political and civil equality of African Americans and whites, and they would never use the legislative process to amend these resolutions. The resolution adopted by this committee helped to entrench the Republican party as a major power in Alabama politics.[57]

Michael Perman writes that African American Republicans were "unsympathetic to proscription."[58] To Richard Hume, "Negro delegates showed little interest in restricting ex-Confederates."[59] Thomas Lee, the lone African American member of the legislative committee, provided an excellent example of the sentiment of an Alabama African American toward proscription. Remarked Lee, "I have no desire to take away any rights of the white man; all I want is equal rights in the court house and equal rights when I go to vote. I think the time has come when charity and moderation should characterize the actions of all. Besides, the minority report is confined strictly to the Reconstruction measures of Congress, which measures define the powers and limit the action of this convention."[60]

69

NEITHER CARPETBAGGERS NOR SCALAWAGS

Inevitably, the minority report differed vastly from the majority report; it opposed the disfranchisement of Southern whites. This minority report gave every man the right to exercise the franchise and further warned the Federal government would refuse to readmit the state if the convention adopted the majority report.[61] Nevertheless, the minority report gained little support from other convention delegates. Convention President Peck favored the majority report and argued, "I believe the majority report while...not rigidly...confined to the letter of the Reconstruction Acts, is framed in the spirit and adheres to their [congressmen's] intent and purpose. The great object which ought to govern the convention is to keep the State out of the control of disloyal men."[62] Thus, tragically, the leniency exemplified by the members of the minority committee went unheeded, because the leadership of the convention showed more interest in punishing former Confederates than in trying to rehabilitate the state.

Proof of the intent of the committee was not hard to find. Albert Griffin, like other Northern Republicans, endorsed the majority report because he wanted to disfranchise the "incarnate fiends who had haunted Union men with blood hounds, who had whipped the wives and daughters and sisters of Union men, who had starved prisoners, and who had violated every moral principle, and acted like devils turned loose from hell."[63] Daniel H. Bingham wished to disfranchise "those merciless wretches who had ruined the country."[64] Other speeches by Northern Republicans also sought to destroy the Southern planter-class, whom they held responsible for the war.

Northern delegates also avoided a serious discussion of African American enfranchisement or African American civil rights in the absence of a congressional mandate. Therefore, these delegates made it clear that what was best for African Americans and what African Americans wanted would be of little importance to them. On the other hand, the position of Southern whites was no more noble, for they sought political supremacy as well. They, too, objected to African American suffrage, since to do so was in vogue. As a representative, Democrat James Howard Hurt based his opposition to African American suffrage on educational grounds. Thus, he offered the suffrage only to educated African Americans.[65] Nearly all Northern and Southern Republicans and Democrats opposed the political and the social equality of Alabama African Americans, and they maintained their positions throughout the convention, as they agreed not to push for any African American advancement beyond the scope of enfranchisement.

African American delegates readily recognized the importance of the report of the franchise committee and offered their reflections. Even so, it was remarkable that none of the African American delegates wanted disfranchisement to exceed the scope of the Reconstruction Acts. One African American delegate and future legislator, John Carraway, argued that he would not disfranchise any whites "except the editors and publishers of rebel presses, who have done more harm than fifty thousand men."[66] For his part, Rapier favored the disfranchisement of only those whites who were denied voting rights by the Reconstruction Acts.[67] These two delegates represented areas where a large contingent of antebellum free African Americans had lived and enjoyed greater freedom than their peers who had lived in the Blackbelt during the antebellum period. Perhaps such an explanation accounts for the leniency of these two delegates toward disfranchisement. Still, it is difficult to clarify why so many African Americans voted for the disfranchisement of whites as outlined in the majority report. The fact remains that when the time arrived to vote on the report of the franchise committee, African American delegates--without any exception--yielded to political pressure and voted for disfranchisement. As a result, the delegates approved the majority report by an overwhelmingly impressive vote of 59-26.[68]

Subsequent debates enabled African American delegates to discern the extent to which other members and factions of the party were willing to vote with them on issues not equally beneficial to all members of the party. Such an issue arose when debate began on an attempt to write into the bill of rights a guarantee of equal rights for African Americans on common carriers and public transportation. John C. Keffer, Alabama Union League president and chairman of the Republican state executive committee, proposed a section to the bill that made no distinction because of color for

72

those who traveled on public carriages. Then, John Carraway, seeking to add greater specificity to the bill, introduced a section that provided for equal access to railroads, steamboats, cars, and hotels, regardless of color. Carraway claimed that "at present the colored man cannot send his wife from one part of the state to another, because she will be placed in a smoking car and exposed to the insults of low and obscene white men. How can any friend of the colored man vote against breaking down such a monopoly?"[69]

Ovide Gregory, Carraway's African American colleague from Mobile, supported the amendment. Argued Gregory, "How can any delegate go home to his constituents, nineteenth-twentieth [sic] of whom are colored, after having voted against their enjoying their rights, in all respects, as white people [would]?"[70] Unionists, on the other hand, wanted a section added that guaranteed separate accommodations, since whites wanted them. Most Unionists, even those who previously had supported the disfranchisement amendment, shied away from any solidarity with African Americans on this point. They then opposed any attempt at all to award African Americans social equality. Montgomery delegate Henry Churchill Semple suggested that Southern men in the convention held no fear of meeting the issue head on. But, Northern Republicans, discerning the accuracy of Semple's admonition, left the defense of the issue to the black delegation. They sought to appease African

73

American delegates by promising to enact such legislation when the next legislature convened. However, these Northern Republicans had their reasons for postponing debate on the issue; by so acting they had also placated the fears of Southern Republicans, who stood prepared to bolt the party had the issue of social integration passed. Thus, the volatile and disappointing debate on the issue of public transportation clearly revealed the fragility of the Republican coalition.[71]

The Constitutional Convention of 1867 was the initial occasion in which the aggregate population in Alabama had been represented, and the Blackbelt possessed a greater voting strength because of the so-recent enfranchisement of African Americans. Yet, this African American voting strength, translated into delegates, merely widened the rift in the Republican coalition, for the measures advanced by African American delegates were at considerable variance with the interests of white Republicans who, African American delegates learned to their regret, were willing to form alliances with Democrats rather than advance legislation of benefit to African Americans.[72]

When the convention decided to proscribe interracial marriage, another impasse developed within the Republican coalition. On this issue Southern Republican Henry Churchill Semple of Montgomery wanted the legislature to enact a law to forbid miscegenation to the fourth generation and to provide penalties for such marriages. Again the delegation from Mobile opposed Semple's resolution.

Accordingly, Carraway amended Semple's amendment and proposed that a white man should receive life imprisonment if he married or cohabitated with an African American woman. Ovide Gregory held another view. He wanted a law to compel a white man to marry an African American woman if authorities found them living together. Each of these amendments provoked considerable discussion, especially from Southern Republicans who considered miscegenation a threat to their way of life. For their part, Northern Republicans again sensed the intensity of the issue, but instead of procrastinating, as they had done on the common carrier issue, they decided to minimize the importance of the issue with the statement that intermarriage did not seem a real possibility in Alabama. Therefore, the convention agreed by a revealing vote of 58-22 that to write a statement on intermarriage into the constitution was unnecessary.[73]

The Alabama constitution, similar to ones passed in Florida and Mississippi, was not a radical one, but it departed from earlier versions in several significant areas. For one, in many ways both black and white Alabamians, not just white Alabamians, became the new source of political power. For another, the governor's authority to pardon was now limited. For a third, the electorate now voted for all executive officers, including secretary of state, treasurer, auditor, and attorney general. For a fourth, the new constitution also provided for a lieutenant governor--an officer who would preside over the Senate and cast his vote to break a tie. For a fifth, the electorate determined who occupied judicial positions.[74] These changes democratized the state's political process.

In creating a free system of public education and a State Board of Education, however, the Constitutional Convention of 1867 produced the most profound change in the state's educational process. Alabama had been moving slowly toward a system of public education since 1854, when the legislature initially provided for public education. Though the war curtailed much of that impetus, the convention made public education a reality when it allocated the initial funding for the board, making it possible to begin fundamental changes in the educational process.[75] Charged with the management of public education, the Board of Education was to receive one-fifth of the annual revenue of the state, including income derived from the tax on industrial and commercial corporations and the exclusive use of a state poll tax of $1.50. The state also was directed to use for educational purposes the revenue derived from all Federal lands. The new constitution further required the governor to sign guidelines passed by the board, but if he failed to do so, a two-thirds vote of the legislature could override his veto. Most of the changes in education bore a striking resemblance to similar educational provisions in the constitutions of Michigan, Indiana, Ohio, and Iowa.[76]

The administrative style of the new board and its average annual allocation of $261,839 for education drew the wrath of Democrats, who emphasized the cost of education and higher taxes and their effect on race relations during the 1874 election campaign. Democrats and other Southern whites opposed African American education because, as historian Walter Lynwood Fleming observes, they found particularly objectionable such history texts as *Freedmen's Readers* and *Freedmen's Histories*. They claimed these books gave African Americans a Northern view of Southern history. Democrats also placed much of the blame for the tone and theme of Southern education at the doorsteps of the Freedmen's Bureau. They preferred Southern white teachers for Alabama's schools, since these teachers would give a view of history favorable to Democrats. They also held a dislike for the "free" schools of Alabama, because they disagreed with spending public monies for education. Accordingly, they found pleasure in the election of fellow Democrat Joseph Hodgson as superintendent of public instruction in 1870. Hodgson replaced Southern white Republican Noah B. Cloud, who lost his bid for reelection. Democrats publicized widely the corruptions and needless expenditures Hodgson claimed to find in the operation of the Board of Education, and they emphasized these charges until they succeeded in overthrowing Republicans in 1874.[77]

In any event, since no public schools existed for African Americans in antebellum Alabama, the convention left an indelible

77

mark on public education with its provision for "one or more schools" in each district. Still, race became an inevitable and important issue in the arrangement of Alabama schools when Republicans sought to include a provision in the constitution for separate schools for black and white students. On this issue Joseph H. Speed of Montgomery suggested white students would not attend school with black students; therefore, it would be impractical to demand that they attend the same school. Albert Griffin, a white Republican of Mobile, reminded Speed that since black and white students played together on the streets of Montgomery, he saw little reason for segregated schools. Carraway maintained that if schools were separate, the bill should provide for an equitable division of school funds between the black and white school in each school district. In the end, neither black nor white Republicans pushed for integrated schools; they merely voted against segregated schools. Thus, they "allowed" the Board of Education to determine school segregation matters.[78] The convention also left to subsequent legislative bodies the task of deciding the nature and kind of funding for black and white schools.[79]

The Convention Adjourns

When the convention adjourned on 6 December, many legislative changes had occurred in Alabama. The convention had proscribed imprisonment for nonpayment of debts and the seizure of property for indebtedness. The delegates enlarged the rights of women with

78

a provision that a married woman's real and personal properties remained in her domain and did not become the common property of her husband. However, beyond the citizenship, suffrage, and education provisions, the convention did little specifically for African Americans. Southern Republicans also saw little reason for celebration, for a narrow interpretation of the disfranchisement provision of the Reconstruction Acts now limited their own continued political participation. White Republicans who had worked fervently to disfranchise white Democrats found themselves disfranchised.[80]

The convention delegates had revealed something even more devastating to Alabama Republicans than the disfranchisement of some Unionists. Too frequently race issues seemed to tear the party asunder. Although they continued as members of the National Republican party, white Alabama Republicans maintained their prewar social attitudes and stood prepared to leave the party rather than allow for social equality. In other words, they subordinated party interests to racial considerations. This meant that in Alabama Republicans were divided between Blackbelt and north Alabama factions, and the two wings vied constantly for party dominance. The result was that factionalism undermined party unity more than Democratic opposition ever could have done. Despite this Republican divisiveness, African American delegates had performed superbly during the constitutional proceedings. Their performance

79

was especially impressive considering their prewar status. Yet, those who spoke most frequently--Carraway, Gregory, and Rapier-- were not natives of the Blackbelt region; instead, Carraway and Gregory lived in Mobile, and Rapier lived in the Tennessee Valley. Although these were the areas where the impact of slavery had been less severe than in the Blackbelt--where most of the state's slave population lived during the antebellum period--they spawned the most vocal African American delegates.

The acrimony that characterized Republican politics after the close of the convention on 6 December began even before Peck sounded the gavel to adjourn. Scalawag James P. Stow disagreed with certain sections of the constitution, and his colleague Henry Churchill Semple of Montgomery argued that the evils of the constitution were greater than any evil the state had ever confronted. Both men concurred that the proposed document proceeded beyond the guidelines of the Reconstruction Acts.[81]

Adoption of the Constitution

Some of the protesting delegates joined the Democratic or Conservative party, largely a fragmented party, in opposing the adoption of the constitution. By standing in clear opposition to the constitution, however, Democrats gained renewed vigor. Realizing that the votes of most of those who registered were required for the constitution to gain approval, James Holt Clanton accepted leadership of the Democratic party and promptly urged voters to boycott the polls in February. Several journalists joined Clanton to defeat the constitution. John Forsyth, editor of the Mobile *Register*, William Wallace Screws of the Montgomery *Advertiser*, Robert McKee of the Selma *Messenger*, Joseph Hodgson's Montgomery *Mail*, Ryland Randolph's Tuscaloosa *Monitor*, and Henry St. Paul of the Mobile *Times* issued broadsides in opposition to the adoption of the constitution. Former provisional governor Lewis E. Parsons; industrialist Daniel Pratt; J. L. M. Curry, educator and politician; and former State Senator Benjamin Fitzpatrick joined the strong opposition to the adoption of the constitution.[82]

Conservatives believed the constitution failed to separate blacks and whites on common carriers and that it did not proscribe interracial marriages. Most important, they opposed the constitution because of its provisions for African American enfranchisement and public education. Allowing African Americans to vote, they claimed, would lead to miscegenation, social equality, and, foremost, African American supremacy. Conservatives further charged that because of the free system of public education, Alabama's citizenry would face additional and needless taxation. This was a telling argument indeed. The ominous impact of additional taxes on people already poverty-stricken was sufficient to send icy shivers through the body of every citizen. Democrats heightened the people's anxiety by charging the new taxes would cost as much as $2 million annually.[83]

81

NEITHER CARPETBAGGERS NOR SCALAWAGS

In vigorous response, Republicans relied on agencies such as the Freedmen's Bureau, the Union League, and most of the press to rally for the constitution. Republicans also spoke often at rallies in areas with large concentrations of African American voters; these sections included the Blackbelt and the Huntsville area. As a ruse to encourage a large turnout at the polls, they even raised the possibility of reenslavement if voters did not ratify the constitution. Their appeal to the poor man and the working man was broadcast in a long list of newspapers at their disposal. Foremost among these were Albert Griffin's Mobile *Nationalist*, John Hardy's Montgomery *Daily State Sentinel*, and William Bibb Figures' Huntsville *Advocate*. Republicans made certain their broadsides were disseminated across the state. These broadsides functioned as the official voice of the state government.[84]

Although the Huntsville *Advocate* wavered in its support of the constitution, the Montgomery *Daily State Sentinel* revealed a deep and sincere interest in the future of the Republican party, especially in the adoption of the constitution and the welfare of African Americans. The Montgomery *Daily State Sentinel* advertised the following catechism:

Do you want Alabama in the Union?
Vote for the Constitution!
Do you want a loyal good government, to protect life,
liberty and property?
Vote for the Constitution!
Do you want the return of peace, order, and prosperity?
Vote for the Constitution!
Do you want railroads built and manufactories erected?
Vote for the Constitution!

Do you want your children educated?
Vote for the Constitution!
Do you want time on your old ante-war and war debts?
Vote for the Constitution!
Do your want the speedy development of all the resources of
the state?
Vote for the Constitution!
Do your want capital to come into the State and money in freer
circulation?
Vote for the Constitution!
Do you want immigration to buy your land and cultivate the
soil properly?
Vote for the Constitution![85]

The day of the election began as strangely as the election would
proceed. The ratification of the constitution began on 4 February
1868, a cold day--one on which a rainstorm swelled rivers and made
travel difficult. In response, General George Meade, who had
replaced General Pope on 28 December 1867, added another day to the
four-day election. Concerned Democrats mused that the election was
the longest one in state history. Besides the weather, the
election held a strange twist: According to the Second
Reconstruction Act, a majority of the 170,631 registered voters--or
85,000--were required for the adoption of the constitution.
Knowing this, Clanton and the Democrats realized how easily they
could defeat the constitution.[86]

When the election had ground to a close, 70,812, had voted for
adoption of the constitution. Only 1,005 voters had opposed the
constitution. Democrats immediately claimed victory, since most of
those registered did not participate in the election.[87] Each side
then charged the other with fraud. For their part, Democrats

assailed Republicans for driving African American voters to the polls by the thousands. Democrats Parsons and Forsyth even traveled to Washington to protect their interest. Republicans, in turn, charged Democrats had used threats of violence to keep African Americans from the polling places.[88]

General Meade investigated the charges of both sides and declared the election free of irregularities. However, his report to Congress also advised that body to reassemble the convention so Alabamians could vote again on the desirability of the constitution. Offsetting this, John Hardy of the *Daily State Sentinel* already had assured his readers Alabama would have been readmitted to the Union if the impeachment trial of President Andrew Johnson had not preoccupied Congress.[89]

Key members of Congress vehemently disagreed with Alabama's Democrats. Under the direction of a vigilant Thaddeus Stevens, the United States House of Representatives approved the Fourth Reconstruction Act, which confirmed the results of the voting majority, and the Senate prepared itself to discuss the readmission bill. Meanwhile, William D. "Pig Iron" Kelley, Steven's colleague in the House, worked for the readmission of Alabama so he could prosper from his investments in iron manufacturing in Alabama. Other reports suggested the Republican party sought an early readmission, since the state's votes were essential in the November election, and Alabama's additional votes were needed to remove President Johnson. Thus, the Fourth Reconstruction Act, passed by

Congress on 11 March 1868, reversed the Democrats' victory. Congress accepted the results of the election because most of those who voted had signalled their approval.[90]

Ohio Senator John Sherman also helped to lead the fight for the readmission of Alabama because, among other reasons, the national party needed the state's electoral votes in the November election. In pushing for Alabama's readmission, he laid the foundation for another charge Democrats used to discredit Republicans in the 1874 election: that National Republicans had forced a constitution upon the people of Alabama. In any event, the Alabama readmission bill passed the Senate in June 1868, and Alabama was readmitted when its legislature ratified the Fourteenth Amendment.[91]

An era had passed in Alabama history and the history of the South--Presidential and Military Reconstruction had ended. General Orders 101, issued by Major General George Meade, mandated "that all civil officers, holding office in the state, whether by military appointment or by failure to have successors qualified, shall promptly yield their offices and turn over to their properly elected and qualified successors, all public property, archives, books, records,&C, belonging to the same."[92] A civil government again ruled the state, although some citizens claimed to prefer a combination of military rule in contrast to the civil government of the Republican party.[93]

Intraparty Factionalism

During the fight for adoption of the constitution, serious divisions had developed within the ranks of the Republican party. Not only did one-third of its members object to the constitution, but--and most alarming to the party--its African American members had seen the party's leadership overlook them as it nominated chairmanships at the constitutional convention. Therefore, they then became much more assertive, openly seeking a more conspicuous role in party affairs. White Republicans did little to help the cause of intraparty unity when they met to nominate the state ticket but didn't nominate any African Americans.[94]

Rapier assailed this all-white ticket, especially the nomination of William Hugh Smith, former supervisor of registration, for governor. Labeling Smith as conservative on the race issue, Rapier preferred Robert M. Patton as the party's gubernatorial nominee. He was even ready to withdraw entirely from the party--much as the Southern Republicans had threatened to do during the convention debates--unless the party changed the slate. Yet, when the slate remained unchanged, Rapier did not resign; so, the volatile relationship between Rapier and Smith continued unabated and later played a fundamental part in future Republican factionalism.[95]

Rapier was far from being the only African American Republican who threatened to leave the party. Caesar Shorter, a former valet of Alabama's wartime governor John Gill Shorter, withdrew and, with Levi Floyd, formed the nucleus for the African American Democratic party of Alabama. Shorter never did return to the Republican party. Another leading African American, future legislator and congressman Jeremiah Haralson of Dallas County refused to support the constitution and supported candidates Horatio Seymour and Francis P. Blair in the 1868 United States presidential campaign.[96]

Summary

As Alabama voters showed their attitudes toward the ratification of the constitution, they concurrently chose state government officials. They picked William Hugh Smith as the state's first Republican governor. Smith said he wanted to place principles above party, and if he could not do much good, at least he would try to prevent much evil.[97] Still, the most dramatic aspect of the 1868 election was not Smith's election. However unaccustomed Alabamians were to a Republican governor, they were even less prepared to receive or accept the 27 African Americans who had won seats in the state house and the one who had been elevated to the state senate. These 28 maligned members of the General Assembly have been the center of much historical attention. Some of this attention has come from careful research, but much of the criticism has blossomed because of partisan politics and racial preference. So it is entirely proper to ask, "Who were these much-maligned men?"

Alabama Constitutional Convention, 1867
Alabama Department of Archives and History, Montgomery

James Thomas Rapier
Springarn Collection, Howard University Washington, D.C.

William Hugh Smith
Alabama Department of Archives and History, Montgomery

CHAPTER 3

SOCIAL ORIGINS OF BLACK OFFICEHOLDERS

Altogether, between 1867 and 1884, 108 African Americans represented Alabama as lawmakers. A large majority of these emergent officeholders had been slaves in antebellum Alabama. After all, free African Americans in Alabama totaled only 2,360 at the close of the war, or less than 1 percent (.005) of the 439,000 slaves emancipated by the war. Compare this to the 5.3 percent for Louisiana, the 2.4 percent for South Carolina, and the 0.8 percent for Georgia. Also, as a class, antebellum free African Americans in Alabama seldom came into contact with their slave brothers. The main reason for this was geographical, since most of the state's free African American population lived either in the Tennessee Valley area of north Alabama or in the coastal area of Mobile, although a sizeable number of free African Americans also lived in the Tuscaloosa area.[1]

Free Blacks

The number of free African Americans in Alabama increased steadily during the decades from 1820 to 1860. However, the rate of increase throughout the South declined after 1830 because of the restrictive legislation enacted after the Nat Turner revolt of 1831. In Alabama the legislature responded by passing the Anti-Immigration Act of 1832. This act, approved on 16 January 1832, stipulated "that from and after the first day of January next, it shall not be lawful for any free person of color to settle within the limits of this State,...they shall, on notice of this act, depart within thirty days, or shall be liable, on conviction, before any justice of the peace, to receive thirty-nine lashes."[2]

The legislature occasionally set aside the Anti-Immigration Act, although there was no general nullification of the law. Of a total of 2,265 free African Americans who lived in Alabama by 1850, 589, or 26 percent, were born in other states. In startling contrast New Orleans was home to 10,939 free African Americans before the war. But, the number of free African Americans in Alabama continued to increase. Such growth, though slow, indicated that "in spite of legal strictures, the free black man was making a place for himself in an order that, apparently, was dedicated to his eradication as an element within that order."[3]

Only three, or possibly four, of the Reconstruction era African American legislators had been free-born. Peyton Finley, a Montgomery County delegate to the Constitutional Convention of 1867, may have been one such person.[4] Future legislator Shandy W. Jones was one of 132 free African American residents of Tuscaloosa in 1850. Having violated an antebellum law designed for free African Americans, Jones came to the attention of civil authorities when he allowed whites to use a room over his barber shop for gambling purposes.[5]

Ovide Gregory, another free-born African American future legislator, was a descendent of the French and Spaniards of the Mobile area. Gregory was known as a Creole.[6] Under the treaties between France and Spain in 1813 and with the United States in 1819, Creoles came into possession of the rights, privileges, and immunities of citizens of the United States.[7] Moreover, Mobile was the home of the state's largest contingent of free African Americans. By 1850, 1,195, or 52 percent, of the state's total free African American population lived in the County of Mobile, and 817 free African Americans lived in the city.[8]

James Thomas Rapier, of Florence, Lauderdale County, was the best-known member of the state's African American delegation. Although situated outside the state's Blackbelt, Lauderdale was one of two Tennessee Valley counties with a sizeable African American populace, both slave and free. Free African Americans drifted toward Florence because there they could pursue occupations other than farming, such as manufacturing and the trades. Free African Americans who lived in other parts of Lauderdale County and the Tennessee Valley engaged mainly in agricultural pursuits. By 1850, 148 of the state's 2,265 free African Americans in the state engaged in agriculture. The remainder of the state's free African Americans worked as carpenters, blacksmiths, barbers, brick masons, shoemakers, cigar makers, shopkeepers, mechanics, painters, and plasterers.[9] Situated close to the State of Tennessee, the Tennessee Valley area more closely identified with its Northern neighbor than with the lower part of Alabama. Many antislavery societies existed in the Tennessee Valley during the antebellum days. James G. Birney, founder and leader of the Liberty party, lived in Huntsville, where he served as mayor for two terms before he departed for Tennessee.[10]

Born in Florence on 13 November 1837, Rapier was the son of Richard Rapier, a white slaveowner who exhibited unusual care for his African American children. John H. Rapier, Sr., his foster father, was freed by an act of the legislature in 1829. The Supreme Court of Alabama ruled that slave children assumed the status of the mother. Thus, because Rapier's mother was free, he was born a free person.[11]

In any event, Richard Rapier provided private tutors for his three mulatto children. Because antebellum law prescribed a penalty for the education of mulatto or African American children, the senior Rapier sent his children to the North to receive an education when the boys reached school age. Therefore, James Thomas Rapier traveled to Canada in 1857 to study at Montreal College and, later, he studied at the University of Glasgow, in Scotland. In both places, because Rapier was a determined student, he frequently studied from 16 to 18 hours a day. The lifetime effect of his study habits were apparent; years after he had completed his studies, his concern for education had not abated. He wrote to George L. White

94

of Fisk University to ask about the status of Thomas, his younger brother: "I wrote to him that I wanted him [Thomas] to remain in school. I am inclined to think he may have gone home without my knowledge. Will send money to pay tuition if Thomas was still at [the] University."[12.]

In one respect, Alabama law was progressive. It provided for manumission through popular subscription. This method allowed local whites to pay the owner for a servant with the understanding that the owner would free the bondsman after purchase. However, none of Alabama's African American legislators received their freedom through such means. The state also provided for manumission because of meritorious service to the state or to the community in which a slave lived.[13]

Manumitted African Americans

Among manumitted African Americans, Horace King, of Russell County, was an outstanding example. The legislature emancipated King largely because of his service to Phenix City, Alabama, and to Columbus, Georgia. He served both cities, working tirelessly as bridge and home builder. Born in the Cheraw District of South Carolina in 1807 to a dying Edmund King, a slave, Horace King and his slave mother soon became the property of John Godwin, who then sent him to the North to receive an education. King's father was a Catawba Indian. Anyhow, when Godwin answered an invitation to build bridges in Alabama in 1832, he brought a well-educated King with him as his foreman.[14]

It was Alabama's good fortune that Godwin decided to do this, because even before coming to Alabama, King's bridges already spanned the Pee Dee River in South Carolina. Upon arriving in Alabama in 1832, King immediately began both to build sturdy bridges and to make a reputation as an outstanding citizen. In his first year in the state, he constructed the Dillingham Street bridge, linking Phenix City and Columbus, Georgia. Between 1832 and 1848 he constructed homes in the Girard section of Phenix City. Working steadily in the approximately 30 years between 1832 and the beginning of the Civil War, he saw his bridges spanning the Chattahoochee River as far south as Eufaula and as far north as Lafayette. King also constructed roads in western Georgia and eastern Alabama before the outbreak of hostilities. In addition, in 1840 he restored the courthouse in Muscogee County, Columbus, Georgia, after a fire had destroyed the structure during the previous year.[15]

As time passed, misfortune dogged Godwin's steps so that by 1846 he had lost nearly all his earnings. He decided to emancipate King instead of selling him to honor debts. His action stemmed from the unusual bond of friendship that had developed between them. Godwin's seniority of nine years undoubtedly made this easier.[16] Later that year, the General Assembly issued Act No. 292, which freed King. The act read:

96

An act to emancipate Horace King. That the said Horace King is hereby declared to be free and his emancipation is hereby confirmed, and the said Horace King shall not be required to leave the State of Alabama upon the condition that the said John Godwin, Ann H. Godwin, and William C. Wright, or any one of them, shall enter into bond with approved security to the Judge of the County Court of Russell, in the sum of one thousand dollars, conditioned that the said Horace King shall never become a charge to this State or any county or town therein. Approved 2nd February 1846.[17]

Despite the amicable relationship between King and Godwin, the legislature refused to compromise on the security bond. It considered a compromise already had been made when it allowed King, now a free man, to remain in Alabama. As a manumitted slave, King's life was an excellent example of productivity and good citizenship. He used his wealth to enhance his chances of upward mobility. King enjoyed complete freedom of movement as he traveled to other parts of the state. Besides, he earned the distinction of being the only African American future lawmaker who received his freedom while residing in Alabama. In addition, he was the only African American future lawmaker--free-born or emancipated--who owned slaves.[18]

Despite the decrease in the number of manumissions in other states after the Nat Turner revolt of 1831, the Alabama legislature continued to emancipate slaves. For example, in 1827 it freed 15 slaves; in 1828, 42; and in 1829, 58. Mulatto John Robinson, of Huntsville, was freed by legislative decree in 1828. By 1830 Robinson was one of the 22 African American heads of household in Madison County. Nine of these heads held a total of

15 slaves. Robinson headed a family of seven and owned four slaves. Three of his slaves were members of his family. Finally, in 1830, the legislature authorized Robinson to set free his wife Ann and her two children, Lelia Ann and Lafayette. Much later, the same Lafayette Robinson served as a delegate to the Constitutional Convention of 1867.[19]

Another manumitted slave, John Dozier, a Virginia native, received instruction in reading. His owner, the president of a college in Virginia, manumitted him soon after that. Nonetheless, the same owner also sold Dozier's wife and sons to a plantation owner in Alabama. After this latter act, Dozier moved to Alabama in search of his family and found them in Perry County. He read Greek even as a slave, something his owner probably taught him while he was a bondsman. Born in 1800 Dozier was the oldest member of the African American delegation upon assumption of office. Also an antebellum minister, Dozier died at the age of 92.[20]

Slaves also could receive their freedom through the bequest of a will. One such person, John Carraway, received his freedom as part of the will of his deceased owner. Born in Newbern, North Carolina, in 1834, Carraway, with his mother and two sisters, was emancipated upon the death of Charles Carraway, his wealthy white father. The same father, in an unusual act of kindness, also had willed to them a portion of his property. However, whether in shock at Charles Carraway's "gift," loss of estate, peer or social pressure, or greed, the white members of the Carraway family, to

98

deny the African American Carraways their inheritance, seized upon a loophole in the will and dissociated themselves from the African American members of the Carraway family. They also separated the African American Carraway family by selling the mother to slavers in Alabama. To confuse matters further, for reasons that are unclear, the white Carraways freed John and his sisters, although they forced them to leave the state without compensation. They had to leave because state law required emancipated slaves to leave the state. Sometimes whites allowed emancipated slaves to remain in the state if they revealed evidence of self-support. The white Carraways chose not to do this for John and his sisters.[21]

Years later, John Carraway stated that his white relatives sold his mother and forced the remainder of his family to leave the state to lay sole claim to their father's inheritance. In any event, whereas the Carraway sisters have disappeared from historical accounts, John traveled to Brooklyn, New York, where he married and later engaged in the tailoring trade. Then, because of the prejudicial reaction of even his Northern white peers, he was forced to leave New York. At this point, he decided to become a sailor.[22]

Future legislator Alexander H. Curtis was the only African American legislator to receive his freedom through self-purchase. Born in Raleigh, North Carolina, on 29 December 1829, Curtis worked there as a waiter in the store of Stockton and Hunt for many years. Because of his frugality, finally, in 1859, drawing on money he had saved, Curtis paid Mrs. E. Haygood, his owner, $2,000 for his freedom. During the same year he, like Carraway, traveled to New York and was emancipated.[23]

Quasi-Free Blacks

However each achieved it, four of the state's black legislators were quasi-free before 1865. The remainder had been slaves until that year, although some of them functioned in privileged capacities. One such person was Thomas Walker, of Dallas County. Walker's father and owner was Samuel M. Hill, an aristocrat whose wealth included several thousand acres of land and nearly a half million dollars in cash. Early on Hill recognized the unusual talents of Walker, so he allowed Walker to serve in a domestic capacity. Thus, Walker did not "mix with the common herd of slaves and was not exposed to the semi-tropical sun as a field hand in the cotton field." Instead, he shrewdly used his elevated position of house servant to acquire many business talents--talents that were to benefit him greatly in postbellum Alabama. His privileged position also allowed him the opportunity to acquaint himself with various members of the Alabama aristocracy. Fortunately for him, Walker knew very little of slavery, for at the age of 15, he saw the Civil War come to a close in Alabama.[24]

Like Walker, Benjamin S.(terling) Turner, also of Dallas County, occupied a privileged position as a slave. Born in March 1825 in Halifax County, North Carolina, Turner was the property of

100

Elizabeth Turner, a widow, who moved to the Southern part of Dallas County when Turner was five. He worked for her until he reached the age of 20, when she sold him to pay off debts. Advantageously for him, Elizabeth Turner sold Turner to Major W. H. Gee, her step-daughter's husband. The Gee family had recently removed from Huntsville to Selma. His new owners placed him in charge of the Gee House Hotel, the Gee family's new business enterprise. Later, upon the death of both of the Gees, Turner became the property of Dr James T. Gee, the brother of W. H. Gee. James T. Gee also operated one of the city's largest hotels and allowed Turner to hire out his time. Thus, Turner operated a livery stable and amassed more than $10,000 worth of property before the war ended.[25]

Thanks to the assistance of his owner's children, Turner learned to read and to write. These children taught him to repeat the letters of the alphabet, but much time elapsed before he recognized the difference between a name and a printed character. He recalled later that he "was mostly educated by reading the New York *Herald*," though occasionally he read the New York *Tribune*, too.[26]

His traits of perseverance, inquisitiveness, diligence, loyalty, and attentiveness enhanced his livery stable business dealings. They were shown further when, after General James H. Wilson's raiders had destroyed much of his property and left him penniless by the close of the war, he doggedly climbed out of economic ruin. By 1870 his resilience had paid such huge dividends that he had reacquired significant property holdings.[27]

NEITHER CARPETBAGGERS NOR SCALAWAGS

Until the beginning of the war Elijah Cook of Montgomery County, another more privileged African American, hired out his time for $25 a month. Born in 1833 as the slave of Dr Algernon Cook, of Wetumpka, Elmore County, he soon became the property of a Mr Stringert, who later sold him at auction to the business firm of Reeves and Battle, apparently a slave-trading organization. After the death of George Reeves, Cook's ownership passed to William H. Reeves, who employed him as a buggy boy. Cook then requested and later received permission to learn carpentry. His new owner placed Cook under the apprenticeship of Montgomery attorney J. T. Jackson. After an apprenticeship of four years, he hired out his time and paid Reeves monthly. Then, when Reeves died as hostilities began, Cook showed his loyalty and honesty by continuing to honor the agreement, paying the full allotment regularly to Reeves' widow. When the war ended, although he was penniless, he had the satisfaction of knowing how his trade would provide for himself, his wife, and his two children.[28]

Field Hands

Most of Alabama's African American legislators had toiled as field hands during the antebellum period. They bore the brunt of slave laws and suffered tremendously because of the absence of legal protection or a religious sanctuary. If few opportunities existed for free African Americans, fewer opportunities were available for slaves. Yet, some slaves managed to acquire skill as artisans,

102

both on plantations and in urban settings. Vocational education for African Americans had begun during slavery, as many plantation owners with foresight helped their slaves to become skilled in carpentry, bricklaying, blacksmithing, and other similar fields. For example, in Sumter County a physically infirm George Houston operated a tailor shop for whites from 1846 to 1860. His owner allowed him to learn this trade, because he considered manual labor too demanding for Houston.[29] Other slaves also acquired skills. Perry countian Thomas Lee, who lived on the Henry C. Lee plantation, learned carpentry.[30]

Not being fortunate enough to learn a trade, John William Jones, who also answered to the name of John William Coleman, succeeded economically after the war. Born as a slave in North Carolina in 1842, Jones came to Alabama as a youth. Although the source of his income is uncertain, after the war he purchased a large plantation and operated a race track and a general store in Hayneville, Lowndes County. Being adept at acquiring property, by 1886 he had built a large hall in Montgomery for society use. He called the large immaculate structure Centennial Hall. He purchased much of his property in the High and Jackson streets area of Montgomery. Whether his wealth or his business acumen led him there, Jones was one of six African Americans who served in the State Senate.[31]

Like Jones, Holland Thompson of Montgomery was emancipated because of the war. He was an Alabama native, but his parents had migrated from South Carolina with William H. Taylor, their owner,

103

who became a wealthy planter in Montgomery. Thompson was born around 1840, and by the close of the war, he was working as a waiter at the Madison House hotel in Montgomery. He relied on his position as a waiter to learn to read and to write. By August 1865 Thompson had legalized his marriage to Binah Yancey, a slave of secessionist leader William Lowndes Yancey. One writer describes Thompson as "pure African, nearly as black as they are ever made, six feet high, and with rather a good-natured expression."[32] With a socially advantageous marriage and sound physical characteristics, there is little surprise that Thompson sought a career in politics.

James K. Greene's expression was typical for former field hands. He remarked that as a slave he had been "entirely ignorant; knew nothing more than to obey his master." Greene remembered that other field hands had been in the same condition; yet, they "didn't know the Lord's prayers, but the tocsin of freedom sounded and knocked at the door and they walked out like free men and met the exigencies as they grew up, and shouldered the responsibilities."[33] Born in North Carolina on 15 December 1823, Greene had resided in Greensboro, Alabama, since 3 January 1857. Though he was a home builder during the antebellum period, he accepted coach-making duties besides his carpentry work after the war ended.[34]

Lloyd Leftwich knew little more than Greene; yet, after slavery he purchased his former owner's plantation. By 1880 he owned 122 acres of tilled land and 20 acres of woodland and forest. The value of his farm, including land, fences, and buildings, was $1,200.00; the value of his farming instruments and machinery was $30.00; and of his livestock, $350.00. Also in 1880 Leftwich paid $18 to repair fences and buildings; $12 for fertilizers; and $41 for labor.[35] Born in Virginia in 1842, he came to Alabama after the close of the war and settled in Forkland. Later, Leftwich would represent Greene County in the Senate.[36]

With Leftwich, other African American future legislators had been ministers during slavery. Of these, Mansfield Tyler, born about 12 miles from Augusta, Georgia, in November 1826, lived as a youth with the family of his great-aunt, whose husband was a minister. Because he was a privileged slave, his owner brought him to Alabama in 1854 and in 1855 permitted him to join the church in Lowndesboro. Even before slavery had ended, Tyler had begun to preach.[37]

Another slave, Jeremiah Haralson, of Selma, was born on a plantation near Columbus, Georgia, in 1846. Haralson was self-educated and became a minister. Politically more successful than Curtis, Royal, Thompson, or Turner, Haralson was the only African American lawmaker to serve in the House, Senate, and Congress.[38]

Educated Officeholders

As just observed, many of Alabama's African American future legislators served as slave-ministers. After the war, others accepted the ministry as an avocation. Few of the state's African American future legislators had received a formal education, including the ministers. Rapier was the best educated of them. Another, Charles Smith, of Bullock County, who had attended Talladega College after his departure from the legislature, had received some schooling. In 1875 J. N. Brown, a teacher at Talladega College, wrote to the Reverend E. M. Cravath, formerly with the Freedmen's Bureau, "A member of the legislature, Rev. Charles Smith, has been here to see us and wishes to enter the class when the legislature adjourns. He is man of some culture, having attended school in Canada in his youth."[39]

Another educated African American officeholder, Charles E. Harris, of Selma, frequently confused with Charles O. Harris, of Montgomery, was one of the legislature's African American lawyers. In 1874 the Marion *Commonwealth* wrote:

> Charles E. Harris [color'd] applied to the Supreme Court on yesterday for license to practice law in the courts of this state. Messrs. Gardner, Jones, and Watts were appointed upon the committee to conduct the necessary examination. He is from Selma. Since the above was written, we have learned that the committee reported favorably and that he was admitted to the bar.[40]

Engrossing clerk William H. Councill also was an attorney. Born in Fayetteville, North Carolina, in July 1848, Councill attended a school for "colored" children in Stevenson, Alabama, immediately after the war. He studied law and was admitted to practice in 1883. However, he never practiced law, because after he returned

106

to his Huntsville home from his engrossing clerk position with the legislature, he founded and became the first president of Alabama Agricultural and Mechanical College.[41]

As a testament to their zest for learning, several of Alabama's African American future lawmakers learned to read and to write between the close of the war and 1870. Of the state's 108 African American lawmakers, the population census of 1870 provides information on the reading ability of 70, or 65 percent. The color variation of African American lawmakers can be classified as either black or mulatto. Forty, or 57 percent, of these lawmakers listed their color variation as black, and 30, or 43 percent, listed their color variation as mulatto. Actually, only 19, or 48 percent, of the state's black delegation claimed the ability to read. Twenty-seven, or 90 percent, of the mulatto delegation, indicated reading abilities. Furthermore, 17, or 43 percent of the black lawmakers, claimed the ability to write, and 27, or 90 percent of the mulatto delegation, indicated the ability to write. Thus, the evidence clearly shows that a greater number of mulattoes than blacks could read and write. Although other lawmakers listed their literacy, their color was unknown. The census reports were not the most reliable sources of information, since they relied to some extent on unverified data; yet, these reports suggest that less than 50 percent of the state's black legislators could read or write, as appendix A indicates.

Military Experience

Whether slave or free, many of Alabama's African Americans had gained military experience by the close of the Civil War. One such person, James H. Alston of Macon County, recalled before a congressional committee his childhood role in the Mexican War. The colorful shoemaker-turned-musician recounted how Confederate General Cullen Battle purchased him in South Carolina and transported him to Tuskegee to serve as a drummer for the city, but when the Mexican War began, Battle forced him to enlist in the army yet refused to give him a musket. Alston thus served throughout the Mexican War as a drummer. He performed a similar role for Battle during the Civil War. Paradoxically, he did not participate in either war as a "fighting" military man.[42]

Two other former military men were Reuben Jones and William D. Gaskin. Jones, alias Reuben P. Morris, served with a Michigan infantry unit before representing Madison County in the General Assembly in 1872.[43] Twenty-year old William D. Gaskin, alias William Turner, enlisted on 1 May 1865 in Macon, Georgia, and served for three years with Company H of the United States Colored Cavalry. Born in Russell County, Alabama, Gaskin received a promotion from private to sergeant on 16 July 1865. He represented Lowndes County twice in the legislature.[44]

Although Robert Smalls of South Carolina was acclaimed as the nation's best-known African American Civil War military hero because he delivered the Confederate steamer, *The Planter*, to Union forces, John Carraway emerged as Alabama's most celebrated African American Union Army veteran. He enlisted on 3 March 1863 at Boston, served for two years, and was discharged on a surgeon's certificate of disability on 30 March 1865 at Camp Meigs, Massachusetts. Carraway served in Company A of the all-black 54th Massachusetts Infantry, the unit Frederick Douglass had persuaded President Lincoln to organize so the nation's African American citizenry could participate in the fight for freedom. Martin R. Delaney, of South Carolina, commanded this group of African American volunteers. While a serviceman, Carraway wrote "Colored Volunteers," the most popular tune among African American troops.[45]

Moses Brown Avery, the assistant secretary of the Alabama Constitutional Convention of 1867, was the sole Alabama African American lawmaker to serve with the Union Navy. Born in Pensacola, Florida, on 22 November 1833, Avery was the son of Frederick J. Avery, a wealthy white citizen of Mobile. The elder Avery purchased the freedom of Avery and his slave mother and brought them to Mobile. As a youth Moses Avery distinguished himself by his rapid progress in English and French. Reared as an Episcopalian, he made his way to the Union gunboat *Clifton*, on which he served until the Battle of Galveston, fought on 1 January 1863, the same day Lincoln issued the Emancipation Proclamation. Because he never did fully recover from injuries he sustained during the Battle of Galveston, Avery received a discharge from the

NEITHER CARPETBAGGERS NOR SCALAWAGS

Navy and departed for his family's new home in New Orleans. There, he organized the "Union Brotherhood," a secret society of which he served as secretary. He attended the first National Convention of Colored Men, held at Syracuse, New York, in 1864, where he may have met Frederick Douglass, Martin R. Delaney, Henry Highland Garnet, and many other nationally prominent African Americans. Returning to New Orleans, Avery became editor of the New Orleans *Tribune*. While organizing congregations in Louisiana, he answered General John Pope's call to serve as a registrar to enroll Alabama's first postwar electorate. He had been a member of the Republican state conventions of both Louisiana and Alabama.[46]

Contrary to some terribly distorted later myths, it was not unusual for African Americans to serve with the Confederacy. One example was Jordan Noble and his 1,440-man Louisiana regiment, the Native Guards. This unit of the Louisiana Militia, Confederate States, protected New Orleans. As early as 1729, long before the Civil War, African Americans in Louisiana had begun their military tradition. They later fought with Andrew Jackson at the Battle of New Orleans in 1815. Jordan Noble had been a drummer boy at the Battle of New Orleans.[47]

Turning to Alabama again, African American future lawmaker Horace King repaired bridges for the Confederacy. In one telegram to Bozeman, probably a bridge construction foreman, John Gill Shorter, Alabama's wartime governor, asked, "Is Horace engaged, if so how long, if not tell him I want him on this river."[48] Bozeman replied, "Horace is driving [a] pile slow down on the Apalaccola [sic] river...will be back in a few day[s]."[49]   As part of the Apalachicola-Chattahoochee river system, the Apalachicola River was of vast importance to the commerce of the area before the war, and during the war it served as an important line of communication for the Confederacy.   King was manumitted and, having repaired the stairwell in the state capitol after it burned in 1849, he was well known by whites in Alabama and Georgia.   He constructed most of his homes and bridges in these states. King also was able to "relate" to the Union Army. According to legend, when Wilson's raiders "employed" King's last two mules without his permission, King displayed to Wilson the masonic signal; then, Wilson returned the mules and apologized![50]

Phillip Joseph also worked for the Confederacy, although his career was not as illustrious as King's.   He was born in July 1846 of Spanish and French ancestry.   His grandfather, also named Phillip Joseph, fought with Andrew Jackson in the War of 1812.   His mother was the daughter of a wealthy Cuban and the beneficiary of a large estate--one that included nearly 900 slaves, whom she later liberated.   Joseph spoke fluent French, Spanish, and English and read classical literature.[51]

In 1872, as Joseph and Benjamin S. Turner competed for a seat in Congress from the Fifth District, Turner recounted Joseph's role in the Civil War.   Berating Joseph for having received remuneration from Democrats, Turner highlighted Joseph's role in the war. Turner argued:

> Phil Joseph was a secret agent of the rebel government and was paid fifty thousands dollars, by said government to poison three thousand colored soldiers who were made prisoners of war by General Forest at Fort Pillow and sent to the prisons in Mobile. In 1865 Joseph decoyed one hundred and seventy-five colored men on board [the] schooner *Neptune*, and shipped them to Cuba, where he sold them into slavery. He was tried on Thursday, the 19th day of December, 1865, in the US District court of Alabama, and convicted of it and sentenced to be hanged on the 12th day of March, 1866, in the city of Mobile.[52]

In what was undoubtedly campaign rhetoric, Turner offered no evidence to support his charge. The combative relationship between Turner and Joseph was characteristic of the time but uncharacteristic of Turner. Whatever were the merits of Turner's accusation, one observation is accurate: The election rivalry between Turner and Joseph paved the way for a Democrat to assume office.[53]

Military participation was advantageous for African Americans and whites. Joining with the latter in military units provided many of them with their first association with whites on a nearly equal footing. In addition, they carried weapons and received pay and health care. African American soldiers could also marvel at the opportunities provided by the military to travel and to demonstrate leadership capabilities. Many prevailing stereotypes crumbled as blacks and whites alike were able to notice undeniable African American bravery and leadership. This was important, because the propensity for leadership should have carried over into postbellum Southern society. Indeed, where their demonstrated leadership in the military was combined with the educational training African American soldiers received, one wonders why they were not more assertive after the war. There is little indication many African American future lawmakers relied on these wartime advantages as guidance in postbellum society.[54]

African Americans such as Horace King received significant benefits from their roles in the war. Already a wealthy man before the war commenced and held in high esteem by his neighbors, King continued to build bridges, homes, and roads in west Georgia and east Alabama after the war. He lived long enough to pass on a legacy of wealth and construction expertise to his sons. In fact, at the turn of the century, the King name represented the best in home construction in Georgia and Alabama. King's bridges also connected the races. Accounts of his attempts to moderate race relations in Alabama were widespread.[55] Were it not for the ascendancy of the disfranchisement movement, his four sons might have continued the King political legacy and established a foundation for other African American leaders of the twentieth century. However, this was not to be.

Political Advantages

The children of the African American legislators didn't inherit political advantages. The Rapier family possessed a greater opportunity to create a political dynasty than the family of Horace

113

King. John H. Rapier, Sr., had served as a registrar for Lauderdale County. When Governor Robert M. Patton made him a notary public in December 1867, James Thomas Rapier, of Florence, Lauderdale County, became the state's first black political appointee. Because none of his brothers engaged in political matters, the political legacy ended with James Thomas Rapier. Also, Rapier never married. One historian writes that Rapier "was a bachelor" who recently toured "Europe without hindrance of wife or pocket."[56] Celibacy was a personal preference.[57] His travel afforded ample opportunity for matrimony, especially in Hayneville, where he had moved his newspaper, the Montgomery *Republican Sentinel*, by the time of the 1872 election. This newspaper was the first African American newsorgan in both Montgomery and Lowndes counties. Later, after he had served out his tenure as congressman, Rapier relocated to Montgomery, where he died in 1883.[58]

Hershel V. Cashin, a respected mulatto attorney and barroom operator in Montgomery, also might have established a political legacy. From 1890 to 1905, he enjoyed Federal patronage as receiver of public lands in Huntsville. Therefore, he relocated his family to the Tennessee Valley. In addition, Cashin possessed the education and the accepted social standing to accomplish such a feat. His sons chose professional careers in medicine instead of politics. Perhaps these sons had the foresight to sniff out the political winds during the late nineteenth century and to see little such opportunity ahead. The Cashin political impulse did manifest itself in the personage of John Cashin, a grandson, who gained considerable public recognition as he, first, unsuccessfully sought a seat on the Huntsville city council in 1966, and second, also unsuccessfully, sought the governor's chair in 1970. Dr Hershel V. Cashin, Jr., the son of Hershel V. Cashin, married Countis Harris, a teacher in the State Normal School and a daughter of Montgomery African American legislator and engrossing clerk Charles O. Harris, thus enhancing the Cashin and Harris families as two of the state's three most politically and socially prominent African American families.[59] Equally advantageous, Ruth, another Harris daughter, married Dr Ralph J. Bunche, a Nobel Peace Prize recipient and one-time under secretary for special political affairs of the United Nations.[60]

The family of Methodist minister Frank H. Threatt attained greater political success than any of the other postbellum African American lawmakers. His grandson-in-law chose a career as a journalist, founding one of the earliest African American newspapers in Birmingham at the turn of the century. Much later, in 1982, his great-grandson, Oscar W. Adams, became the first African American to occupy a seat on the state's supreme court.[61] In passing, note the irony in the statement of Greene Shadrack Washington Lewis who had predicted in 1873 that "the day is not too far distant when you will find on the bench of the Supreme Court of the state a man as black as I am."[62] Only 109 years had to pass before the state apparently became enlightened and mature enough to recognize such individual merit untainted by color.

Financial Gains

Alabama's African American legislators didn't make significant financial gains during the immediate postbellum period. Neither prewar status nor color admixture significantly affected economic elevation. For example, the agricultural census of 1870 lists only one black legislator or future legislator (from the free-born or manumitted group) as a property owner. This one, John Dozier, owned 320 acres with a cash value of $1,600. In addition, the same census lists one member of the mulatto class (from the free-born or manumitted group) as an economic gainer. This was mulatto James Thomas Rapier. Of the manumitted or free-born class, five had received freedom through manumission (four mulattoes and one black), and four were free-born (three mulattoes and one black). Of the 10 lawmakers listed in the agricultural census of 1870, seven are listed as mulatto, two as black, and the color variation of one remains unknown.[63]

The population census of 1870 identifies three property owners from the ranks of the free-born or manumitted. Already identified as mulatto and free-born, James Thomas Rapier, a thirty-four years old resident of Montgomery, owned $500 worth of real property and $1,100 in personal property. Black and free-born Peyton Finley owned personal property valued at $1,000. As already stated, John

116

Dozier owned 320 acres of land, valued of $1,600, according to the census of 1870. Already in 1850 Horace King owned real properties valued at $300. King was not listed in the Federal census of 1870. The number of free-born or manumitted black members of the Reconstruction legislature was too small to make a valid comparison with the number of those members of the legislature who were freed by the war.[64]

The population census of 1870 reveals that 21 black legislators had amassed real property valued at $19,538 for an average of $938. Among these, Lawson Steele held property valued at $5,836, the largest real property holdings among black legislators. Second among the black lawmakers, Nimrod Snoddy of Greene County claimed holdings valued at $1,800. Fifteen members of the mulatto group owned real properties valued at $45,770 for an average of $3,051. Altogether, black legislators as a group did not fare as well with real property holdings as did the mulatto group, although more of the former held such property.

Seventeen of the black lawmakers owned personal property valued at $14,980, for an average of $881. Dallas County livery stable owner Benjamin S. Turner emerged as the wealthiest black legislator with personal property holdings valued at $10,000 in 1870. In contrast, 14 of the 39 persons identified as mulattoes amassed personal property valued at $8,375 in 1870 for an average value of $598.[65] Nathan A. Brewington clearly exceeded all other mulattoes. His real wealth was valued at $30,000. Benjamin F. Royal occupies

117

a distant second place with holdings valued at $6,600. These figures do not reflect the real advantage mulattoes held; mulattoes acquired more real property than they did personal property. In turn, this fact is a testament to the lack of opportunities for blacks in postbellum Alabama. Their holdings suggest mulattoes reaped significant financial advantages because of their lighter complexion or color variation. Although more blacks than mulattoes owned personal properties, the value of personal properties owned by mulattoes far exceeded the holdings of black legislators. The wealth of these legislators notwithstanding, a significant change, or even a noticeable trend upward in the financial standing of blacks nor mulattoes in Alabama, did not occur.

Occupation, Age, Nativity

The occupations of these legislators do not fully account for their individual or aggregate lack of affluence. The evidence suggests mulatto lawmakers were more numerous than black lawmakers in six categories: shoemakers, clerks, policemen, bridgebuilders, attorneys, and dill merchants. In contrast, blacks were more prominent as farmers, teachers, grocers, livery stable owners, and carpenters. Each group had equal representation as ministers, blacksmiths, and railroad mail agents. Except for the teaching vocation, mulatto lawmakers were clearly more numerous in the professions.[66]

The age of these legislators enhances our understanding of their affluence. The population census of 1870 reveals the age for 79 of Alabama's 108 black legislators; their average age emerges as 39. Of these 79 politicians, 46, or 58 percent, listed their color variation as black. Their average age was 41. On the other hand, 33, or 42 percent of the 79 lawmakers, listed their color variation as mulatto. They averaged 36 years, showing that mulattoes assumed office significantly earlier than did black lawmakers. Also, the evidence suggests that either mulattoes were more eager to seek office or such agencies as the Freedmen's Bureau were more prone to push them to seek office than they were to push blacks. Another possibility is that the black electorate was more eager to vote for a mulatto candidate than it was to vote for a black candidate.[67]

Most of the state's black delegation were natives to the state. Of the 86 lawmakers on whom information was available, 34, or 39 percent, were native Alabamians. In declining order among the remaining, 14, or 16 percent, were natives of North Carolina and Georgia; 13, or 15 percent, were born in Virginia; 10, or 11 percent, were born in South Carolina; and one, or 1 percent, was born in Maryland and Kentucky, respectively.[68]

Summary

Blacks in Alabama did not have such a publicly and socially respected institution as Roman Catholicism or any widely fraternal society to protect and advance their individual or public interests or patiently to instruct them in the rudiments of reading or writing. King and Carraway were members of a Masonic order, but there is no evidence the Masonic order either proliferated in antebellum Alabama or that King was a driving influence in establishing the order in Alabama. As for Carraway, even if he had lived in antebellum Alabama, he would have been unable to establish such an order there because of his youth, since his political views would scarcely have gained him prestige among whites in antebellum Southern society. Instead, curious onlookers would have monitored his movements much more closely than they would have watched those of Horace King. Still, had Carraway possessed King's driving influence, he would have been more successful in establishing such an order in Mobile because of its sizeable free black population and its cosmopolitan atmosphere. As for King himself, although he was mobile, few free blacks lived in his home area, the Russell County area. Contrast the educational opportunities in the Palmetto State for free blacks with those in postbellum Alabama: In South Carolina educational possibilities--coupled with the presence of a sizeable group of emancipated slaves--afforded both free blacks and manumitted blacks distinct advantages in postbellum society. On the other hand, look at conditions in Alabama at the same time. Neither its black nor its manumitted slave population approximated Louisiana's free black population--nor South Carolina's free black class. This fact was a testament to the rigidity of slavery--and its aftermath--in Alabama. Also, economic opportunities were few for Alabama's free blacks and for its emancipated class. In postbellum society mulattoes held an advantage.[69]

Like black politicians in South Carolina, most of Alabama's black legislators gained their freedom because of the Civil War. Unlike Louisiana and South Carolina, where many of the state's postbellum black lawmakers had been free before the war, few of Alabama's politicians had known freedom before the war. Still, because most of the black delegation had been educated in the vocational skills before the war, the background of Alabama's black delegation compares favorably to Georgia, where four of its 69 black lawmakers were free-born and where another four had been manumitted before the war. Paradoxically, most of the South's postwar black congressional delegation came from the ranks of mulattoes who were better educated and wealthier than the black ones were.[70]

Fleshing out the biographical profiles of Alabama's black officeholders in many ways significantly enhances our understanding of these men. Doing so also helps to silence some of the abusive criticisms they have had heaped on them. After all, most of these men marched out of slavery with a few earthly belongings and even fewer other advantages. It is altogether likely their mistakes would have been made by any other group with similar preparation. Their shortcomings were many, but so were their achievements.

Benjamin Sterling Turner
Alabama Department of Archives and History, Montgomery

A young
Horace King
Courtesy of Thomas L.
French, Jr.

ing, during later life

Samuel J. Patterson
Courtesy of the Tyus Family

Chapter 4

Between 1865 and 1870 the American Missionary Association (AMA), the Pittsburgh Relief Association, and other similar benevolent societies descended upon Alabama and other parts of the South. Their pronounced purpose was to relieve hunger and suffering and to build educational institutions. These agencies did not set out to train blacks for leadership, and although a coterie of the state's black future officeholders joined these agencies and later rose to political prominence, they did not view their affiliation with such benevolent agencies as a prerequisite for leadership. Most Southern whites envisioned these organizations as radical vehicles for change, and for that reason they rejected them--sometimes violently, sometimes more subtly, but most of the time relentlessly. They were especially intolerant of and outspoken regarding the American Missionary Association, the most significant of these organizations.

Although a select group of blacks gained leadership experience from their affiliation with the Bureau and the American Missionary Association, several other successful politicians relied on minor officeholding instead as an avenue to political prominence. Examples include James H. Alston of Macon County, who counted on his affiliation with the Union League to gain valuable experience. A second, Benjamin F. Royal, one of the state's most successful officeholders, also worked with the Union League. In contrast, James Thomas Rapier of Lauderdale County did not work with a benevolent agency; instead, Rapier's minor political position, wealth, and education account for his rise to prominence.

One would have expected most of Alabama's black lawmakers to have begun their careers with church-related agencies, since the church was the only institution Southern whites permitted slaves to associate with. Besides, black males who worked with religious agencies were the only group the black masses viewed as models. Surprisingly, only a few of the state's antebellum ministers worked with church-related agencies, and an even smaller number participated in postbellum political affairs as legislators.

With a background deeply rooted in the Baptist persuasion, future black officeholders in Alabama seldom chose to work with the Congregationalist American Missionary Association. However, motivation lay at the core of the matter: Blacks who did join the American Missionary Association fervently wanted to provide an education for their people. Also, their association with such organizations as the Freedmen's Bureau and the Union League reflected an attempt on their part to politicize the black masses by preparing them for enfranchisement and its privileges. Still,

126

most black future officeholders did not associate with these organizations to reshape Southern society as some officials of these agencies would have desired.

The Freedmen's Bureau

As we have already seen, some black officials did gain invaluable leadership experience through their association with the Freedmen's Bureau. The Bureau provided most of the financial assistance for black education in Alabama. Bureau Commissioner Oliver Otis Howard informed General Swayne of "$25,000 for Expenditure for rental and repairs of school buildings and asylums in your State" besides whatever Swayne may have secured from the sale of "Confederate property."[1] Most of the whites who worked with the Bureau had served as chaplains during the war.

Blacks decidedly did not view their work with the Bureau as a link or a prerequisite to officeholding. This disposition was a natural result from the opposition of many whites in the form of physical violence and economic reprisals. In fact, their vehement opposition partly accounted for the association of only a few blacks with the Bureau. Yet, the altruistic desire to help educate the black masses was the reason African Americans gave for working with the Bureau and its schools. One observer noted that Alabama's African Americans "have scarcely a leisure moment that you cannot see them with a book in their hand learning to read."[2] A writer of the period offered further evidence when he observed that "the whole race wanted to go to school; none were too old, few too young."[3]   John Alvord, the Bureau's general superintendent of education, concluded that African Americans wanted to go to school because "they had seen knowledge equated with power; now that they were free, they sought knowledge so that they could exercise power as free men."[4]

Many African Americans worked as Bureau teachers. Some of them worked as assistants to white teachers; others showed their dedication by teaching in primary capacities. Of the latter, Richard Burke taught 22 primary grade-level students in a small structure in rural Gainesville. His students paid a small tuition. Both to help his students and to excite and build their interest, Burke, a Baptist minister, read to them regularly from the newspaper and the Bible. He later represented rural Sumter County in the legislature of 1868.[5]

William V. Turner, another primary teacher, taught both a day and a night school in Wetumpka, in south-central Alabama. He, too, moved on to the legislature, later representing Elmore County in the State House. An articulate speaker, he involved himself in political and social affairs more fully than any other of the African American Bureau teachers who became lawmakers.[6]

A third, Alexander E. Williams, served as a Bureau teacher in Eufaula.   In 1871 he taught 62 students in the primary and intermediate grades.   Barbour countians sent Williams to the legislature in 1870.[7]

The Union League and the Mobile *Nationalist*

Fewer African American legislators worked with the Union League or the Mobile *Nationalist*. One, Phillip Joseph, a future engrossing clerk in the legislature, was chosen as president of the Mobile Union League. Joseph also presided over many political conventions held in the county.[8] Although Mobile County sent two African Americans to the legislature, neither of them served with the Union League. Joseph was the only African American Mobile County politician of note who worked with the Bureau or the Union League.

Most of the future African American lawmakers who associated with the Freedmen's Bureau and the League came from the Blackbelt. Benjamin F. Royal of Bullock County was one of these persons. The Montgomery *Daily State Sentinel* wrote that Royal was "one of the most sensible and, on account of his influence, most hated freedmen in the vicinity. His political proclivities are well known and have resulted in threats made against his life by a number of white men."[9] The *Daily State Journal* identified Royal as "one of the starters of the Union League which, through his untiring efforts, now numbers over 400 members. Ben is a peaceful man and avoids...impertinent inquisitives in the best manner possible."[10] Royal himself insisted that the "Union League was merely a moral and benevolent society which did not interfere with any man's political or religious opinions." In September 1867 he shared the platform at a Union League meeting with state president John C.

Keffer and stressed the importance of voting and officeholding; he did not view the League as a vehicle to punish the white South.[11]

Future legislator James H. Alston also was instrumental as a League organizer. He had come to Tuskegee from South Carolina before the Mexican War to fulfill the need of a local military company for a drummer. Having been the slave of Cullen Battle, Alston served him as his drummer during both the Mexican and Civil wars. After the Civil War ended, Battle considered Alston a changed man. He was especially displeased when Alston led the formation of the Macon County League. Later, Alston was to testify during the congressional Ku Klux Klan Hearings that Battle, a Democrat, led the effort to drive him from the county. Thus, political events at Tuskegee became heated following Alston's formation of the Union League there. The intensity of white opposition became obvious as Alston and his pregnant wife prepared for bed one night; someone fired several shots into the Alston home. Although no one received injuries, this incident marked the beginning of a volatile period for African American Republicans in Macon County. Still later, Alston fled to safety in Montgomery when Robert Johnson and seven or eight Democrats (probably Klansmen or members of a Klan-like organization) visited him at his home and told him that, if he wished to live, he must leave Tuskegee. Because Johnson, Alston's white father-in-law, and others had offered him $3,000 to campaign for the Democrats, Alston and other Macon County African Americans considered Johnson and the others as the unidentified Democrats who had fired the shots into the Alston home.[12]

Alston's participation with the Macon County League catapulted him to a leadership position, and his advancement to the legislature suggests that Alston used his advantage well. However, determined Democratic opposition made Alston a one-term legislator. Also, despite its heavy African American majority, Macon County sent only four African Americans to the legislature during Reconstruction. Alston was the only one of the lawmakers who held membership in the League.[13]

George Houston, another Union League-associated African American, suffered a fate similar to Alston's. Houston represented Sumter County in the legislature of 1868. Then he testified during the congressional Klan Hearings that wealthy whites looked upon him as the most prominent African American person in the Sumter County area. He also recounted that whites wanted him to deny his Union League membership. Yet, he maintained that before the war whites in the area had befriended him, largely because of his 16-year service as a tailor.[14] A witness at the hearings remembered the African American lawmaker as "kind, well disposed, and orderly until he began to associate with Republicans-Then [he] began to drink too much."[15] Later, during the summer of 1869, a band of outlaws fired into the Houston home. After returning the fire, he was wounded in the thigh. Perhaps this assault caused Houston· to migrate to Montgomery when he had recovered.[16]

131

NEITHER CARPETBAGGERS NOR SCALAWAGS

Whatever else one says of the League's influence among African Americans, one must agree that the Union League provided leadership opportunities for only a handful of them. Obviously, the intimidating reaction of many area whites precluded any long-lasting influence. Few whites considered the League as an organization without political ends. On the contrary, most of state's white citizenry considered the League as just another threatening Northern intrusion into Southern affairs. Similar to their clearly negative position toward the Union Army, the American Missionary Association, and the Bureau, most Southern (and Alabama) whites' reaction to the Union League and other Northern agencies suggests that they rejected the efforts of these agencies to restore political and social stability.

Several future legislators who had secured employment with the Bureau, the Union League, or the American Missionary Association found employment with the Mobile *Nationalist*, the state's first African American newspaper. This organ had the distinction of being the only nonpolitical agency African Americans made use of in their rise to political prominence. For example, John Carraway served as its assistant editor. Because of its existence, those who read the *Nationalist* learned of events as African American writers saw them. African American future lawmakers William V. Turner of Wetumpka and Holland Thompson of Montgomery informed readers of local and state events through this newsorgan. Jordan Hatcher of Selma and Hales Ellsworth of Montgomery distributed

132

copies of the paper in their communities. No wonder, then, the *Nationalist* exerted such a powerful influence in the African American community.[17] Despite the presence of the Freedmen's Bureau, the Union League, and the *Nationalist*, few future African American officeholders ascended to political prominence through these agencies.

The American Missionary Association

The American Missionary Association, more than any other organization, paved the way for ascendancy of black leadership. The Freedmen's Bureau paid teachers' salaries, but the American Missionary Association provided teachers for the Bureau. The American Missionary Association began during the 1840s, participating in an attempt to secure the release of 42 slaves who had revolted against Spanish captors on the *Amistad*.[18] Then, after the war's conclusion, the American Missionary Association, the Peabody Agency, and other agencies came South and established schools and churches. They also provided food, clothing, and books.[19] These organizations were part of a national movement intent on aiding freedmen in the South. The American Missionary Association dispatched many teachers to the South to educate African Americans. Bureau officials accepted the humanitarian spirit of the American Missionary Association, whose teachings were replete with the New England Sunday School style: "You now have the sympathy of all humane and Christian people. There is nothing that

133

makes people so beautiful, whether they are white or black, as virtue."[20]

Understandably, most Northern teachers approached African American education with a spirit of benevolent paternalism. They also sought vigorously to share their idealism. One such teacher, the Reverend William Fiske, wrote from Mobile, "I have found it difficult to get at a Colored audience to say anything to them in this city. There is still so much acrimony in the minds of the ruling class, that there is no confidence in their former masters."[21] Northern teachers also considered the freedmen unprepared for an education. Noted AMA teacher John Silsby stated, "The colored population lack organization and cohesion--a defect of course resulting from their previous condition of slavery. They need education and lack the experience and mutual confidence which are needed in successful cooperation."[22]

At first glance these statements by Fiske and Silsby seem to offer little insight into the attitude of Northerners toward African American education. On a closer observation, however, these statements clearly reveal Northerners--like their Southern white contemporaries--assumed they truly knew what was best for African Americans. Significantly, there is little or no evidence either group consulted with freedmen themselves about such matters. Much of the acrimony of the post-Civil War period could have been averted had either group given African Americans a voice in their educational destiny. Missionaries also believed that freedmen could not care for their finances. Wrote the Reverend Fiske to the Reverend George O. Whipple, the corresponding secretary of the American Missionary Association, "I have a high opinion of Savings banks, for freedmen in any section that has a central point, with a dense population. Savings banks would do an immense amount of good in preventing the frittering away of their earnings in small amounts...but your influence would be necessary."[23]

William Fiske clearly revealed an acute awareness of the Southern disposition toward the work of the American Missionary Association and how missionaries sought to camouflage their intentions. His letters revealed much more; they highlighted the attitudes of missionaries toward freedmen, the people whose condition they sought to improve. Their benevolent paternalism was beneficial, but it was also deficient in its assumptions and execution. It is also undeniable the missionaries sought to improve the living conditions of African Americans. Unfortunately, they began their work with the unproven and false assumption that freedmen lacked moral fiber. This was indistinguishable from the attitude of most Southern whites. On the one hand, missionaries did not hold the people they sought to help in high esteem. On the other hand, Southern whites feared any intercourse between former slaves and Northern whites. Between them, without consulting African Americans, both groups denied that the personal dignity of African Americans might have minimized internal state acrimony and won respect and cooperation.[24]

135

NEITHER CARPETBAGGERS NOR SCALAWAGS

Despite the opposition of Southern whites, AMA schools spread throughout the state. By 1867 the American Missionary Association had sent 39 missionaries to Valhermosa Springs, Talladega, Selma, Girard, Athens, Demopolis, Marion, Mobile, and Montgomery.[25] Emerson Institute, located in Mobile, was one of the earliest institutions established in Alabama by the American Missionary Association. The Northwestern Freedmen's Aid Society, later a branch of the American Missionary Association, helped to establish this school in Mobile within two weeks after the close of the war. Its curriculum included reading, arithmetic, advanced English, and geography.[26]

In January 1868 Ralph Emerson (not to be confused with the Transcendentalist poet) made a large donation for the establishment of Emerson Institute. The American Missionary Association then purchased a brick building four stories high. By late 1868, George L. Putnam, superintendent of education in Mobile, reported to the Reverend E. P. Smith, the general agent at New York, that the institute was more than full and was turning away students because it employed only six teachers.[27] The lack of space at Emerson Institute underscores the concern of General Superintendent of Education John Alvord as he wrote to the Reverend R. D. Harper, superintendent of education for Alabama, "We hope it will not be long before Alabama has a public free school system and is able to actually accomplish all which her uneducated population deserves."[28] Yet, though the constitution of 1868 established the state's

136

earliest public school, meanwhile Emerson Institute and other AMA schools continued to function. Within a decade and under adverse conditions, the institute, also known to students as the Blue College, had taught more than 3,000 African American students. In summation, however, Emerson Institute laid the foundation for Alabama's public school system.[29]

The American Missionary Association also established successful schools at Talladega and Selma. The institution established at Talladega was the most successful of the AMA schools, but no future African American legislator was instrumental in its success. On the other hand, William Savery, a former slave, helped in the founding of Talladega College. Fully realizing the role education played in society, Savery convinced Bureau officials of the need for a school in the area.[30] Joe M. Richardson writes cogently of Savery's role in the school's founding and how the Bureau and the American Missionary Association purchased an unoccupied Baptist College building in which to locate the school.[31] According to the Talladega faculty, Savery "sawed the first plank and chipped the first shaving" for the original building.[32] Quite fittingly Savery also became a trustee of the school and "saw three of his children receive diplomas at Talladega."[33]

Doing what he could to help Savery and other area African Americans realize their dream, Henry E. Brown, AMA director of the school, met with interested African Americans in log churches and instructed them to "pick out the best specimen of a young man you

137

have for a teacher, and bring to church with you next Sunday all the corn and bacon you can spare for his living and I will make him a teacher."[34] This approach apparently worked well, because no other AMA institution enjoyed a similar tranquility during its early development. Though there were no dormitories, Talladega College began its legacy in African American education in November 1867 with four teachers and 140 students. They all worked faithfully under the direction of Henry E. Brown.[35]

The institution established by the American Missionary Association in Marion gave future African American lawmakers their greatest opportunity for leadership. Its incorporation papers listed the names of Ivey Parrish, Thomas Speed, Nicholas Dale, James Childs, John Freeman, and future African American lawmakers Alexander H. Curtis and Thomas Lee, two important persons in AMA work. These original trustees were to serve for a two-year period. They named the school the Lincoln School of Marion, and by incorporating the school on 18 July 1867, the trustees laid the foundation for one of the earliest school for African Americans in Perry County. Despite its later state affiliation, a series of name changes, and its removal to Montgomery, the Lincoln School of Marion also laid the foundation for the state's oldest African American educational institution.[36] On 10 September 1868 the trustees signed to transfer the school's property to the American Missionary Association. By this time, D. Harris had replaced Thomas Lee as a trustee. Curtis served as the agent for John

138

Freeman and Ivey Parish during the transferral.[37] On 11 April 1869
AMA missionary Thomas Steward dedicated a school building in
Marion. The Bureau contributed approximately $2,800 of the $4,200
cost for the school; the African American citizens of Marion and
the American Missionary Association contributed the remainder.[38]

Lee died prematurely in 1869; so, it is impossible to measure
his possible influence. Yet, he lived long enough to represent
Perry County at the Constitutional Convention of 1867. As events
would unfold, the educational climate also revealed the interaction
between African Americans and the American Missionary Association.
Future legislator Alexander H. Curtis emerged as the leading
African American educator in the Marion area and the guiding force
behind the Lincoln School.[39] African American education in Perry
County reflected a constant battle between AMA missionaries and
Curtis. For example, in 1872 Steward wrote to the Reverend E. M.
Cravath, "One of the trustees [Curtis] will call on you in New
York...he is looked upon by the people here as a scoundrel."[40]
Steward's letter offered no explanation for his attitude toward
Curtis, but Helen M. Leonard, an instructor, touched on the center
of the matter in a letter to Cravath. She based her letter on a
conversation with Stephen Childs. She had learned through Childs
of a recent trustee meeting in which Curtis suggested "it would not
be honorable for them [the AMA] to get teachers from the North
unless they were sure of paying all their expenses."[41] Curtis
allegedly told Childs as far he was concerned, his older children

139

could attend the school of George N. Card and his younger children could receive instructions at home. She asked Cravath for advice and concluded her letter, "Our people are afraid that if they propose anything the others will think it a Congregational trap."[42] The seat of the problem was that most of the African Americans of the Marion community adhered to the Baptist persuasion, which contributed to the problem. This speculation remains unproven to date.

In any event, a letter from Leonard four days later offered much more information about the African American community in Marion. She claimed that although Curtis threatened to dismiss the AMA board, the African American community desired to retain its affiliation with the American Missionary Association. Apparently, Curtis had engineered the separation of the Lincoln School from the American Missionary Association, but the community then sought to reassociate with the American Missionary Association. Her letter suggested that the trustees, except a Mr. Hall, wanted to return Lincoln School to AMA control.[43]

Leonard wrote to Cravath again one month later. She lamented at the prospect of "selling the church to the Baptists and emigrating to Montgomery." By this time, the American Missionary Association had lost control of the school to the state, and the small state appropriation was not enough to support the large student-age population of Marion. She bemoaned, "It seems as though their children ought to suffer with the rest. Really don't you think others ought to have a chance to attend before the Trustees' children?"[44]

The next year, N. E. Willis, an AMA teacher, wrote to Cravath, but his letter revealed a tone much different from the tone of the Leonard letters. Willis had met Curtis at a Sunday School convention in Montgomery. He found Curtis willing to cooperate with the American Missionary Association, which had begun to court Curtis for educational favors;[45] six days after the Willis meeting, G. W. Andrews wrote to Cravath that he (Cravath) had made a good impression on Curtis. By May, Willis had told Cravath of a conversation with Joseph H. Speed, the state superintendent of education. Speed indicated that although the governor had pocket vetoed a bill designed to pay for teacher salaries, the legislature had passed a measure to create normal or teacher training schools. Such an act pleased Curtis, since it meant the American Missionary Association would not control African American education at Marion.[46]

Events were moving fast and favorably toward the establishment of a public school at Marion. Still, the American Missionary Association did not relinquish its quest to provide teachers and to control the school.[47] Then, by August, they discerned that state aid, though small, was forthcoming.[48] Finally, they and African American Marionites realized their dream when the General Assembly created normal schools in Florence, Marion, and Huntsville. The schools at Marion and Huntsville operated as African American institutions. The new board of trustees for Lincoln Normal included Porter King, John Harris, John Dozier, J. H. Sears, and John T. Foster. Dozier already was a member of the General Assembly. His role as founder and pastor of one of the largest churches in Uniontown accounted for his political prominence.[49] James W. Steele, Joseph C. Bradley, and Lafayette Robinson served on the Huntsville school board. Robinson already had served as a delegate to the Constitutional Convention of 1867.[50]

Passage of the acts to create normal or teacher institutions was largely the work of Peyton Finley, the only African American to serve on the State Board of Education during the nineteenth century. Finley served on the board from 1871 to 1873 and attempted to create normal schools during his tenure. His final attempt ended with the vote tied at three because of the opposition of the board's Democratic members. After his departure from the board, however, he continued to work with board member John Sears to gain passage of his proposal. Thus, with Sears casting the decisive vote on 3 December 1873, Finley's proposal created teacher institutions for African Americans and whites for the first time in Alabama history. This activity is hardly surprising, since Finley was no newcomer to political affairs; he had served as a registrar and later as a delegate to the Constitutional Convention of 1867.[51]

Whatever the cause, the creation of the African American school at Marion gave several area African Americans opportunities for leadership. Unfortunately, within one year of the passage of the act to create black normal schools, the Democrats had returned to power. By December 1874 the State Board of Education had removed Speed, Sears, Dozier, and Foster from the Lincoln College Board of Trustees and replaced them with Democrats. John Silsby wrote to Cravath and indicated that some of the leading citizens of Selma had written letters to the new board to support his candidacy as an additional board member. He identified his supporters as Democrats, Baptists, and Presbyterians: "Dr. Ward, J. Haralson, Esq., Dr. Black and Ex chancellor Holloway."[52]

Although AMA activities at Marion provided opportunities for Curtis, Dozier, and Lee, Holland Thompson relied on his work with the American Missionary Association in Montgomery to ascend to a position of leadership. Thompson was the city's most important religious leader from 1866 to 1876. He had been a member of the integrated First Baptist Church, and when its African American members separated, Thompson helped them to organize the all-black First Colored Baptist Church. Black parishioners who had separated from the parent church laid the cornerstone for this new church in May 1867. He served as church clerk and as superintendent of the Sabbath School of the new church, which they named, as previously noted, the First Colored Baptist Church. In 1869, two years later, Thompson became president of the missionary society attached to the school. As a religious leader, he also helped to found the Second Colored Baptist Church, which later became known as the Dexter Avenue Baptist Church and was located one block from the state

143

capitol.[53]   Martin Luther King, Jr., would bring national acclaim to this church nearly a century later. Despite the preceding, Thompson did not limit his religious activities to the capital city; his activities spanned the state. He helped to convene the state's first Convention of Colored Baptist churches that assembled at the First Colored Baptist Church in December 1868. The Colored Baptist State Convention grew out of this meeting. Its delegates chose Thompson as secretary, and for several years he served as superintendent of the Sunday School division. Nearly 27 churches sent 100 delegates to this convention. The convention, comprised primarily of former bondsmen, raised nearly $50. Future African American legislators such as Mansfield Tyler of Lowndesboro and John Dozier of Uniontown also attended this convention, and like Thompson, they relied on the church as a vehicle for political advancement.[54]

Because of his religious activities, Thompson's relationship with AMA officials is easily understood. Charles Buckley, the superintendent of education for the Bureau, wrote to the Reverend George O. Whipple, the corresponding secretary of the American Missionary Association, on 13 March 1866, about the need to have a man at Montgomery to serve as the teacher at the normal school and as an "organizer and conductor of our colored Sabbath Schools. These freedmen need a standard of action in such matters."[55] One year later Buckley wrote to Cravath, "We need therefore, and must have in Montgomery a colored school of the highest order."[56]

144

The American Missionary Association found success in both instances. The same Holland Thompson became an agent for the missionary society. Then, after the Bureau appropriated $10,000 for a school building within walking distance of the capitol in 1868, local African Americans purchased the property and named George Stanley Pope as the first principal of the school. They chose to name the school Swayne School in honor of Wager Swayne, the head of the Alabama Bureau.[57] In this way, educational opportunities became a reality for African Americans in the capital city.

The amicable relationship between the American Missionary Association and Thompson was not a lasting one. Thompson later charged the American Missionary Association with trying to convert members of his Sabbath School to the Congregationalist persuasion; then, he severed ties with it. Fortunately, future legislators Elijah Cook and Hales Ellsworth helped to fill the void caused by his departure. Yet, neither of them possessed Thompson's broad concerns nor his vast support.

Of the two, Cook had helped to establish the first school for African Americans in the basement of Montgomery's Old Ship Church. He also had helped Thompson to establish Swayne School. Even after his retirement Cook served on the board of trustees for Swayne School.[58] He also worked to advance African American education across the state. On the other hand, Ellsworth sat as a member of the county board of education. Additionally, Ellsworth was the earliest African American to serve on Montgomery's county

145

commission, and he continued close contacts with the American Missionary Association after 1873.[59]

Though it provided the greatest opportunities for leadership for the state's African American future officeholders, the American Missionary Association, like the Bureau, did not intentionally set out to prepare them for officeholding.[60] It came to Alabama to provide educational opportunities for African Americans. Regrettably, it soon found itself embroiled in controversy, first, with state officials, and second, with African Americans themselves. Oddly enough, this very controversy gave former slaves leadership opportunities. Through it all, religious differences existed; even though they were secondary to personality differences, these religious differences further exacerbated a slowly developing divergence of opinion of what was best for area African Americans.[61]

The church was the most important institution in the African American community both during slavery and during the immediate postbellum period. Although a state law of 1833 had prescribed that five whites must be present when slaves gathered for religious services, slaves still managed to have such services. Then, when the Civil War ended slavery, African Americans sought to establish their independent institutions. Against this background the Congregationalist American Missionary Association and other Northern agencies considered the newly emancipated slaves as prime targets for conversion. AMA logic simply did not appeal to former slaves. If Willis, Cravath, Leonard, and other AMA officials had only studied African American attitudes--and benefitted from it--before or even while trying to reach them, they would have discovered quickly that the logic of Congregationalism held little interest for African Americans. Hence, it was not surprising that few African Americans--future political leaders or laymen--worked closely with the American Missionary Association.[62]

Other Northern religious agencies also came South immediately after the war and sought to convert former bondsmen. They, too, were unsuccessful. Northern Methodist missionaries came to Alabama and, expectantly, they received the most vehement opposition from Southern Methodists--all of whom were white. For their part, Southern Methodists charged that their Northern peers intended to spread hatred among Alabama's African Americans. Yet, despite the opposition of these Southern whites--which they likely expected to help their missionary work among African Americans--Northern Methodism still found few adherents among the latter. True, future Constitutional Convention of 1867 delegate Benjamin Inge, of rural Sumter County, accepted the Methodist doctrine, but he died in 1869, too early to determine the impact of Northern Methodism. Frank H. Threatt also accepted Northern Methodism. Threatt represented Demopolis, Marengo County, for one term in the House of Representatives.[63]

Relatively few institutions sought to help African Americans after the Civil War; still, fewer agreed wholeheartedly with the idea of African American independence. Northern agencies, such as those identified earlier, failed in Alabama because they sought to shape the lives of African Americans to their liking and therefore gave little or no consideration to the African American's quest for independence. It is not surprising, then, that few African American ministers willingly worked with them. Several of the African American ministers who worked with these agencies enjoyed political careers. Nonetheless, those African Americans who worked with the American Missionary Association, the Union League, and the Freedman's Bureau represented only a few of the total number of future African American lawmakers. As a result, few of the state's future African American lawmakers possessed any significant training before accepting major legislative responsibilities, and this stark fact had far-reaching and, for the most part, discouraging-to-tragic consequences.

The influence of the American Missionary Association aside, the numbers and terms of black elected officials highlight the lack of impact of the agencies just discussed. Those same numbers and terms clearly reveal that, despite their earlier experiences, few black lawmakers won reelection bids. That only two members, or less than 2 percent of the state's African American elected officials, served for the duration of the period supports this earlier contention.

James K. Greene of Perry County served for four consecutive terms in the legislature. He was first elected as a delegate to the Constitutional Convention of 1867. Or consider Benjamin F.

148

Royal of Bullock County, the most successful African American lawmaker. He began the first of his four Senate terms in 1870. Two other African Americans--Greene Shadrack Washington Lewis of Perry County and Lawrence Speed of Bullock County--served for three terms in the legislature.[64] Although 38, or 36 percent, were reelected, an overwhelming 70, or 64 percent, served only single terms. Of the successful African American lawmakers of the era, only Benjamin F. Royal was associated with the American Missionary Association, the Freedmen's Bureau, or the League. Furthermore, nearly all African American lawmakers didn't learn the art of reelection politics, largely because most of them ascended to their political positions after having known freedom for less than three years. Indeed, few agencies or allies were available--or really willing-- to instruct them in the rudiments of political affairs.[65]

Most of the state's Reconstruction congressmen were equally unsuccessful at winning reelection. Thus, five, or 20 percent, of the Reconstruction congressmen served for a single term. In contrast, scalawag Charles Hays was the state's most successful congressman; he served for four consecutive terms. Northern Republican and former Bureau agent Charles Buckley served for three terms. Then, too, Democrats Peter M. Dox and John H. Caldwell and scalawag Joseph H. Sloss served for two terms.[66]

None of the congressmen elected at large won renomination. In fact, few Reconstruction era lawmakers were reelected. The lack of a meaningful political experience was a central characteristic distinguishing both African American and white lawmakers in Alabama. The result was that, although an astounding 84 percent of the state's congressmen had held other political offices prior to their election to Congress, an equally depressing 80 percent didn't maintain their seats for a second term.[67]

Military Service

Paradoxically, the Civil War gave four of Alabama's African American future lawmakers an opportunity to serve in limited leadership capacities, although they did not excel in these roles. One, John Carraway of Mobile, served with the 54th Massachusetts Regiment; yet, there is no evidence that he assumed a leadership role with this all-black group. Also, there is no evidence that he excelled--or even participated--with the 54th Massachusetts in the battle of Fort Wagner, South Carolina--a battle in which black future South Carolina legislator William H. Carney excelled. On 18 July 1863 Carney and other members of the 54th Massachusetts began to draw near the fort. Carney stood alone as the other members of his unit fell victim, one by one, to enemy gunfire. When rescued, he boasted, "The old flag never touched the ground, boys."[68] Carney's actions were in sharp contrast to the role of John Carraway in the same battle. Having entered the Union Army on 12 March 1863 and having served with Company A, John Carraway probably fought in this battle. If he did distinguish himself, there is no record of heroism.[69]

150

Carraway's military service provided him the opportunity to see African Americans in leadership roles. Even without a position of leadership, he probably considered such African American military leaders as William H. Carney, Martin R. Delaney, and Robert Smalls as role models.[70] In any event, it is clear the army never intentionally set out to train African Americans as leaders, nor did it set out to mitigate the "sambo" image or its impact by giving African Americans role models. Despite the original intent of military agencies, African Americans gained immensely from their military careers through travel, through the opportunity to work away from the plantation and, through the chance to see other African Americans as leaders.

Unlike other branches of the military, the Navy provided excellent opportunities for African Americans, having permitted African American enlistment since the War of 1812. Moses Brown Avery of Mobile was among the 5 percent of African Americans who served in the Union Navy during the Civil War. A naval order rescinding an earlier order limiting rank and the near-complete absence of discrimination and segregation was especially appealing to African American recruits. Avery served on the gunboat *Clifton*, where the pleasant atmosphere of naval services impressed him favorably.[71] Yet, Avery, too, did not excel as a military leader. Although, in the Battle of Galveston, he received crippling wounds that caused him to terminate his military career, his role in that battle was very small. But, he applied the tremendous experience he gained from his military service to his political career.

Travel was one of the benefits of military service, and Avery traveled in the Southwest, especially in Texas. Such travel gave African American servicemen a cosmopolitan perspective that they could gain in no other way. As an emancipated mulatto, Avery--like Carraway--had known freedom and the advantages of travel before the war. His wartime travel gave him unique and exciting experience.

The opportunity to see armed African Americans also later influenced the perspective of many African Americans. Mobile, the area with the state's largest contingent of antebellum free African Americans and its most vocal African American officials, was also the area in Alabama where the Reconstruction era had ended earliest. Oddly enough, none of Mobile's African American lawmakers served after 1870, despite its African American representatives having been either free-born or emancipated by the close of the war. Also, the area's African American representatives were well traveled. Yet, it appears the cosmopolitan perspectives derived from wide travel proved insufficient to overcome the political and social obstacles facing African American politicians of the Reconstruction era.[72]

Minor Officeholding

As events unfolded, most of the state's African American future officeholders relied initially on minor political roles to get later major political positions. After the war, Alabama's African American lawmakers assumed leadership positions for the first time. The life of Benjamin S. Turner shows the path followed by a privileged former slave as he rose to become an officeholder. Turner was privileged to be one of Selma's wealthiest and most influential African Americans both before and after the war. He relied on his ownership of a livery stable and his role as operator of one of Selma's largest hotels for whites to acquaint himself with some of the city's most prominent white citizens and some of its most influential African Americans, although African Americans did not visit the hotel as patrons. Then, on 2 April 1865, when it appeared some of the city's residents would escape the ravages of war, General James H. Wilson and his raiders marched into Selma and destroyed their property, taking 2,700 prisoners, more than 100 pieces of equipment, and hundreds of horses and war supplies. Turner did not escape the ravaging; he, too, lost much property. Drawing on his resilience, however, Turner soon regained some of his wealth through sound business dealings.[73]

Obviously, Turner was more fortunate than the African Americans who came to Selma after the war without visible means of support. Anyhow, he and John H. Henry, a prominent white Selma physician, addressing a group of freedmen at Weaver's Grove, located in rural Dallas County, urged the former slaves to return to work. This, among things, caused white residents to pay attention to Turner's rapidly rising influence. They credited him with the return to order in the area.   In turn, his position of influence propelled him to a position of leadership. Consequently, after the passage of the Reconstruction Acts of March 1867, the citizens of Selma called on Turner to accept the position of tax collector for Dallas County. That he resigned this position one year later for personal reasons did not hurt his public image.[74]

Therefore, when Turner returned to political affairs in 1869, his campaign as an independent candidate for the city council was successful. Later, when the Republicans nominated him for Congress in 1870, he sold his horse to finance his campaign.   Yet, his election as the first African American officeholder to represent Alabama in Congress was also his last major office.   Whatever the reason, he decided not to seek reelection in 1872, preferring instead to return to Selma to manage his newly purchased farm.[75]

He could have gained other elective offices, because he was a favorite among the electorate of Dallas County. Perhaps one can find a clue to his political retirement in his temperament, for he refused to engage in political acrimony. Observers noted he "was too gentle a man for political infighting, even if he had not lived in a state where the Ku Klux Klan thrived."[76]   A Washington correspondent of the New York *Globe* described Turner as "a big broad-shouldered man with a large nose and curly hair.   He is very quiet, seldom seen conversing, always present, never speaks, and among Republican colleagues, has a considerable reputation for good sense and political sagacity."[77]

Many other African American future legislators also relied on minor officeholding to gain the attention of the public.[78] James Thomas Rapier, the second African American to represent Alabama in Congress and the state's most prolific African American officeholder, was appointed as a notary public on 6 December 1867.[79] Rapier had served as a delegate to the Nashville Convention of Freedmen two years earlier. Therefore, he and Moses Brown Avery, former recording secretary of the Louisiana state executive committee, were the only African American delegates at the Constitutional Convention of 1867 with extensive political experience inside or outside Alabama.[80]

Rapier possessed other experiences that enhanced his political future. As a student in Canada, he had recited before King Edward IV of England, who was visiting the United States and Canada. Rapier's articulation had impressed the king. After the war began, he had wanted to travel to his family home in Alabama, but the wide-ranging hostilities of war made such travel impossible. Therefore, he settled in Nashville and gained employment there as a teacher. When the war ended, he traveled to other parts of the South as a correspondent for a Northern newspaper.[81]

Later embroiled in politics, Rapier found that political exhortations came easy for him, because he could draw from his earlier addresses, especially his Nashville convention plea to white citizens of Tennessee. In that speech, he emphasized the importance of African American suffrage. Success at the polls also was easier for Rapier than it was for other African American legislators, because he could rely on the support of his 100 employees in Alabama. This alone could not account for his success, since he had to gain the support of the white electorate in his district, too. The white majority vote exceeded that of African Americans by more than 600. This fact led him to assume he would receive white support on the state level and so drove him to seek statewide office. Accordingly, he campaigned unsuccessfully for the Office of Secretary of State in 1870. This campaign made him the only African American to seek statewide office during the nineteenth century.[82]

Rapier was not the only African American lawmaker awarded a minor appointment; others were appointed as justices of the peace or constables. Elijah Baldwin served as a constable in Wilcox County.[83] George Braxdell accepted a justice of the peace position in Talladega on 4 September 1868.[84] Two others became justices of the peace. Of these, John Dozier combined his ministerial duties with his new duties as justice of the peace, assuming that position on 5 December 1868.[85] The other, Greene Shadrack Washington Lewis, one of the Blackbelt's most outspoken lawmakers, received his justice of the peace appointment on 12 December 1871.[86]

For reasons unknown, African Americans falsely assumed winning a justice of the peace position would lead to a rich political future and increased personal prestige. For these same reasons, many of the state's future African American lawmakers gravitated toward these positions. Since they could travel in an official capacity, they became role models for other African Americans. Then, as they performed marriage ceremonies and carried out other routine duties of the office, they began to give greater import to the official capacity in which they then served. Also, their being informed of social and political events of state-wide and national importance sooner than nonpoliticians of their region also contributed to their overestimating the position's value as a political power base.

However, if their serving in an official capacity and their acquiring a knowledge of state and national events earlier than their peers were the only reasons motivating African Americans to aspire to these positions before their ascendancy to the General Assembly, then they do not explain why they continued to seek these and similar minor positions after they had left higher office and Reconstruction had ended. Former legislator G. W. Allen was appointed and commissioned as a justice of the peace for Precinct 2 of Opelika, in Lee County, on 13 April 1885.[87] Thomas J. Clarke served as a constable at Lincoln, Precinct 1, in Talladega from March 1885 to November 1886.[88] Jacob Martin was appointed as a justice of the peace for Dallas County on 27 November 1881.[89] Former engrossing clerk William H. Councill--then president of a Huntsville, Alabama, college--received his commission as notary public for Madison County on 24 January 1881.[90] African Americans continued to accept these minor positions regularly, suggesting they considered such positions to have purpose other than as a means to higher leadership levels. That no African American held an administrative position in state government should have provided sufficient proof to them that such positions as justice of the peace and constable would not lead to major officeholding. A more practical explanation for their seeking these minor positions is that they needed the income.

Summary

African Americans in both Louisiana and South Carolina were far better prepared for leadership positions than were their Alabama peers.[91] The experiences of North Carolina's black lawmakers were much the same.[92] Alabama Reconstruction, then, provides a splendid example of an area where postwar leadership was deficient and where allies were few. African Americans associated with the Bureau or the American Missionary Association despite unrelenting white opposition and the paternalistic attitudes of agency personnel. Black future officeholders gained invaluable leadership experience largely through minor officeholding rather than through their relationships with benevolent agencies.

First Colored Baptist Church
Alabama Department of Archives and History, Montgomery

Dexter—Then—1895

Zelia S. Evans and J. T. Alexander, eds., *Dexter Avenue Baptist Church, 1877-1977: One-Hundred-Year History of A Famous Religious Institution* (Montgomery, Ala.: Dexter Avenue Baptist Church, 1978), ii.

CHAPTER 5

EDUCATION, LAND, AND ECONOMIC DEVELOPMENT

The Civil War ended slavery in Alabama, left the state a wasteland of economic devastation, and forced most Alabamians to reorder their lives. With amazing swiftness African Americans could move about nearly at will, make valid contracts, receive the rudiments of an education, vote for the first time, and legalize their antebellum marriages. In stark contrast, however, because most African Americans could survive only by engaging in agricultural labor, they found their aspirations for economic independence quickly squelched. This situation resembled slavery in many respects. Finally, although both poor African Americans and whites found it extremely difficult to carve out a livelihood after the war, blacks found it more difficult to survive because of overt and covert racism.[1]

Most African Americans saw the end of the war as an excellent opportunity to stabilize their lives. The words of historian W. E. B. DuBois are especially insightful. He believes the three "essential features of slavery were the absence of legal marriage, family, and control over children."[2] DuBois continues, "During slavery his [a slave husband's] wife could be made his master's concubine, his daughter could be outraged, his son whipped, or himself sold away without being able to protest or lift a preventing finger."[3] However, since all Alabama slaves did not live in an organized community, as slaves did on the Henry Watson plantation in Blackbelt Greene County, Alabama blacks immediately set out to rectify the adverse impact slavery had had on their families. These families now had a chance to come together; mother-child relations could be strengthened; and men could become responsible for the livelihood of their families.[4]

One writer of the period suggests the "most important manifestation of this change in the condition of the Negro family was the result of the legalization of slave marriages."[5] Commented the Mobile *Nationalist*, "Slavery taught us that the marriage relation was a thing of no sacredness, to be abolished at the will of another. It subverted the authority of parents."[6] C. Peter Ripley writes that in Louisiana "some planters acknowledged slave marriages" and encouraged both marriage and the family as much as possible "within the context of slavery."[7] In contrast to antebellum times, the weight of the law supported African American marriages during the postbellum period.[8] Therefore, General Wager Swayne of the Freedmen's Bureau ordered a general remarriage of persons who had married without license or had lived together without license and required that all employers enforce it. He later perceived the impracticality of enforcing his regulation, although the constitutional conventions of 1865 and 1867 both adopted resolutions calling for the legalization of African American marriages. Many Southern states in both the antebellum and the immediate postbellum periods did not require the registration of slaves marriages; instead, they required only the legalization of marriages.[9]

More importantly, African Americans themselves were not without a sense of responsibility. Herbert G. Gutman writes that former slave Cato Carter believed Alabama's African Americans "had their mar'age put in the book...after the breakin' up, plenty had grown children."[10] Indeed, most African Americans, including many future African American politicians, sought to legalize their informal marriages. Some even legalized slave marriages immediately after slavery. One such person, Holland Thompson of Montgomery, legalized his antebellum marriage to Binah Yancey in August 1865, although the couple had given birth to a son in 1862. She had lived on the plantation of secessionist leader William Lowndes Yancey.[11] John Carraway proudly introduced a resolution at the Constitutional Convention of 1867 to declare "all freedmen and women living together [be] recognized as man and wife." Samuel S. Gardner of Maine amended Carraway's resolution on 30 November 1867 so that it declared "null and void all prosecutions for bigamy, adultery, or fornification instituted against any persons [sic]...who had married another."[12]

Emphasis on Education

Future African American lawmakers also worried about educational concerns. At Montgomery's first New Year's Day Emancipation Proclamation program, Holland Thompson reflected on the life of President Abraham Lincoln and then turned his attention to the future of African Americans in Alabama. He sought to allay the fears of whites by admonishing his fellows to "show by good conduct, by industry and fidelity to duty, that the year 1866 was a year of jubilee, instead of insurrection."[13]

Thompson emphasized that "Providence had denied them learning, but it was now in their [African Americans'] power to secure education for their little ones."[14] Not only did Thompson express a concern for the education of African American youth, but he also revealed an equal concern for the religious training of his people. Acknowledged Thompson, "They must lay aside their prejudices and unite together--Methodists, Presbyterians, Baptists, and Catholics--to make one good school for all."[15] Thompson also paused to reflect on the new postbellum condition of African Americans when he exclaimed, "No man, today, was to be torn from his wife and children; no wife sold from those nearer and dearer to her than life; no child torn from its weeping parents."[16] Before closing his speech, Thompson urged African Americans to show thrift and economy. He also wanted every African American to own land and a home.[17]

164

One could have easily dismissed Thompson's remarks or overlooked them, as did the local newspaper. Yet, other key African American politicians articulated Thompson's well-orchestrated concerns as time progressed. First, he sought to dispel the fears of whites of an insurrection on New Year's Day. Second, he discussed issues of importance to African Americans, such as landownership, education, family, and wage contracts. His comments earned him the respect of local whites and the admiration of his African American contemporaries. More importantly, Thompson's remarks helped to set the tone for African Americans as they sought to carve an existence for themselves in postbellum Alabama. Most of all, his speech revealed a strong sense of optimism.[18]

Thompson was not alone in his prescience. The next year, as African Americans prepared to select registrars, who comprised the state's first group of African American public officials, James Thomas Rapier addressed a meeting of African Americans in the Tennessee Valley town of Florence. He explained the meaning of the recently passed Reconstruction Acts and ended his speech with the caveat: "In our first act of participation in the politics of the State, [let us] proceed with calmness, moderation, and intelligence."[19]

Rapier received the opportunity to proceed according to his wishes. With calmness he helped to draft a document at the 1867 meeting of the Alabama Republican State Convention that called for "free speech, free press, free schools, and equal rights for all

165

men without distinction on account of color."[20] With moderation, he urged the delegates at the Constitutional Convention of 1867 to remove the political disabilities of former Confederates and to secure equal rights for African Americans. With intelligence, he pleaded to these delegates for a moderate disfranchisement clause, a lenient oath of office, and a common carrier section in the bill of rights.[21]

Paradoxically, neither Thompson nor Rapier expected opposition to their views on landownership, education, employment, voting rights, and social equality. They, like most other African Americans, held fast to a dream of democracy and freedom, which was not unlike the dream of most other Americans. They dreamed of owning a home and land, getting an education, and receiving recompense for their labors. But, economic, social, and political circumstances continually dashed the dreams and aspirations African Americans held as they disembarked from slavery.[22]

Educational achievement was central to African American advancement. Other field hands had been in the same predicament as future African American legislator James K. Greene of Hale County, who recalled that during slavery "he had been entirely ignorant; knew nothing more than to obey [his master]."[23] He recounted that others (African Americans) "didn't know the Lord's prayer, but the tocsin of freedom sounded and knocked at the door, and they walked out like free men and met the exigencies as they grew up, and shouldered the responsibilities."[24] The Mobile *Nationalist* further

166

enlightened African Americans about the meaning of an education, "Let us all strive to have all our people learn to read and to write and to obtain all the knowledge we can; and especially, let us be untiring in wise efforts for the education of our children."[25]

In similar fashion, future African American lawmaker William V. Turner of Wetumpka reminded a largely African American gathering of its indebtedness to God, Abraham Lincoln, and the Republican party for breaking the shackles of slavery. He explained that freedom would be worthless, if they didn't improve that freedom, and insisted that thrift, politeness, work, and education helped to sustain freedom. Foremost, he impressed his listeners with the importance of education. "Without this," he stressed, "you can never enjoy liberty in its fullness."[26] Turner's emphasis on the need for an education was no less emphatic than James K. Greene's.

African Americans had other motives for wanting an education. They wanted an education to increase the power of the African American family, especially the father. They also considered education as a way of extricating their children from the control of former masters. To African Americans, education was nearly synonymous with freedom.[27] However, in antebellum Alabama, schools for blacks had existed only in the Mobile area. As one writer of the period notes, "The record showed that there were no colored children attending any sort of school in Greensboro."[28] In 1854 the legislature enacted a school law and passed a statute entitled, "To Prohibit the Teaching of Slaves to Read and Write." The sentiment of whites toward African American education did not change significantly during the postbellum period; they, too, realized education would place the African American child beyond their control.[29]

The apprentice system, already discussed, also significantly inhibited the stability of the African American family. An act of the legislature of 1865 gave the probate judge the authority to apprentice African American children if their parents could not provide adequate financial support. Two provisions of this act gave the probate judge extraordinary power. First, he had the right to a compensation of one dollar, payable to the former master or mistress to whom the child was apprenticed; second, the other provision gave the former owner preference for the service of the child. Therefore, many children found themselves bound to former owners in a system similar to slavery.[30]

For example, one African American woman complained to General Swayne that her granddaughter had been apprenticed before the body of the girl's father was hardly cold.[31] The Mobile *Nationalist* wrote that African American orphans were placed in the custody of whites until the girls reached 18 and the boys reached 21. This tactic, lamented the newspaper, allowed these orphans to grow up in ignorance.[32] Despite the vehement protestations of African American parents to the Freedmen's Bureau, probate judges continued to apprentice African American children.[33]

The burning of their schools and churches also deterred the growth of educational institutions.[34] Southern whites claimed they burned African American churches because Northern whites used them as headquarters for area Union League meetings.[35]

African American education received its initial support from the state when the Constitution of 1868 provided for the state's first system of public education. Proceeding beyond the proscriptive laws of 1854 and 1856, this constitution provided for the education of youth between the ages of six and 20.[36] Still, this educational mandate didn't suggest whether the school system would be integrated or segregated; therefore, the Board of Education declared in August 1868 that "in no case shall it be lawful to unite in one school both colored and white children, unless it be by the unanimous consent of the parents and guardians of such children."[37] Obviously, Southern whites still feared educated African Americans. Walter Lynwood Fleming points that out "an educated negro was even more obnoxious to the slave-holding Southerner than a free Negro."[38]

Funding provided an excellent method of educational control. Because Alabama was emerging from the devastation of the war, the state found it impossible to provide large sums of money for public education. However, African American and white schools, although separate, received nearly equal funding. Educational opportunities became the greatest success of the Reconstruction era. Table 2 is a list of funding from 1869 to 1874. Diversion of funds, not

169

appropriations, did more to impede the growth of education in Alabama than did white opposition. That whites continued to burn school buildings attests to their persistent opposition.[39]

The educational provisions of the constitution of 1875 required the General Assembly to establish and maintain a separate system of education for children between the ages of seven and 21. The constitution continued the trend set by its predecessor of providing equal funding for African American and white schools. Continuing their quest for an independent educational system,

Table 2

School Statistics of Alabama, 1869-1874

Year	Money Appropriated	Money Received	Money Diverted
1869-70	500,407	306,872	187,872
1870-71	571,389	320,480	260,908
1871-72	604,978	166,303	438,675
1872-73	522,810	68,313	454,496
1873-74	474,346	-----	474,346

Source: Bond, *Negro Education in Alabama*, 99.

members of the Colored Baptist State Convention--the same body hat African American religious leaders established in Montgomery in December 1868--decided at its annual meeting in Tuscaloosa in 1873 to build a school for African Americans. In this way, they established the Alabama Normal and Baptist Theological School in 1878 as a denominational school with courses in the theological, normal, college preparatory, grammar, and primary departments. This school attracted a small but influential segment of the state's African American population. The school was renamed Selma University in 1908.[40]

Concern for Landownership

African Americans in Alabama showed an equal concern for landownership and education. Indeed, their aspirations paralleled those of other nineteenth-century Americans who held fast to the thesis that landownership provided the basis for wealth. They envisioned no rags-to-riches elevation for themselves; yet, they considered landownership necessary to control their educational institutions, families, and lives. They also firmly believed American citizenship entitled them to landownership if they could afford it. Their interest in landownership underwent a turning point after 1869, for when Congress passed the Fifteenth Amendment, African Americans shifted their emphasis from political agitation to agitation for landownership, education, homesteading, migration from the South, civil rights, and economic concerns.[41] After 1869 African American leaders espoused a more militant tone. Greene Shadrack Washington Lewis of Perry County articulated the mood of African Americans as he exclaimed in 1874, "We are done begging and pleading for our rights. Hereafter, we intend to demand them and

171

press [for] them on every occasion."[42]

Difficulties in owning land severely affected the ability of African Americans to support their educational institutions. They made their greatest accomplishments in education and received their most overwhelming disappointment in economics, largely because of their failure to purchase land. To address this shortcoming, Congress passed the Southern Homestead Act, which provided for homesteading in Alabama, Arkansas, Florida, Louisiana, and Mississippi. This act, passed in 1866, made landownership seem possible, something unprecedented for former servants.[43]

The Homestead Act was moderately successful in Florida, but it failed miserably in Alabama. Few freedmen knew of the availability of land, and by 1870 92 percent of the state's African American population lived in rural areas, far removed from the Mobile, Montgomery, and Huntsville offices. The Homestead Act failed because African Americans lacked the experience to operate a farm independently and because of the opposition of Alabama whites, who feared the loss of a cheap labor force. The failure of no other single act of Congress held greater meaning for the advancement of African American independence--and, at the same time, the failure of Reconstruction--than this act. The Louisiana Constitutional Convention discussed a plan by which land would be sold in small parcels if forfeited by defaulting taxpayers. South Carolina's African Americans petitioned Congress for a $1 million loan to make land available to the landless. The South Carolina delegates also created a land commission to buy land for African Americans.[44] Nothing of this nature occurred in Alabama.

To make matters worse, when African Americans possessed the financial means to reach land offices, they found the application fees of $4.00, and the patent fees of $5.00, exorbitant. In addition, homesteaders also paid a surveyor's fees that ranged from $15 to $20. The total costs to a freedman frequently ranged from $27 to $37. Holland Thompson suggested that for a freedman the "expenses of traveling to these offices and back again is often greater than the value of the land he would obtain."[45]

The Homestead Act restricted landownership to a small class of affluent African Americans, a class that could have secured land even without the assistance of the act.[46] Whereas the Homestead Act of 1862 made available 160 acres of land, the act of 1866 made available only 80 acres to each applicant. Paradoxically, John Silsby, the editor of the Mobile *Nationalist*, bubbled with enthusiasm when he initially learned of the Homestead Act. He incorrectly assumed a freedman needed only $5 to own land.[47]

In short, the act didn't help most African Americans--black officeholders, notwithstanding--to purchase land. Alabama's coterie of African American landowners were scattered across the state, mostly in areas where few other blacks lived and where the land was poor. Thus, the Homestead Act didn't help African Americans advance from chattel slavery to economic freedom.[48] Indeed, the acquisition of land would not give complete freedom to

173

African Americans; however, the failure of the act of 1866 and the advent of an ill-defined labor system meant African American freedom would not advance beyond emancipation.

Another roadblock for many African Americans was the difficulty they had in securing adequate wages. Yet, while much of this deficiency can be attributed to the sharecropping system, African Americans themselves preferred sharecropping because they believed it offered them greater control of their lives and it gave them the basis to obtain cash or the credit necessary to purchase land. But, they didn't recognize the scarcity of cash for African Americans or whites in postbellum Alabama.[49] Even when rural African Americans possessed the means to purchase real property, they could not sell their crops between sunset and sunrise until Green T. Johnston of Dallas County introduced a bill in the 1876-77 session of the legislature that was specifically designed to achieved that purpose.[50] The proscription on selling crops after sunset severely limited African Americans from enhancing their economic status, since few of them could afford to leave the field during the day to sell crops.

Need For Financial Institutions

A financial institution that provided credit and enabled African Americans to accumulate savings would have been beneficial. The national government initiated the first step in this direction in

March 1865 when it created the Freedmen's Savings and Trust Company Bank. Since many of its incorporators worked for the Bureau, these banks maintained a close connection with the Freedmen's Bureau.[51] Its headquarters were located in Washington, D.C., and branches proliferated in the Southern states. The first Alabama Freedmen's Savings Bank branch was established in Huntsville in December 1865, and other branches were located in Montgomery and Mobile during the next year. The Mobile branch was housed on the ground floor of the same building that housed the Mobile *Nationalist*. Each depositor received a bank book with a copy of the regulations enclosed. The directions suggested that President Lincoln had endorsed these financial institutions and that he had signed a bill to establish the Freedmen's Savings Company as his final act as president. The cover of the book also listed an attractive table that showed how rapidly daily savings of ten cents accumulated at an annual interest rate of 6 percent.[52]

Optimism was the central reaction of African Americans toward these financial institutions. In 1866 William Fiske of the American Missionary Association wrote, "Savings banks would do an immense amount of good in preventing the freedmen from frittering away their earnings in small amounts and worse still, for whiskey."[53] By 1870 the *New National Era*, the nation's leading black newspaper, wrote that freedmen were earning, saving, and investing, and "the time is not very far ahead when they will be an extremely comfortable well to do class."[54]

175

NEITHER CARPETBAGGERS NOR SCALAWAGS

The branches of the Freedmen's Savings Bank were immensely popular with Alabama blacks who lived at or near the offices. Few other blacks were aware of their existence, but those who deposited did so enthusiastically. Mobile blacks sacrificed from meager postwar earnings and deposited $4,809 during January 1866. By May 1869 the deposits in Mobile amounted to $50,111.66 and to $17,603.29 in Huntsville.[55] In all, the deposits for the Alabama banks ranged from $305,167 in 1866 to a high of $31,260,499 in 1872, the final year the branches were in full operation. The total deposit for the period was $55,000,000; the average annual deposit was $7,857,143. The average deposit for the period amounted to $284. In time, their deposits increased, reflecting a similar increase of confidence in freedmen banks.[56]

Because of these financial institutions, African American depositors could save enough money to sustain them through the winter months or through other difficult periods. Most of all, Freedmen's Saving Banks provided an opportunity for African Americans to make economic progress. For African Americans, both depositors and the African American population at large, these banks symbolized hope and reflected a commitment of the national government to help make for a better life.[57]

Freedmen's Savings Banks also gave African Americans the opportunity to finance mortgages and to buy land, but for several reasons these banks were short lived. Many failed because of mismanagement and fraud. Whatever the reason, because they bore the brunt of the experiment, African American depositors lost more than $160,850. Still, by 1886, depositors received late dividends amounting to 60 percent, although only a few depositors benefitted from the late payments.[58]

One African American, Lafayette Robinson, served as the first cashier of the Huntsville bank. He took leave of his duties to serve as a delegate to the Constitutional Convention of 1867. Robinson was not responsible for the failure of the Huntsville branch, nor were any of the other branch managers responsible for the loss to depositors.[59] The Depression of 1873 and speculation by incorporators caused the bank's failure. These same incorporators sought to restore the confidence of African Americans by appointing Frederick Douglass, former abolitionist and America's then best-known African American, as caretaker for the bank. Douglass not only failed to restore the stability of the bank, he also did not successfully renew the confidence African Americans had held for these banks.[60]

The Freedmen's Savings and Trust Company Bank was the final economic program initiated for African Americans during Reconstruction. By 1873 the Bureau had been dismantled, and the Thirteenth, Fourteenth, and Fifteenth amendments were ineffective. Federal programs--the Homestead Act, the Civil Rights Act of 1866, and the Freedmen's Bureau--had provided limited success for a race whose livelihood depended on the success and continuation of Federal legislation. When Federal programs failed, African

177

Americans in Alabama became disillusioned and considered emigration. Still, many more optimistic ones decided to remain in Alabama and to carve out a better way of life there for themselves and their families. Although African Americans had held conventions earlier and, also, had considered emigration before the failure of the Freedmen's Savings and Trust Bank, the period after its failure in 1872 marked a rise in the intensity of black interest in conventions and emigration.[61]

Impetus for Conventions

The decade of the 1870s signalled a turning point in the activities and interest of Alabama blacks, for even before the failure of the Freedmen's bank, African Americans correctly predicted the repeal of beneficial Federal legislation. Accordingly, they began to hold conventions to advance their cause. The spirit of optimism continued to dim as some pessimistic African Americans envisioned emigration to the Midwest as an alternative to remaining in the South and facing alone the wrath of whites.[62]

Therefore, in proportion to their numbers and the potential of American society, Alabama blacks had gained few benefits from Federally-sponsored programs. In other parts of the South, African Americans experienced an equal sense of neglect. They considered it paramount to support themselves. Pursuant to this end, they convened a series of conventions, all designed to provide a surrogate for government-sponsored programs. The interest in conventions was not a new experience; Northern African Americans had sponsored conventions since the 1830s, when they emphasized moral suasion to end slavery. The convention movement of the 1870s combined political activity with economics, something the previous movements had not done. Nonetheless, convention movements sought to enable African Americans to enjoy the rights and privileges of American citizenship.[63]

The tone of the conventions of the 1870s differed from the tone of their predecessors. Whereas earlier conventions had stressed conciliation, those of the 1870s gained impetus from congressional Radicals, who, in turn, steered passage of the Thirteenth, Fourteenth, and Fifteenth amendments. If the Bureau and other government-sponsored agencies had continued, perhaps the convention movement would not have occurred, or it might have taken a different course. Despite the passage of these amendments and civil rights legislation, such as the Civil Rights Act of 1866, African Americans continued to hold their conventions. Between 1869 and 1874, African American conventioneers focused on working conditions; in other words, they emphasized economic concerns.[64]

Stimulus for Labor Movement

James Thomas Rapier was one who had long recognized the need for the educational, political, and economic development of African Americans in the South. His interest in the economic development of the state's African American community began during the

179

antebellum period, when all efforts toward African American development seemed futile. As early as 1858, he had vowed, "If God is willing, I will do [my] part in solving the problems [of African American poverty and illiteracy] in my native land."[65] When the war ended, Rapier received his long-awaited opportunity. Within a short but frantic eight years, he would witness the shortcomings of the Freedmen's Bureau, the Civil Rights Act, the Homestead Act of 1866, financial support for the public schools, and the devastating impact of the Depression of 1873 on public education in Alabama.

To enhance African American financial independence, he accepted an appointment as director of the Freedmen's Savings Bank in Montgomery. At first the Montgomery branch bank was a thriving institution; then, the Depression of 1873 led to its regrettable end, even as it also destroyed the public system of education. Rapier used personal funds to build schools and churches. This generosity prompted J. N. Fitzpatrick, one well-traveled black Montgomerian, to exclaim, "No man in the state has more cheerfully aided our church in erecting places of worship and building than he."[66] Rapier could use as a model the work of the Louisiana's Freedmen's Aid Association, an agency designed to help African Americans with loans, agricultural equipment, land, and legal counsel.[67] More specifically, New Orleans blacks relied on unions to gain near-complete independence. Here, too, was a model for Rapier.[68]

180

He realized quite early that the dismal economic performance of Alabama blacks resulted in large part from their exclusion from the mainstream labor unions, although some of them occasionally managed to gain admission to craft unions. Indeed, the leadership ranks of the National Labor Union invited African American membership, but strong opposition from other members kept black participation at a minimum. In response, black skilled workers were forced to form their protective and benevolent associations. This split in labor's ranks was only one manifestation of the curse of the segregationist impulse that characterized the antebellum period--a curse that continued unabated during the 1870s, 1880s, 1890s, and well into the twentieth century.[69]

African Americans like Rapier came to realize the value of a labor organization, if they were to get economic independence. The *New National Era* noted, "In a word, without organization, you stand in danger of being exterminated. With organization you will find employment, you will force opposite [illegible] to recognize your claim to work without restriction because of your color and open the way for your children to learn trades and [to] move forward in the enjoyment of all the rights of American citizenship."[70]

The Colored National Labor Convention

As a response to their exclusion, African Americans convened the Colored National Labor Convention. Isaac Myers, the Baltimore ship-caulker, organized the assembly that met in Washington, D. C.,

181

in December 1869. Myers contended that "we are here to seek the amelioration and advancement of those who labor for a living."[71] The 155 other delegates chose George Downing, a delegate from Rhode Island, as permanent chairman. He urged the United States government to secure land for freedmen.[72] Other delegates asked for an eight-hour work day, the organization of state and local labor unions, and a graduated income tax. One delegate proposed that this tax sought "to make the burdens of taxation heaviest upon those who have reaped the lion's share of the American toll."[73] Many delegates did not represent the African American labor movement; instead, they were politicians, religious leaders, and perennial conventioneers.[74]

Rapier served as the sole representative from Alabama, and the evidence suggests he was self-appointed, reflecting his acute interest in the welfare of African Americans in Alabama. Naturally, then, as he had walked toward the podium in his new position as vice president of the National Negro Labor Union, he revealed a strong concern for many issues affecting his brethren. Still, he did not agree with the pledge for a graduated income tax, nor did he accept the idea of an eight-hour work day. However, he favored the resolution on African American landownership.[75]

Rapier considered it important for the Federal government immediately to provide African Americans with 50 million acres of land for homesteading in the South or in Kansas, Nebraska, or the Dakotas. He believed this scheme would make blacks independent and place them beyond the reach of Southern white landowners. His report the next day as a member of the Committee on Homesteading contained a more detailed analysis of his plans. The delegates unanimously accepted his report, which included a plan for the establishment of a Federal land bureau for blacks.[76]

Rapier and several other members of the convention sent a memorial to Congress for Southern blacks. They urged Congress to subdivide a portion of the 47 million acres of public lands located in the Southern states into homesteads. Their plan was simple: homesteaders would receive a deed to the land if they remained there for one year. Further, the efficacy of homesteading was economic independence for Southern blacks. With Joseph Rainey of South Carolina, John Harris of North Carolina, J. Sella Martin of Massachusetts, and other delegates, Rapier asked President Ulysses S. Grant to protect African American sharecroppers from their landlords, sanction African American landownership, and help them establish a Federal land bureau.[77] In response, the president promised his support, but with the passage of several months, Rapier realized he and the other delegates had received empty promises.[78]

Returning to Alabama, he fully perceived the task that lay before him. Most assuredly, he understood African Americans needed an effective labor union if they were to find success in politics or if they wanted to build a strong educational system. Also, he realized the need for the continued presence of the African

183

American father as head of the family if African Americans were to organize an effective labor organization.[79]

In effect this meant if blacks were to move forward, a strong labor union in Alabama was mandatory. To build the needed labor association, Rapier saddled his horse and rode across the state, talking to farmers and all others who would listen to an enthusiastic incipient labor organizer. He also carried with him a bundle of labor literature and urged African Americans to gather information about their churches, schools, and wages. Then he issued a call in the 16 December 1870 issue of the Montgomery *Alabama State Journal* for a state labor convention to assemble in Montgomery.[80] He issued this call as vice president of the National Negro Labor Union. African Americans all over the state then selected delegates to a three-day union convention--one scheduled for noon in the House of Representatives, beginning on 2 January 1871. Ninety-eight African American farmers, representing 42 counties, answered his call. He also asked the delegates to choose delegates to the National Negro Labor Convention, scheduled to assemble in Washington, D.C., the next week.[81]

Once convened, the delegation of carpenters, mechanics, cotton pickers, and sharecroppers selected Rapier as its permanent chairman. A lively discussion of the state of African American affairs followed. Several sharecroppers recounted how their white landlords had cultivated crops at their expense. Other sharecroppers related how they had contracted in January, assuming

184

they had sufficient protection for the remainder of the year, only to discover in December they were as poor as they were at the beginning of the year. They also explained the difficulties they had encountered in trying to purchase land and how the activities of the Klan had retarded their economic progress.[82]

More specifically, former African American legislator George W. (ashington) Cox of Montgomery, chairman of the Homesteads Committee, asked African Americans to leave Alabama. He exclaimed, "Here huddled as we are, so much of the same kind of labor in the market, wages down to starving rates, without land, or a house that we can call our own, nothing is in store for the masses."[83] Cox refused to consider homesteading in Alabama, because the sites for possible homesteading were found in areas frequently visited by terrorist bands. He suggested African Americans remove to Kansas and other Western states, where they could buy land and live as free men.[84] Cox had become disgruntled with the policies of the state Republican party, and by 1872 he no longer worked for the party of Lincoln; he joined Caesar Shorter and other blacks who believed Democrats offered better opportunities.[85]

African American former state legislator William V. Turner of Wetumpka in Elmore County chaired the Committee on the Condition of Colored People and agreed with Cox. Turner declared the conditions of African Americans in Alabama were worse than those in any other section of the United States. He emphasized that African American schools received inadequate funding and revealed that, in some

185

areas of the state, African American schools were dilapidated; in other areas of the state, their schools were not tolerated.[86] Turner, Rapier, and Cox recommended emigration to the West as a cure for the ills of Alabama society.[87] The delegates recommended that "each owner of 160 tillable acres of land spend $1,000 to furnish better homes, tools, and other improvements for his tenants; that the convention set up wage standards; that the convention appeal to Federal authorities for aid in education and for protection against the Klan; and that members support the Freedmen's Savings and Trust Companies."[88]

The convention rejected the resolution that called for emigration to the Midwest, but it endorsed the reports on the economy and on education. A rejection of the call for emigration was aimed at Turner and Cox. The Barbour County *Bluff City Times* reminded African Americans to think for themselves and to disregard the advice of men like Cox and Turner. The Montgomery *Advertiser* wrote that emigration was a carpetbagger idea, manufactured by Northerners, and cautioned African Americans to beware of this scheme and to remain at home and work zealously. Even some white friends counseled African Americans to remain at home. The editor of the Montgomery *Alabama State Journal* wanted them to consider settling among a more liberal people only if denied all opportunity for improvement at home. The Selma *Press* asked them not to act hastily.[89] Paradoxically, these newspapers didn't offer solutions to the remonstrances of these African American delegates, nor did they address whites about black concerns.

As the convention came to a close, the Committee on Permanent Organization issued its report and named the association the Labor Union of Alabama, making it an affiliate of the National Negro Labor Union. This committee designated offices and established an executive and a constitution committee. The Constitution Committee suggested the purpose of the organization was "to further the welfare and education of the laboring people of the state."[90]

Then the delegates chose state representative Jeremiah Haralson of Selma as its first president. In addition, they chose Rapier, Hale County representative James K. Greene, and Montgomery County representative Latty J. Williams to represent the Alabama affiliate at the second annual meeting of the National Negro Labor Convention that assembled in Washington, D. C., the following week. Before adjourning, the delegates appropriately applauded Rapier for his untiring efforts for the laboring people of Alabama.[91]

Rapier, Williams, and Greene arrived in the nation's capital one week after the Montgomery convention. Again, Rapier was among the first group to address the body, and for the second time he asked Congress to establish an agency to help African Americans to purchase land. On this occasion Rapier proceeded beyond his earlier request; he now specifically requested that Congress create a bureau of labor to help African Americans locate homesteads in the public domain. Rapier's ideas appealed to other delegates.

187

NEITHER CARPETBAGGERS NOR SCALAWAGS

Isaac Myers considered the organization a vehicle to distribute information. George Downing accepted Rapier's plan for improving the condition of American blacks. The black labor group decided to establish local affiliates in the Southern states except Alabama, where Rapier already had established such an organization.[92]

The Alabama delegation agreed to reassemble the state affiliate upon their return home. They believed they should gather and coordinate more information about the condition of the African American wage earner in Alabama. To this end, 50 delegates met again at Montgomery for two days. The body assembled on 14 December 1873, nearly one year after the first meeting of the Labor Union of Alabama, and discussed earnings of tenant farmers, educational opportunities, and homesteading. The Committee on Labor and Wages reported the tenant farmer's average earning of $387 a year allowed little with which to purchase food, medical supplies, clothing and feed. This committee wanted Congress to create a joint stock company to purchase land for African Americans. The Committee on Emigration recommended emigration, just as a similar convention did in Georgia.[93]

Still, the report on education received most of the attention from the delegates. Chairman J. B. Simpson of Montgomery reported that African American school attendance was impressive and that the State Board of Education had done all it could to provide a sound education for black students. Rapier agreed with the reports on wages and emigration, but he took strong exception to the report on

188

education. He pointed out that the black student did not receive a good education because of inadequate funding; Alabama allocated only $1.20 per student in comparison to $16.45 in Massachusetts. Rapier further commented that Alabama employed teachers with deficient skills in mathematics and grammar. As a solution, he recommended the creation of a board to screen teachers. The most striking aspect of his report was his suggestion that the Federal government assume the responsibility for educating Alabama's children by using the $115 million a year it received from internal revenue, which, if divided among the Southern states, would allow the schools in Alabama to remain open at least for nine months each year.[94]

The emigration idea didn't subside because of the votes of the delegates. To be sure, the notion of emigration began immediately after the war. Noted the Mobile *Nationalist*, "Without advising anyone to leave the South, we will say to those who are resolved to emigrate, that Kansas is one of the best states of the North to go to."[95] The Jacksonville *Republican* was the only white organ to propose black emigration: "The funds expended by the Freedmen's Bureau [should] be applied to paying the expenses of any of the colored population who may desire to go where they can better their conditions."[96] The next year, the Gadsden *Times* reported that an average of 50 wagons a week had passed through town.[97] The emigration impulse was so intense that emigration agents roamed through Barbour, Russell, Lee, Macon, Bullock, Chambers, Sumter,

189

Pickens, Pike, Conecuh, Clarke, Talladega, and Montgomery counties to entice African Americans to leave these areas. Local authorities compelled them to pay a fee of $100 for solicitation.[98]

AMA officials in north Alabama complained that "emigration [will take] away the greater part of the present church as soon as the members can sell their property."[99] Two months later they reported that "five families, numbering 18 people, will leave Florence for Kansas, leaving about half the numerical equivalent but not the strength."[100] James Thomas Rapier visited Kansas in 1880 and made large investments in real estate. Upon his return to Alabama, the politically oriented Rapier declared that "Kansas will go fifty thousand for Garfield and Arthur."[101]

Though many African Americans expressed an interest in emigration, few of them migrated, despite the threats they received for trying to vote. The Montgomery *Daily State Journal* noted that many of the best black laborers "have emigrated to Missouri and Arkansas under the impression their rights as citizens would be more likely to be respected there than here."[102] Montgomerian Robert H. Knox testified that blacks should remain in Alabama a while longer and pray for protection from Klan violence at the polls and enforcement of the Unites States Constitution and laws.[103] Enforcement, however, was not on the agenda of officials in Washington or Montgomery.

EDUCATION, LAND, AND ECONOMIC DEVELOPMENT

Summary

By the end of the Reconstruction era, despite the soundness of the pleas of black Alabamians, the discouraging response to their grievances was uniform. Even many white members of the Republican party remained indifferent to the pleas of the black masses and their spokesmen. When Arthur Bingham barely mentioned the events of the African American labor convention in his *Alabama State Journal*, the conclusion was inevitable.

It appeared Alabama blacks had gone full circle. They had enthusiastically joined the party of Lincoln by the thousands only to see their aspirations dashed by mass indifference or hostility; they had gone to Washington to speak with the president; they had held conventions to advance their cause in the absence of governmental support; they had considered emigration, in turn, only to have friends and foes tell them to remain in Alabama; and they had listened to Rapier's admonition that they proceed with caution. The results had been the same.

Therefore, after the Reconstruction period, African Americans began to retreat. They had to reconsider politics as a vehicle for their development. They asked but received few trustworthy answers to their question, "Why are white Republicans indifferent to blacks?"

191

PART 2

THAT SUN ALSO SETS

CHAPTER 6

VIOLENCE, FRAUD, AND INTRAPARTY STRIFE

SECTION 1

Three important elections occurred in Alabama between February 1868 and November 1870. Partisan politics surfaced in each of these elections when Democrats and Republicans sought the right and legitimacy to officeholding. On one hand, Klan violence helped Democrats to win elections. Through a reign of terror in western and northern Alabama, Klansmen tortured, murdered, and drove black and white Republicans from their homes and families. On the other hand, Republicans called on Federal troops to monitor elections when they feared violence would interfere with proper voting procedures. From their relentless attempts to control elections, both parties saw varying degrees of factionalism emerge.

The Reconstruction government that met in Montgomery on 13 July 1868 was an unstable coalition of Republicans--Northern and native-born whites and former slaves--and a handful of Democrats. The success of the experiment depended on the ability of these Republicans to minimize their differences.

NEITHER CARPETBAGGERS NOR SCALAWAGS

First Republican Governor

Alabama elected its first Republican governor on 4 February 1868. Confident in victory, Republicans lacked the prescience to discern that by 1874, a period of only six years, a Republican governor would leave office for the last time. Republicans had every reason to feel secure in 1868. In power for only 18 months, they had rewritten the constitution of every Southern state government except Mississippi, Virginia, and Texas. They would do these three the next year. In addition, Ulysses S. Grant, a Republican, had been elected president. Despite their success, Republicans would be the last persons to admit the role of intraparty strife in their fall from power in Alabama.[1] Alabama Reconstruction failed in part because the Republican coalition found few reasons to work in unison.

There was little evidence during the early months of 1868 that the Republican ascendancy would be brief. The ability of Republicans to win major offices after the adoption of the Constitution of 1868 astounded even Democrats. The Democratic, or Conservative, party, comprised mainly of former Whigs, Know Nothings, and some native pro-Union men, and led by James Holt Clanton, opposed the work of the Republican party.[2] Democrats' dislike for Republicans was underscored by one contemporary newspaper that claimed Democrats hated Republicans themselves, their dogs, horses, and the grounds that yielded them reward for their labor. They said, "There is nothing that a Republican has that is any good except his money, and they say he stole that."[3]

After the Republican victory at the polls in 1868, Democrats responded by seeking the African American vote because they realized the voting power of former slaves had enabled the Republican party to win elections.[4] Some Democrats found it expedient to "get up huge barbeques" to attract the black vote.[5] Democrats were optimistic at their chances to woo black votes. Immediately after the Constitutional Convention of 1867 adjourned, Caesar Shorter, a former body servant of former Governor John Gill Shorter, bolted from the convention and formed the nucleus for a black faction of the Democratic party. Shorter, Levi Floyd, and their group made campaign speeches for Horatio Seymour and Francis P. Blair in the presidential campaign of 1868. At one stop, the Montgomery *Mail* commented that Shorter "made a short, intelligent speech."[6] So pleased were Democrats with their African American supporters that they considered offering financial support to all African Americans who would join the campaign. Democrats advised, "Whenever you find a Democratic colored man who can speak, take him away from his crop! Pay his expenses."[7] Shorter and Floyd became the state's first African American Democrats and by doing so clearly revealed the tendency of some African Americans to identify with their former masters despite the efforts of the Union League and the instructions of Bureau teachers.[8]

Democrats did not view the Shorter movement as an indication of black disenchantment with the Republican party; instead, they regarded Shorter as a disgruntled individual with a small following that joined the Democratic party late in 1868. By December 1868, while African Americans were becoming associated with the Democratic party, several prominent Democrats renounced their party for the Republican party. One such Democrat was Samuel F. Rice, a lawyer, who had moved from his native South Carolina to Talladega in 1838. Rice had been a typical Democrat; he was a secessionist, an opponent of the Constitution of 1868, and an opponent of African American enfranchisement.[9] Alexander White, also of Dallas and Talladega counties, had joined Rice in renouncing Democrats. The son of an Alabama Supreme Court Justice, White had fought at the side of native fellow Tennesseeans during the Civil War and had joined the Republican party after an unsuccessful attempt to form a third party movement in Alabama.[10]

Other Democratic dissidents included David Peter Lewis, Alexander McKinstry, and former Provisional Governor Lewis E. Parsons. A Huntsville attorney, David Peter Lewis had come to Alabama from Virginia. He had been elected to the Provisional Confederate Congress but resigned and later fled to the security of the Union Army. McKinstry, too, had sympathized with the secessionist movement, but unlike Lewis, he had served in the Confederate Army. Their departure took on added significance when, in 1872, Lewis was elected governor and McKinstry became the state's second Republican lieutenant governor. Native-born

Republicans welcomed these fellow Alabamians to their fold.

Alabama Democrats rejected the new movement tactic of Democrats in Texas, Virginia, Tennessee, and Mississippi. This political strategy sought to defuse and undermine Republican policies.[11] If one assumes Democrats joined the Republican party mainly to increase their political opportunities, one also can infer that had they known the Republican regime in Alabama would be a short-lived experiment, they would have maintained their allegiance to the Democratic party.

Unprecedented Republican Rule

The unprecedented rule of the Alabama Republican party began when executive officials were sworn in on 14 July 1868 under the leadership of William Hugh Smith. As the first of two Republican governors, Smith incurred the wrath of white Alabamians, who despised the party of Lincoln. In many ways, his administration did not receive a chance to rule fairly. Smith did not go far enough to please fellow Republicans, and he went too far to satisfy Democrats. Paradoxically, Democrats and Republicans endorsed Smith's economic policies, especially his proposal for aid to railway construction. Smith's economic posture was decidedly different from former Governor Patton's stance, as revealed in Smith's decision to promote the sale of the Northeast and Southwest Railroad, which owed the state for a loan contracted in 1860. An increase in the rate of endorsement to $16,000 per mile enhanced such Democratic-controlled railroads as the North and South, the Montgomery and Eufaula, the Mobile and Montgomery, and the Republican-controlled East Alabama and Cincinnati Railroad. Governor Smith had helped to organize the last-named company.[12]

Railroad bonds procurement during the Smith administration went hand in hand with the Alabama and Chattanooga Railroad and its financiers, J. C. and Daniel N. Stanton. Smith held high regard for sound economic procedures and, in seeking capital to pay the interest on Alabama's debt, he relied on the Stanton brothers. Smith informed his secretary that the brothers promised to lend him $100,000, which to Smith was an alternative to selling bonds. J. C. Stanton was also inclined to lend $80,000 for the construction of the East Alabama and Cincinnati Railroad. Stanton had received the confidence of Northern financier Henry Clews. Several Alabama politicians, including the governor, served on the board of directors of the East Alabama and Cincinnati Railroad. Stanton used his influence to persuade the legislature to merge the bankrupt Wills Valley Railroad with the Northeast and Southwest Railroad under the name of the Alabama and Chattanooga Railroad. This line was to be 295 miles long and was entitled to $4.8 million in state bonds upon completion.[13]

The plight of the Alabama and Chattanooga Railroad best illustrates the pattern of railway financing in Alabama. At no point did lawmakers skirt the law in merging these lines, but on 2

198

March, when they made a special loan of $2 million of state securities without an endorsement of company bonds, a strong case for bribery had been made. African American lawmakers Jeremiah Haralson and John Carraway allegedly received $50 and $500, respectively.[14] John Hardy, scalawag and chairman of the House Internal Improvement Committee, supposedly took a bribe for pushing the bill, which received bipartisan support from leading Republicans, such as scalawags Frederick G. Bromberg and Green T. McAfee, and Democrats such as J. J. Parker and J. P. Hubbard. In its original form, the bill gave the Alabama and Chattanooga $3 million in state bonds for first and second mortgages, whereas other companies finishing 20 miles of track by March 1871 were scheduled to receive only $20,000 per mile.[15] Historian Mark Summers reports, however, that unified Democratic opposition could have killed the bill's chances of passage.[16] In its final version, the omnibus railroad bill, as the proposal for the financial support for the Alabama and Chattanooga was called, was well conceived and cautious.[17]

Few observers could complain about the Alabama and Chattanooga, since the company was making exceptional progress. African American, Irish, German, and later Chinese laborers could be seen working along the tracks and earning as much as $1.75 a day. The Stantons were expecting $4.8 million from the state to offset the $6 million they would need to complete the road, and they planned to sell $2.8 million in second-mortgage bonds. Nearly all observers overlooked the fact the bonds would sell for under par or not be marketable at all. The company also overrated the selling price of the 480,000 acres it owned. In addition, J. C. Stanton used company funds to help the East Alabama and Cincinnati Railroad to lease part of the track of the Selma and Meridian and to buy stock in the Vicksburg and Meridian. To make matters worse, the Stantons again used company funds to build a hotel and an opera house in Chattanooga. Alabama law required that first-mortgage bonds be used only on construction of railroad lines. Realizing that Smith was responsible for protecting the state against fraud, Democrats used these expenditures as a rallying cry in the election of 1870. They also knew Smith could appoint a committee whenever he suspected instances of fraud and that the law itself was defective in allowing too much aid.[18] Summers proposes that a Republican victory in the 1870 election might have vindicated their policies, but Republicans were not to be victorious in that election, and Democrats began to seize on Republican railroad policies.[19]

Factionalism

Leading up to the 1870 election, Republicans not only had to deal with allegations from Democrats, they also had to cope with intraparty discord. The railroad bond was one of the few issues on which both parties agreed, but it was also one of the few issues in which Republicans themselves cooperated. Republican dissension was evident as scalawags and carpetbaggers differed on several other key issues. Although Alabama carpetbaggers sought a strong state militia, native-born whites opposed a militia. Whereas carpetbaggers advocated disfranchisement, scalawags wanted to remove all political disabilities. Carpetbaggers usually supported restrictive legislation, and scalawags routinely opposed such measures. Nowhere was this divisiveness more evident than on the common carrier bill and the disability bill.[20]

John Carraway and Ovide Gregory, the Mobile mulatto delegation, pushed the Republican-sponsored measure that was designed to end discriminatory practices on common carriers. Not all of the African American delegation endorsed this bill. One African American, George Houston of Sumter County, moved to table it with the Democrat-sponsored disability bill, designed to relieve the political disabilities of disfranchised whites. Houston's motion failed, yet it revealed a split in African American opinion that was overshadowed by the course of events as the bills proceeded for approval. John Carraway, maneuvered to push his common carrier bill out of the Judiciary Committee to which it had been assigned. Each bill passed the House, but Carraway's bill failed in the Senate. Each bill later was either lost or stolen. One writer of the period suggests carpetbaggers engineered the theft of the common carrier bill, since they were not enamored with the bill and considered the African American vote securely in the fold of the

Republican party.[21] Passage of the common carrier bill and defeat of the disability bill would have posed no difficulty, for the Republicans—33 scalawags, 14 carpetbaggers, and 27 African Americans—comprised most of the membership in the lower chamber.[22]

The strife between native- and Northern-born white Republicans caused greater harm to unity than did their reluctance to advance legislation of benefit to African Americans. The relationship between Governor William Hugh Smith and Senators George E. Spencer and Willard Warner personified intraparty strife. More specifically, these men were the principal movers during Reconstruction. As the Democrats could rely on the Klan to suppress the African American vote, Spencer used the Klan's terrorist activities to enhance Republican power in Alabama by requesting Federal troops whenever there was violence or the threat of violence, especially immediately prior to an election.[23] As time progressed, Spencer found it difficult to rely on the presence of Federal troops because Democrats had begun to denounce the Klan. Democrats, then, were able to defeat Republicans despite the presence of troops. They achieved this victory by getting African Americans to vote the Democratic ticket through duress.[24]

Smith, Warner, and Spencer were well acquainted. During the war Smith had recruited north Alabamians to serve under Spencer's command; Warner had served in Spencer's army.[25] Therefore, these principal actors could have found some middle ground for cooperation, but as events unfolded in Alabama, the opposite was true. Intraparty strife was at a high point in 1870, and George E. Spencer's attempts to control Federal patronage in Alabama were at the heart of the strife. Spencer, a native of New York, came to Alabama with the Union Army in 1862, and after the war, he set up a law practice in the Tennessee Valley town of Decatur. His election by the Alabama legislature to the United States Senate in 1868 was his first political office. Paradoxically, the first sign of intraparty strife appeared between carpetbag senators Spencer and Willard Warner, an Ohio native, who had served in the Ohio Senate before moving to Alabama. A cotton planter, Warner was also picked by the same legislative body that had elected Spencer, but he lost his bid for reelection in 1870. He continued to participate in party politics but later moved to Tennessee, where he served in the State House until the 1890s.[26] Their feud played a major role in the decline of the Republican party in the State of Alabama.

Spencer relied on his intimate friendship with President Grant to lessen Warner's reelection chances and to defeat Smith. Although Warner's term did not expire until 3 March 1871, Spencer began to block Warner's prospects for reelection in 1870. Without question, both men endorsed the presence of Federal troops in the state to maintain law and order, but there the similarity ended and the differences began. Warner favored the removal of political disabilities, yet Spencer sought to limit amnesty to those who had been obedient to the laws of the Federal government.[27]

Spencer's reason for seeking Warner's defeat was a simple one: As the sole Republican congressman from Alabama, he could use the Federal patronage system to defeat the Democratic opposition in the election of 1872. His scheme went beyond a mere elimination of Democratic opposition; it included replacing scalawag officeholders with carpetbag officeholders who agreed with him.[28] The first step in undermining Warner was to defeat Governor Smith in the 1870 election.[29] Meanwhile, scalawags again chose Smith as the standard bearer for the party. To defeat Smith, Spencer relied on his speeches in the Senate, where he berated Smith for not keeping terrorist activities in check. The Republican party, he insisted, existed in Alabama "by a tender thread," because they were "hampered by weak-kneed officials."[30] Smith was aware of Spencer's efforts to oust him, but the governor never retaliated. Smith admitted the existence of terrorist activities in Alabama, for he too realized whites would not swear an affidavit and were unwilling to accept African American militiamen. Smith's idea of deterring terrorism was to urge individual citizens to join a posse and then to seek out terrorists. Yet, in so doing, Smith was concerned with whether he was acting within the limits of Alabama law.[31]

Why did Governor Smith refuse to institute marital law as Governors P. Clayton, W. W. Holden, and W. Brownlow had done, despite Alabama having more Klan violence in 1869 and 1870 than any other Southern state except perhaps North Carolina? Although Smith did refuse to institute martial law, he did not refuse to send more troops, something he had done in Sumter County. His view that the primary responsibility for controlling violence rested with local officials made him feel comfortable in appointing a new sheriff such as Daniel Price for Sumter County. However, even Smith agreed that sheriffs and other local officials had not used the powers they already possessed in the courts. Smith astutely recognized the power to suspend habeas corpus was within the purview of the legislature and, therefore, was not within the purview of the governor.[32] Like Governor Henry C. Warmoth in Louisiana, Smith called on troops when necessary, but as violence escalated, he should have realized the futility of his efforts. Throughout his administration, Smith continuously sought a way out.[33] Smith's legal or constitutional reasoning aside, to understand his rationale for refusing to issue martial law, we must consider his character. Historian Allen W. Trelease argues that in passing the buck, Smith was "a weak executive, almost wholly lacking in crowd appeal." When he took "the course of least resistance to combat the terror, he was doing what came naturally."[34] At the expense of allowing, if not encouraging, the suffering of fellow Republicans, Smith refused to recognize that violence was being perpetrated upon several members of his party. It is not surprising, then, that Senator Spencer opposed Governor Smith's renomination.[35]

NEITHER CARPETBAGGERS NOR SCALAWAGS

Republican Convention

With high expectations of defeating their democratic foes for a second consecutive time, Republicans assembled their convention in the midst of Spencer's efforts to unseat the incumbent Smith. They met in Selma, in the heart of the Blackbelt, on 30 August and chose Smith again as their standard bearer. Party leaders played down internal differences by commending the Smith administration for its past deeds. The party's platform endorsed transportation improvements, universal amnesty, and an efficient public school system. Republicans resolved "that as the party of peace and of equal rights for all men, we demand from our opponents submission to law and the cessation of all intolerance, violence, and outrage."[36] The scalawag faction of the party favored the removal of political liabilities because doing so would increase the number of eligible white voters and retrieve the party from the control of outside whites. Although the party met in the heart of the Blackbelt, undoubtedly to woo native white voters from the Democratic fold, the Republican platform overlooked race or civil rights issues. Astutely omitting these issues certainly pleased the carpetbag faction of the party also, for they, too, had little appetite for such issues.[37] Consequently, neither carpetbaggers nor scalawags had an appetite for the role African Americans wished to play in Republican affairs.

Strategy of Democrats

The Democratic party was fully aware of the momentum Republicans had built during their two years in office and decided to implement a strategy of their own. The central executive committee assembled party members in Montgomery on 1 September. They pledged to "stand ready to obey the United States Constitution; oppose unjust, extravagant, and unnecessary taxation, both state and Federal, and wasteful squandering and embezzlement of the public property; favor law and order, fair and peaceful elections, free from fraud and corruption; and favor conferring the government to Southerners, to men of known capacity and integrity who do not seek official position for public plunder."[38] Democrats also accused Republicans of obtaining power by usurpation; of imposing unnecessary and useless offices; of proliferate extravagance and corruption, and of other enormities in legislation.[39] To this list Democrats added allegations of Republican bribery. Incensed at the possibility of state aid for railroad construction and angered because of the Stantons' support for Smith, Robert Burns Lindsay, later governor, traveled to Montgomery and unsuccessfully sought "to defeat the bill for the $2,000,000 loan to the Alabama and Chattanooga."[40]

Following the example of Republicans, Democrats vigorously deliberated the importance of the African American vote. They, no doubt, realized Republican strength emanated from black enfranchisement, apparently something Republicans either had forgotten or had tried to circumvent. Democrats held an ambivalent disposition toward black suffrage. Some party members suggested that "mixing up with negro suffrage [would] drive away ten white votes for every negro vote."[41] One Democrat suggested the party should support African American candidates in black districts and support white candidates in white districts. But, Democrats almost universally accepted the premise that the best interests of the black man were with those whose lands he had tilled.[42] This position of benevolent paternalism characterized the black-white relationship once the overthrow of Reconstruction was complete and the Democratic party was free of competition from the Republican party, locally or nationally.

Democrats nominated Lindsay for governor; Edward H. Moren for lieutenant governor; J. J. Parker, secretary of state; and L. F. McCoy, treasurer.[43] For the time being, Democrats handled African American suffrage as awkwardly as Republicans. For example, when Benjamin S. Turner, one of two African American candidates on the state ticket, sought a congressional seat as a Republican, the Republican party didn't finance his campaign. He, therefore, sold a horse to finance his campaign. The reason for lack of support from the party seemed clear: he had attacked carpetbaggers for not providing him with funds or speeches. Turner won the election and became the state's first African American congressman because of the support of blacks and native whites.[44] Democrats obviously had passed up an excellent opportunity to woo a successful black

208

Republican candidate. These events revealed that Democrats and Republicans handled black suffrage with ineptitude; that the election provided Democrats with an equal chance to appeal to African American voters; and that African American candidates were forced to campaign without the support of the Republican party.

Republican Failure to Close Ranks

The Republican convention was a splendid place to close ranks and atone for past indiscretions. The Republican slate, chosen in district convention, included Pierce Burton for lieutenant governor, James Thomas Rapier for secretary of state, and Arthur Bingham for treasurer.[45] The election gave the party the chance to support two African American candidates, and in each instance, the candidates were veterans in political affairs. Rapier, the second African American candidate, had been appointed as a notary public by Governor Robert M. Patton in December 1867; he had served as a delegate to the Constitutional Convention of 1867; and he was the best-known and most influential African American lawmaker in the state.[46]

Rapier wanted black candidates to seek statewide office and the Republican party to recognize their just claims. Rapier argued, "Let us elect such of our number as are worthy and competent to places of honor, profit, and trust."[47] He was one of the optimistic members of the Republican party.

Rapier accepted the nomination for secretary of state because he considered it an occasion for white members of the party to show their sincerity toward the principle of political equality. Rapier did not accept a passive role in party politics. At the Selma convention Rapier and Spencer accused Smith of appointing Democrats to high offices, failing to protect African Americans from the Klan, appointing no African Americans to high office, and making corrupt railroad bargains. Acrimony continued unabated for two days and, as one writer of the period notes, it was intensified by the ninety-five degree heat.[48] Then, on the second day, Madison County's Nicholas Davis, a staunch opponent of Smith, struck a bargain with Smith by nominating Rapier for secretary of state. Judge Joshua Morse endorsed the nomination and insisted to the convention delegates, "I recognize him [Rapier] as a man of efficiency, practical ability, and good qualifications."[49]

The opposition to the Rapier nomination was equally swift and decisive. Circuit Judge J. H. Haralson, another scalawag, lamented that the Rapier nomination would doom the party, "It will be killed so dead that the hand of resurrection will never reach it."[50] Shortly after the convention ended, a major defection of native whites occurred. Prominent among these persons were Montgomery Postmaster W. J. Bibb, former Third District Congressman Robert S. Heflin, and Judge Milton J. Saffold, who justified his decision in a newspaper article, saying he preferred to abandon the party than to give unwilling countenance to the party's present course and nominees. Before Rapier departed Selma, he received an offer of $10,000 from railroad magnate J. C. Stanton to withdraw from the ticket. Stanton feared the Rapier nomination would defeat the party and hurt his chances to secure additional railroad legislation for his Alabama and Chattanooga railway system. One editor noted that had Rapier held out, he could have received much more than what Stanton had offered. Instead, Rapier reported the bribe to the local district attorney, who took no action against Stanton.[51] Stanton probably had assumed Rapier was as corrupt as other politicians whom he purportedly bribed at Montgomery's Exchange Hotel.[52]

Republicans handled the Rapier nomination about as poorly as they did the Turner candidacy. Smith refused to acknowledge Rapier's presence on the ticket during his campaign speeches in white areas. At Ashland and Gadsden, Smith didn't mention Rapier's name. In Blackbelt counties, such as Dallas, Perry, and Marengo, however, Smith astutely highlighted Rapier's name. Scalawag Judge Saffold sensed the inconsistency and forced Smith to admit at the Piedmont town of Columbia that Rapier was part of the ticket. Several Republican organs, such as the Stanton-financed Attalla *Union* and the Opelika *Era*, refused to print Rapier's name with the other party candidates, and the Demopolis *Southern Republican* and the *Alabama State Journal* refused to reprint his speeches. In refusing to print Rapier's speeches, William Bibb Figures'

211

NEITHER CARPETBAGGERS NOR SCALAWAGS

Huntsville *Advocate* mirrored the same disdain for Rapier several newspapers held for Benjamin S. Turner, the African American candidate for Congress.[53]

Rapier suspected that newspapers didn't provide advance notice of his speeches. He had campaigned across the state and had spoken successfully at Huntsville, Decatur, Montgomery, Union Springs, Wetumpka, and Eufaula. At Opelika, in east Alabama, Rapier stared at an empty depot as he stepped from the train. More than once fights in the audience interrupted his speeches, but he persevered because he did have supporters. William Loftin's *Alabama State Journal* claimed that "Rapier would represent the rights and interests of the WHOLE PEOPLE of Alabama."[54] Pierce Burton's *Southern Republican* called Rapier "a gentleman of great ability and finished education."[55] From south Alabama, Phillip Joseph's Mobile *Republican* suggested Rapier would represent the claims of black Republicans.[56]

J. J. Parker, Rapier's Democratic opponent, emphasized race in his campaign. A Monroe County lawyer, Parker had served in the Confederate Army. Several newspapers echoed Parker's sentiments. The Troy (Pike County) *Messenger* commented that Rapier was a "full-blooded nigger."[57] Another newspaper classified Rapier as a bright mulatto who would make a fine dining room servant.[58] These sentiments reflected the fears of Alabama's larger white community during Reconstruction.

Klan Violence

One writer of the period considers violence as part of the frontier legacy and the only alternative available to Southern whites. Undoubtedly, Reconstruction violence was a response to the new postwar black-white social order and a reaction by whites who felt threatened by the new black voter and compared black enfranchisement to a slave uprising.[59] Whatever the reason for the violence, African Americans suffered tremendously because of it. By 1870 the Ku Klux Klan had been particularly active in the western Blackbelt, an area where black voters outnumbered white voters by sizeable margins.

More specifically, several persons died at the hands of the Klan in Greene and Sumter counties. African American lawmaker Greene Shadrack Washington Lewis of Perry County informed Governor Smith of the death of Bettie Bradford, a young girl who had traveled to visit her mother in neighboring Marengo County. Her body was found "hanging to a tree with garment stripped off and eyes plucked out."[60] Lewis acknowledged his dissatisfaction with the lynching by saying, "This act was done by unknown parties. And no arrests have been made as yet. As a representative of this county the people complain to me. I refer them to you and pray that something be done to preserve the peace in this section of the county."[61] The sheriff of Marengo County, no doubt in response to a request by Governor Smith to investigate Lewis' charges, wrote to the governor

213

that "no such outrage has ever been committed in Marengo." The sheriff called Lewis' complaint "a fabulous creation of the brain emanating from [illegible]."[62]

Quite active during the months leading up to the presidential election of 1868, the Klan was equally active during the months before the election of 1870. Politically active blacks and whites who would participate in the election of a governor, a legislature, and congressmen were the targets of Klan violence. For example, Alexander Boyd was one of the most prominent whites to die at the hands of terrorists during that year. As Greene County solicitor, Boyd had presented incriminating evidence against the Klan. On 31 March at eleven o'clock in the evening, 30 or 40 disguised men rode their horses to the Cleveland House in Eutaw, where Boyd was staying, roused him from his bed, shot him in the head several times, and galloped out of town. Trelease points out that Boyd's fate was similar to the fate of Daniel Price in Sumter County, Alabama, George W. Smith in Jefferson, Texas, and John W. Stephens in North Carolina--they were all white Republicans of influence and power who had mingled with African Americans. Trelease adds that Boyd's role as county prosecutor probably helped him to learn enough about the Klan to render himself a dangerous man in the area.[63] Jim Martin, a prominent African American member of the Union League, met a similar fate later that night.[64]

Nearly six months after the deaths of Boyd and Martin, sixty years old Richard Burke, a former League leader, Bureau teacher in

214

Gainesville in Sumter County, and state representative, was shot and killed at his home because he worked with the League. Testifying later before a congressional subcommittee, one witness described Burke as "a very clever, harmless, honest, old negro man who was killed because he was a member of the legislature."[65] Although Turner Reavis, his former owner, and several other whites praised his character, Burke also was described by another witness as the "ring leader" who brought "one hundred men to Gainesville," and this witness felt whites acted only in defense.[66]

Governor Smith promptly dispatched Federal Prosecutor John Minnis to bring the murderers to trial, but Minnis didn't find sufficient evidence to make arrests. He learned that Boyd's murder had been committed by a Klan organization from outside the county, acting in collusion with the local Klan. Minnis also learned that a Klan organization from the Pickens County or Tuscaloosa County area had murdered Martin. The grand jury later ruled that because Boyd's killers came from a distance, their identity could not be discovered. The same grand jury ignored the Martin killing.[67] Klansmen also threatened Democratic Congressman Peter M. Dox of Huntsville, in Madison County, when his wife offered academic instructions to area blacks.[68]

One month after the murder of Burke, three key black politicians lost their lives because of their prominence and their work for Rapier. On the night of 13 September, terrorists approached the

215

Guilford Coleman residence, took the quiet and respected Coleman from his bed, murdered him, threw his body into a well shaft, and rode away beyond the reach of the law. Coleman's sin was that he disobeyed verbal threats against attending the Selma convention, where Rapier had been nominated for secretary of state.[69] Louisiana Klansmen took a cue from their brethren in Alabama when, on 29 October, about 40 of them rode into the town of Tangipahoa in search of General J. Hale Sypher, the Republican congressman from that district. Not finding him, they sought out John Kemp, the black Republican coroner. They tore down Kemp's door, dragged him from his house, and shot him dead. Unlike Louisiana, where Klan violence disappeared for three years after the 1868 presidential election, violence in Alabama continued, despite the desire of some Klansmen to disband in 1869.[70]

Klansmen also killed Samuel Clovis and Henry Miller, who had campaigned for Rapier.[71] In November 1870, less than a month later, an unidentified white man approached the Selma and Meridian train and called out for Frank Diggs, a black mail agent whose train had stopped just inside the Mississippi line. When the black lawmaker answered, the unidentified white assailant shot Diggs twice, thus ending his life.[72] Kentucky Klansmen harbored a strikingly similar dislike for African American postal route agents.[73]

The election of 1870 raises two questions: What was Spencer's role in the defeat of the party? and what was the impact of the Klan? A response to the first question reveals some connection

216

between Spencer and the Democrats. The extent of Spencer's activities is open to speculation; yet, evidence suggests that the senator solicited support from Democrats of north Alabama, a Smith stronghold. Spencer's criticism during the campaign undermined Smith.[74] By helping to defeat key party members, Spencer significantly enhanced his chances of controlling Federal patronage in Alabama; nonetheless, Democrats gained control of the governor's office and the House. The Democratic legislature elected George T. Goldthwaite of Montgomery as Warner's successor. By defeating the scalawag faction of his party, Spencer became the sole dispenser of patronage in Alabama, but in the process he wrecked the chances of a Republican victory in 1872.[75]

The general defeat of African American officeholders in 1870 shows Klan violence had taken its toll. Twenty-three African Americans represented 16 counties in the 1868 legislature, but two years later, only 10 counties sent 16 African American representatives to Montgomery. Blackbelt counties such as Sumter, Elmore, and Greene, where black voters outnumbered whites by more than two to one, did not elect black representatives in 1870. These counties had been Republican strongholds; for example, in 1868, Republicans carried Greene County by 2,927 to the Democrats' 869. In Sumter County, Republicans cast 2,516 votes to the Democrats' 1,469. In 1870 Democrats carried Greene County with 1,825 votes to the Republicans' 1,790. Republicans had lost 1,137 votes, while the Democrats had gained 956, nearly as many votes as the Republicans lost. In 1868 Republicans cast 2,516 in Sumter County to the Democrats' 1,469. In 1870 Democrats received 2,055 votes to the Republicans' 1,438, a Republican loss of 1078, a Democratic gain of 586, and perhaps an indication that some Republicans didn't cast ballots.[76]

Although the Klan was responsible for the Democratic victory in North Carolina in the election of 1870, John Z. Sloan absolves the Klan of responsibility for the decline in the number of African American voters in Alabama. Surely, there was a decrease in the number of African Americans in the state by 1870; the African American population stood at 475,510 and the number of African American voters at 95,000. The Montgomery *Mail*, relying on the 1870 census, concludes that 10,000 African Americans had left the state.[77] Sloan's contention that more voters went to the polls in the 1870 election than in the 1868 election gives more credence to Spencer's plot than to Democratic or terrorist intrigues.[78]

Trelease tenders a far different argument. He suggests that troops had been stationed wherever state officials deemed necessary, but there was little correlation between the presence of troops and the election of Republican officeholders. Little violence occurred on election day, 8 November, since hundreds, perhaps thousands, of African Americans voted the Democratic ticket because of threats of violence or actual violence. Some African Americans merely stayed away from the polls. This result was

218

particularly true for Sumter and Greene counties in the western Blackbelt and Macon County in the eastern Blackbelt. Had elections been free and open in Greene, Sumter, and Macon counties, Democrats would not have captured state government by a margin of 1,400 of the 150,000 votes cast.[79] Tuscaloosa Klansman Ryland Randolph put the election in perspective when he noted that "a row occasionally does no little good."[80]

The outcome of the election made it clear most blacks and many whites did not vote for Rapier; instead, blacks stayed away from the polls and, whites, while voting for other members of the party, didn't vote for Rapier. For example, in Greene County, where Grant won by an overwhelming majority, Rapier received only 1,790 votes to 1,825 for Parker. More than 2,000 blacks had not voted. Their votes for Rapier would have given him a victory. In Sumter County Rapier received only 1,435 votes to 2,055 for his opponent. Where freedmen could vote without fear of intimidation, Rapier out-polled Parker by more than a two-to-one margin, but in 10 white counties fewer than one hundred persons cast ballots for Rapier. In these counties his Republican counterparts received over 4,000 more votes than he did. He received fewer votes than any other member of his party, suggesting native-born whites preferred to defeat a black candidate than to see their party win at the polls.[81]

Despite the results of racism, violence, or the chicanery of Senator Spencer in the election of 1870, Benjamin S. Turner of

219

Dallas County became the state's first African American congressman. As congressman, Turner tended to cast partisan votes while voting against the wishes of the carpetbag faction of the party. He voted to remove the political and legal disabilities of native whites and advocated a refund of the cotton tax, for example. Phillip Joseph, editor of the Mobile *Watchman*, challenged Turner's renomination in 1872 and both lost because they split the African American vote. This defeat led Turner to accuse the Democrats of financing Joseph's campaign.[82] That Democrats would want to replace the mild-mannered Turner seems ludicrous. Few African Americans sided with native-born whites more frequently than Turner did.

Republicans were not as fortunate in their quest for the governor's office. Whether it was because of the intrigues of Spencer or the terrorism of the Klan, Democrats gained control of state government, especially the governor's office, although the election had ended in dispute. R. N. Barr of Ohio presided over the state senate and counted the votes for all the offices except governor and treasurer. The House qualified the lieutenant governor-elect, who then counted the returns and declared Lindsay the winner.[83]

Democratic Resurgence

In the Democratic resurgence, Lindsay had tallied 79,670 votes to Smith's 77,760. Although he had defeated Smith, Lindsay's margin of victory stood at only 1,910 votes. Lindsay marched triumphantly into Montgomery on 19 November, but the election results so incensed Smith that he hinted that violence and intimidation had precipitated the results, and he refused to abdicate. Smith then called on Federal troops to maintain his office; earlier, he had vehemently refused to use troops to protect black voters and white members of his party. The reign of the two governors ended on 9 December, when Democrats asked Judge James Q. Smith to adjudicate the issue. Judge Smith, a scalawag, was holding court in neighboring Autauga County but came to Montgomery immediately and gave Smith exactly 30 minutes to appear in his court and to show why he should not hand over the reigns of government to Lindsay. On the morning of 10 December, attorneys for Governor Smith indicated that he had decided to relinquish his office but not his claim to the office. The joint reign of the two governors had ended, with Lindsay becoming the state's first post-Civil War Democratic governor.[84]

Lindsay's Economic Policy

Lindsay followed the course of his predecessor, especially in economic matters and in matters of concern to African Americans.[85] With a Republican Senate and a Democratic House, Lindsay also experienced some of the same difficulties Smith had endured. On 1 January 1871 the Republican-controlled Alabama and Chattanooga

Railroad didn't meet the interest due on its bonds. Lindsay considered this occasion opportune for the state to take over the debt-ridden company. Republicans hired prominent Democrat and former Confederate General John Tyler Morgan to press their claims. Lindsay relied on former Klansman and prominent Democrat James Holt Clanton to represent the state. The United States Circuit Court ruled anyone with a valid claim could sue the Alabama and Chattanooga Railroad, a significant setback for Republicans and a victory for Democrats.[86]

However, the merger did little to improve interparty relationships. Immediately after learning of the Alabama and Chattanooga's lack of immunity from litigation, Lindsay seized its property in Alabama and tried unsuccessfully to seize its property in Georgia, Tennessee, and Mississippi.[87] The company had completed only 225 miles of track and, despite a small debt, could not raise the money to pay its January 1870 interest. Investors refused to advance financing for bonds. Realizing their inability to meet their interest deadline, company officials unsuccessfully petitioned Lindsay for a four-month reprieve. Lindsay's recalcitrance was another blow to Republicans, but he was unable to bask in victory for long, because his seizure of the Alabama and Chattanooga created more problems than he would have faced had he extended the deadline for paying the interest. Also, Alabama could do little with an incomplete line. Although the governor lacked the legal authority to complete the line, the state had incurred a legal responsibility to pay interest on a defaulted line.[88]

Powerless to help the Alabama and Chattanooga because he was uncertain how many bonds Smith had sold, Lindsay began to blame his predecessor for poor recordkeeping. Although House Democrats manifested little affection for the Alabama and Chattanooga, many did not want to do anything to harm the South and North, the other rail line in the state. Senate Republicans were as ambivalent as Democrats; some wanted to uphold the state's credit, and some saw an opportunity to damage the reputation of Democrats.[89]

House Democrats, including several Confederate brigadier generals, established a committee to investigate the Alabama and Chattanooga. The committee found that Smith, in a display of gross incompetence, had given the Stanton faction the $2 million installment all at once. The committee could not determine how many illegal bonds Smith had made, nor could it specify instances of bribery. Satisfied with the embarrassment it had caused Republicans and afraid of the implications other findings could have for other lines in the state, the committee ended its investigation, despite the pleas of Republicans that it continue.[90]

Lindsay compromised by making three of the interest payments. The state purchased the road at a bankruptcy auction for $321,000. Lindsay and his successors--Governors David Peter Lewis and George Smith Houston--tried to sell the company but without success.[91] In

1877 J. C. Stanton purchased the road. He then sold it to John Swann, who was organizing the Alabama Great Southern Railroad Company.[92] The litigation continued, and in the process many observers began to question railroad financing in Alabama. Politics surrounding the Alabama and Chattanooga clearly showed House members were willing to criticize other Democrats if doing so helped to overthrow the Republican party.[93]

To be sure, as one historian notes, railroad aid fostered a spirit of political division in Texas; in Florida such aid promoted political unity.[94] Few Alabama observers would have been shocked to learn Democrats were willing to criticize members of their party to embarrass Republicans. In the first place, when Governor Smith and later Governor Lindsay failed to make certain railroad tracks were in compliance with the law, they were guilty of fraud. Secondly, railroad financing itself became problematic, as supporters came South without much money but with plenty of speculative schemes to get financial advantages. These speculators found railroad support easy to purchase. Thirdly, whatever corrupt activities occurred in Alabama were part of a nationwide phenomenon.[95]

Summary

African Americans were dazed by the callous attitude fellow Republicans held toward their aspirations. They wanted a share in

224

the spoils of office; they believed white Republicans owed them such an opportunity. To their dismay, they found that not only would their fellows fail to support them in their candidacy for office, but that they would not support them against Klan violence or Democratic opposition. Still, African Americans remained loyal to the Republican party in the hope that eventually it would champion their cause. As events began to unfold, however, they found little cause for such optimism.

Hon. George E. Spencer
Alabama Department of Archives & History
Montgomery

Senator Willard Warner
Alabama Department of Archives and History,
Montgomery

David Peter Lewis
Alabama Department of Archives and History,
Montgomery

CHAPTER 7

SECTION 2

Events in Alabama already had shown that Republican strength was precarious at best. Republicans incorrectly assumed the months preceding an election offered sufficient time to coalesce and to defeat Democrats. Continuing to take black members of the party for granted, white Republicans also falsely assumed blacks would remain loyal and that they would continue to have the right to vote. With the progression of time, events in Alabama showed that white Republicans could not have been more wrong on all counts. The tragedy of the Republicans' miscalculations is that they could have retained power much longer had they not taken for granted their early successes at the polls and the allegiance of their black members.

Factional Strife in 1872

Republicans found themselves again embroiled in factional strife as they geared up for the 1872 presidential election. Apparently, George E. Spencer still wanted to increase the number of carpetbagger officeholders in Alabama at the expense of scalawags. Spencer considered it paramount that carpetbaggers should enjoy the fruits of Federal patronage, if not control of the party. Nowhere was Spencer's thirst for control of patronage better illustrated than in Mobile. In May 1871 he sought to reward Postmaster Frederick G. Bromberg with the vacant position of George L. Putnam, replaced for misappropriating funds. Putnam was replaced in May 1872 with scalawag John J. Moulton, a defeat for Spencer.[1]

The litmus test of Spencer's strength came in June 1871, when he urged the somewhat noncontroversial appointment of carpetbagger Timothy Pearson to replace scalawag William Miller. The scenario changed dramatically when Lewis E. Parsons, former Governor Smith, and John Larkin, leaders of the Republican conservative wing, nominated former Senator Warner to replace Miller. Spencer successfully urged President Grant to withdraw the nomination and to offer Warner the governorship of New Mexico. Warner refused the nomination amidst rumors of Miller's reinstatement.[2]

Rapier joined the opposition to the Warner nomination. In a letter to Secretary of the Treasury George Boutwell, Rapier opined that the Spencer-Warner feud had harmed the party in Alabama. Regarding the Warner nomination, Rapier reasoned that Warner's appointment would destroy the party. He continued, "The only solution was for Warner to leave Alabama. With the head of the one, by far the weaker, faction removed, the wing probably would disband. This, in turn, would mean the integration of the Spencer group, and the result would be a unified party."[3]

Blacks such as Benjamin S. Turner, who declared that Warner had few colored friends, joined the chorus of opposition. In Mobile

3,000 African Americans interrupted their celebration of the Fourth of July to support a resolution opposing the nomination of Warner and concluded by saying, "We will never endorse Willard Warner."[4] Instead of endorsing Warner, they praised President Grant for nominating Rapier as assessor of internal revenue. Although the president withdrew the Warner nomination, he didn't do so before the Spencer-Warner feud had greatly damaged the Alabama Republican party.[5]

The appointment of James Thomas Rapier as assessor of internal revenue in April 1871, with the support of United States Congressman Benjamin S. Turner and Montgomery Representative Charles Buckley, further tested the growing influence of Senator Spencer. Charles Buckley, Charles Hays, and Spencer recommended Rapier to President Grant as a replacement for George P. Rex and praised Rapier as "the leading colored man of our state and a gentleman of the highest character and acquirement whose standing in the community in every essential is unimpeachable."[6] Their letter also noted that "Mr. Rapier is an educated man and is a thorough business man. His honesty and integrity are proverbial and his appointment would reflect credit upon and be satisfactory to the Republican party of Alabama."[7] Hays further emphasized Rapier's honesty and ability in a letter to Treasury Secretary George Boutwell.[8]

Rapier assumed his duties as assessor of internal revenue in April 1871, making him the state's first African American recipient of Federal patronage. His appointment did not calm intraparty hostility, especially the opposition from Smith, Warner, and Parsons, who intimated that Rapier was nominated because of his color. Infuriated whites in Selma also disagreed with the selection of a black assessor and placed Rapier in constant danger of his life, which prevented him from opening his office. One newspaper noted that Rapier's appointment was an attempt by Grant and other Republicans to goad opposing whites into action so Grant could make their action a campaign issue.[9] One Selma newspaper reached a similar conclusion, contending that Republicans hoped to use the Rapier appointment to political advantage.[10]

White opposition in Selma forced Rapier to move his office to Montgomery, where he assumed conditions would be more amenable. He opened his office at 39 Market Street, only three blocks from the capitol and clearly within sight of the building. His hired staff included Henry Hunter Craig, a local black politician, and four whites--William W. Hammel, Eugene A. Cory, William Loftin, editor of the Montgomery *Alabama State Journal*, and John Hendricks, a leader of Republican politics in the county. By the standards of the times, Rapier had employed an impressive array of employees. Still, Rapier did not impress his opposition, as he later discovered.[11]

Meanwhile, the plight of African Americans continued to deteriorate, and black politicians continued to hold conventions. Rapier, Josiah Walls of Florida, John Quarles of Georgia, and other black leaders met in Columbia, South Carolina, as part of the Southern States Negro Convention. There was little consensus among the delegates at the October 1871 assembly. Rapier asked the delegates to endorse the Grant administration's policies and to show that Grant was the choice of African Americans. South Carolina's John Boseman declared that the body did not assemble in a political capacity and asked the group to reject Rapier's proposals.[12] The assembly adjourned, giving every appearance of the same ineptitude in charting a course for the nation's African Americans as the major parties did.

Back in Alabama, Assistant Assessor Eugene Cory wrote to Rapier that on the first day of November, Treasury Department Supervisor M. D. Stanwood came to the office and accosted him in a loud and insulting manner, saying, regarding the manner in which Rapier was handling his duties, "This is a damned imposition, what do you think of it, Cory?" Cory replied that he had nothing to do with it, whereupon Stanwood responded, "I'll summon you to my office and see what you think of it." Cory wrote that Stanwood summoned him to his office and, without stating any case, took several pages of testimony regarding various matters, showing eagerness to implicate Rapier in some violation of the law. Cory said Stanwood concluded by stating that Dr George P. Rex should not have been removed.[13]

Three days after receiving Cory's letter, Rapier wrote to Commissioner of Internal Revenue J. D. Douglass and asked for a leave of absence to prepare a response to Stanwood's allegations.

233

He defended his assistants and himself in the Douglass letter. Rapier alleged that the trouble with Stanwood, an anti-Spencer man, began when Rapier challenged Stanwood's authority to take possession of a list of cotton claims. If Stanwood held a list of cotton claims, no assessor could successfully levy taxes on the cotton of Southern planters. Rapier said he had invited Stanwood to join him in an investigation, but Stanwood had refused. Rapier charged that his officers had performed admirably, despite Stanwood's unwillingness to issue instructions.[14] Apparently, Rapier's letter convinced the commissioner, since no action was taken on the matter.[15]

Violence and Bipartisan Politics

The letter didn't settle the matter, however, and Rapier, a victim of partisan politics, resigned on 4 March 1873, having served for only 23 months. Said Rapier in a letter to Commissioner Douglass, "Please accept thanks for the kindness and courtesy shown by your office during the time that I have acted as an Internal Revenue Officer."[16] The failure of the Rapier appointment and his resignation severely vitiated the strength of Alabama republicanism, exemplified the downfall of an officeholder for pparently bipartisan political reasons, and revealed the paradoxical nature of African American membership in the party.

Several African American leaders lost their lives during the months preceding the 1872 election. Klansmen lynched Zeke High of

Sumter County after he had spent "almost a year in jail for killing a marauder who had broken into his home in 1870."[17] Democrats had promised a decline in violence if they won the 1870 election. To a degree they kept their word, but lawless bands from eastern Mississippi counties continued to roam the state in 1871, particularly western Alabama.[18] In 1871 Federal officials arrested more than 300 Klansmen but convicted only 10. Although the Enforcement Act of 1870 protected the right of a person to vote, empowered Federal judges to appoint election supervisors, and provided for imprisonment of convicted Klansmen, some officials considered them dead letters and decided to chart a different course of enforcement. Federal Marshal Robert Healy, Federal Prosecutor John Minnis, Middle District Judge Richard Busteed, and Montgomery sheriff and Austrian native Paul Strobach successfully prosecuted many Klansmen, prompting Healy to predict that, because of the indictments, he expected little trouble from the Klan in the future. Rapier predicted that with the protection of the Federal courts, Republicans could carry the state by over 5,000 to 6,000 votes.[19]

Minnis touched on the essence of the matter when he wrote to Attorney General George H. Williams, "I think a few convictions would entirely break it up, but as long as a hope is entertained of an entire change of policy, we may look for a continuation of these KKK intimidations and outrages."[20] Minnis expanded his concern for African American rights when he identified the weaknesses of the

235

Fourteenth and Fifteenth amendments as "limitations of the states that confer no power on Congress to legislate directly for the protection of blacks."[21] Four months later Minnis echoed Healy's view and remarked that "the Ku Klux convictions and other indictments have done immense good in Alabama, and there is some probability of a free and fair election in the state."[22] Still, Minnis had been correct, because the Supreme Court later ruled the Enforcement Act unconstitutional.[23]

Charges of terrorism did not enhance nor hinder the viability of the two parties in the upcoming election, and as the election neared, bipartisan factionalism became rampant. Republicans were divided into three camps: black, carpetbagger, and scalawag; and Democrats were split between those who cooperated with the Republicans and those who refused to advance African American rights. Those who sought cooperation with Republicans adopted a policy known as the "New Departure." Differing from the new movement, the New Departure sought to undermine Republicans "through the appropriation of their policies and not by organizational maneuvers."[24] Their Democratic opponents, known as Bourbons, refused to endorse African American rights on any level or to cooperate with carpetbaggers. In time, the New Departure was discredited in Alabama, unlike Georgia. The death of General James Holt Clanton, killed during an argument with a drunk in Knoxville, Tennessee, further dimmed the Democrats' chances to retain power.[25]

Despite the efforts of Senator Spencer, the divided Republican party had fallen into the hands of scalawags, who, like Democrats, sought to limit black officeholding. Indeed, Jeremiah Haralson was "howled down" when he attempted to nominate Benjamin S. Turner as temporary chairman of the Republican State Convention.[26]

Regarding their state ticket, Democrats considered Lindsay a liability and instead endorsed Thomas Hord Herndon as the party's standard bearer. A resident of Mobile in South Alabama, Herndon, a former secessionist and representative to the Constitutional Convention of 1867, reflected the party's conservative leanings, a tendency that became more manifest in the next election. Democrats claimed to stand for law and order and opposed the stationing of troops in Alabama. Herndon boasted at a political rally that few differences existed between himself and David Peter Lewis, his Republican opponent.[27]

Democrats again appealed to the African American electorate, and again Caesar Shorter led the Democratic effort to recruit African American voters. Because Shorter and his friends said blacks were too ignorant to vote and wanted Congress to postpone action on the proposed Fifteenth Amendment for a few years, Democrats recruited George W. Cox, a former Republican state representative, and asked him to seek black votes.[28] Cox, the only Republican of note to join the Democratic fold that year, urged African Americans to vote for Democratic presidential nominee Horace Greeley.[29] The Republican Montgomery *Alabama State Journal* called him a renegade for organizing a Colored (Horace) Greeley Club.[30] Although Republicans knew Shorter and Cox actively solicited black support for Democrats, they continued to take the black vote for granted.[31]

Republicans met in Montgomery to nominate their state ticket. Party leaders agreed before the convention to nominate only scalawags from north Alabama for major offices, sensing that was the best way to defeat Democrats. Since he had few enemies among the members of either party, David Peter Lewis of Huntsville was chosen to head the state ticket. Republicans pledged to support public education and internal improvement and endorsed the Fourteenth and Fifteenth amendments. The platform again adroitly evaded controversy or the appearance that the party sought to advance the rights of African Americans.[32]

Much to the chagrin of white Republicans, black political aspirants proved a nemesis to the party: Congressman Turner sought renomination, and Rapier, resilient from his earlier defeat, sought to join Benjamin S. Turner in Congress. Unlike the election of 1870, when Turner was more successful than Rapier, this time Rapier was more successful than Turner. Turner received the party nomination, but another African American, Phillip Joseph of Mobile, received the backing of the conservative pro-Warner faction. Joseph refused to support Turner, ran as an independent and, in the process, gave the election to Frederick G. Bromberg, who ran as a Democrat and Liberal Republican. When the Forty-second Congress ended, Turner returned to Selma and took up farming.[33]

Meanwhile, to enhance his election chances, Rapier rented a small office within walking distance of the state capitol and his residence, made a down payment on a used printing press, and on Thursday, 1 April 1872, released the initial issue of the Montgomery *Republican Sentinel*, the state's earliest black-owned, operated, and edited newspaper.[34] Violence marred the campaign as Conservative Robert Knox led a Charles Buckley faction of 50 to a Rapier meeting at the Old Elam Church in Montgomery. When the shooting ended, one black person had been killed.[35]

When Second District Republicans met in Union Springs on 15 May 1872, Rapier advanced his political fortunes with his selection as a delegate to the national nominating convention in Philadelphia. The delegates also selected Rapier as permanent chairman of the Committee on Credentials. Montgomery Representative Holland Thompson, the state's second most powerful African American official in the 1870s and himself an aspirant for higher office, opposed Rapier's selection as permanent chairman. He correctly believed the selection was a significant step toward Rapier's securing a seat in Congress. Incumbent Charles Buckley also opposed the Rapier nomination, although he claimed to be a friend of the freedman.[36] Thompson was not the only African American politician to oppose Rapier; former Republican state representative George W. Cox, also of Montgomery, objected to the Rapier nomination and exclaimed, "We should not fight the breast that

239

gives us milk. Vote for Greeley."[37] However, Rapier received the nomination in Eufaula on 16 August.[38]

The election of 1872 was a complete success for Republicans, who won every state office. Because Klan activity was at a minimum, the election proceeded quietly. African Americans did not vote with the Democrats, despite the efforts of Shorter, Cox, and other black Democrats. Lewis received 89,020 votes, while 78,524 Alabamians endorsed Herndon. Republicans received 10,000 more votes than they did in 1870. They did not win a majority of the white votes in any of the white counties in either 1870 or 1872; the black vote carried the day for the Republican party by providing the margin of victory. This fact was made clear as 55 percent of the 167,544 votes cast in the election came from the ballots of black counties, where many blacks no doubt considered themselves members of the party of Lincoln.[39] Rapier received 19,397 votes to former Confederate General William Calvin Oates' 16,622; Rapier, the state's second African American congressman, had defeated Oates as decisively as Oates' forces had been defeated at Gettysburg.[40] Though the celebrations were short lived, the election had made it seem like a glorious day to hold membership in the Republican party.

The election for state representatives was much closer. Because of disputed returns from Barbour and Marengo counties, two rival legislatures assembled, and the arrangement continued for two months. The Republican legislature met at the United States

240

Courthouse, and the Democratic body assembled at the state capitol. The United States attorney general adjudicated the case and gave Republicans a majority of two in the House and the Democrats a majority in the Senate.[41]

When the legislative issue ended, a Republican split resurfaced as the party divided between those loyal to Lewis E. Parsons and those loyal to Spencer. African Americans held membership in both factions. Unlike previous divisions, Republicans never overcame the results of this split. Nowhere was the split more visible than in the First District of Mobile, where the Republicans nominated Louis H. Mayer as collector of internal revenue, a position to which Rapier would receive an appointment in 1878. The Democrats wanted to nominate a member of the conservative wing of the party. Black politician Jeremiah Haralson called the nomination an "ill-considered appointment."[42] Another Republican wanted, as a substitute, a "man of higher moral character."[43] Spencer, Rapier, and Third District Congressman Charles Pelham joined in the chorus of praise for Mayer. This group requested an extension on the time for paying Mayer's bond of $60,000, which they considered exorbitant.[44] The eventual appointment of Mayer reflected the influence of the Spencer faction, but neither group worked to mend the split in the Republican coalition. That mending was not done and done soon worked to the detriment of Republican hegemony in Alabama.

241

NEITHER CARPETBAGGERS NOR SCALAWAGS

The Civil Rights Bill

This new Republican rift, pitting scalawags against scalawags, carpetbaggers against carpetbaggers, and blacks against blacks, continued to widen. This alignment was evidenced in the legislature's handling of the civil rights bill, introduced in 1873. According to historian Arthur Williams, it was "the most controversial problem to face the General Assembly."[45] On 2 February 1873 black Representative Latty J. Williams of Montgomery introduced a civil rights bill designed to discourage racial discrimination on common carriers and in hotels, schools, and amusement places such as theaters. Calling it the social equality bill, the Selma *Southern Argus* charged the bill entitled citizens of Alabama, without distinction of race, color, or previous condition of servitude, to accommodation, advantage, facility, or privilege furnished by common carrier, by licensed innkeepers or places of amusement; provided a compensation of $500 to the aggrieved party; empowered the court with powers to act; and annulled all other municipal laws inconsistent with it.[46] The Judiciary Committee, chaired by scalawag Alexander White of Dallas and Talladega counties, reported adversely on the bill, having been pressured by a coterie of lawmakers to issue a report. A volatile debate followed, and on March 10 the House failed to return a favorable vote on the bill.[47]

Jeremiah Haralson, also of Dallas County, introduced a similar civil rights bill in the Senate on 19 February 1873. The Judiciary

Committee made some substitutions and submitted for the approval of the body a bill that entitled all citizens to equal accommodation on common carriers. Alexander H. Curtis of Perry County sought passage of the original bill but accepted the substitute bill, considering it the "best that he could get."[48] He opposed social equality and suggested that the social aspect of the bill had been exaggerated, since that matter "would regulate itself," and that he "would not force himself where he thought he was not wanted."[49] Curtis envisioned little trouble between the races in the Blackbelt, because as a slave he had been provided for at the best hotels, had traveled in the first-class conveyances with his master, and didn't understand why he should not enjoy the same privileges as a freedman he had enjoyed as a slave.[50]

Hales Ellsworth of Montgomery opposed both civil rights bills and was sorry they had been introduced. Ellsworth stated that "colored people should not thrust themselves where they are not accepted. They should exercise more pride."[51] Ellsworth reasoned that the substitute bill was "the best thing that could be done under the circumstances."[52] He did not want to offend the prejudices of whites, especially since his old master had reared him and never in his life struck a blow, and he expected to love him as long as he lived.[53] Haralson's substitute bill passed on 4 April, but the legislature adjourned without having voted on the measure. Thus, African Americans had proposed civil rights legislation in each chamber, and the bill, paradoxically, failed in the Republican House and passed in the Democratic Senate.[54]

The death of the civil rights bills clearly showed the reluctance of the scalawag majority in the House to champion the cause of their African American peers. It further illustrated the failure of carpetbaggers to provide leadership in the party, despite the efforts of some of their members, including W. H. Hunter of Lowndes County, who demanded the passage of the bill, arguing that "the 4,000 colored voters of Lowndes County are unanimously in favor of the civil rights bill. They are my constituents; they demand the guarantees afforded by this bill, and as their Representative, I shall vote to protect their interests."[55] Yet, the bill failed in the House, because scalawags voted with Democrats to secure its defeat. This coalition captured the attention of Greene Shadrack Washington Lewis, black lawmaker from Perry County, who chastised scalawags for not voting to pass the bill. Exclaimed Lewis, "Why, when the war was going on, you stripped-jeans [sic] fellows from north Alabama came down here supplicating for corn, and I have known colored people to steal corn from their own masters to keep your women and children from starving; and yet you vote against this bill."[56] Lewis, one of a handful of African Americans who was willing to dissociate from the party because of its disregard for the civil rights of African Americans, "wanted no miscegenation." His color "was fair enough

244

for him." Neither had he "any desire to thrust the colored race in the way of the white." He wanted "nothing but justice."[57]

Henry E. Cobb suggests that blacks "did possess enough strength to block passage of other bills until they won passage of a civil rights bill."[58] The bill passed the Senate, clearly pleasing the Democrats, who expected it to embarrass white Republicans. Democrats also believed Republicans would find it difficult to explain their actions to whites of north Alabama and to blacks of the Blackbelt.[59]

The reluctance of white Republicans to advance civil rights and the insensitivity of Democrats toward their political participation propelled African Americans to practice what Michael Perman calls "ethnic politics."[60] Rejection by white Republicans also drove blacks politicians to plan their political future through the Equal Rights Association (ERA) convention that met in Montgomery on 26 and 27 June 1874. The delegates included Phillip Joseph and Robert W. Whitaker, elected at large; Jeremiah Haralson and Thomas Walker, representing the First District; Holland Thompson and Allen E. Williams, Second District; William V. Turner and Henry St. Clair, Third District; Alexander H. Curtis and Frank H. Threatt, Fourth District; and Patrick Mosley and Robert Chardavoyne, Sixth district. In an address to the colored people of Alabama, these conventioneers held Republicans responsible for their rejection "at public inns and eating houses."[61] Still, the ERA conventioneers refused to support the Democratic party.[62]

NEITHER CARPETBAGGERS NOR SCALAWAGS

Those who sought civil rights legislation at the expense of the Republican party and those who placed party before principles divided the convention. William H.(ooper) Councill, Huntsville resident and former assistant engrossing clerk for the state legislature, Representatives Charles Smith of Bullock County and William H. Blevins and Jeremiah Haralson of Dallas County wanted to enjoy equal rights in all places. Councill, who played a large role in the educational affairs of the state well past the turn of the century and competed with Booker T. Washington for Democratic favors, claimed he wanted justice first, party or race notwithstanding. Haralson, understanding the strength of his race, favored some form of a civil rights bill but opposed the idea of mixed schools. He sought foremost to advance the cause of his race.[63]

On the other hand, George Patterson and Henry St. Clair, both of Macon County, and former Elmore County Representative William V. Turner endorsed the civil rights bill and adopted a policy of gradualism. The position of the two Macon countians is important in that it presaged the disposition of black educators as Macon County blacks sought someone to head Tuskegee Institute during the late 1870s.[64] Alexander H. Curtis and John Dozier of Perry County and John William Jones of Lowndes County favored the bill but not at the expense of the party. Dozier "favored Civil Rights 'up to the hub'" but opposed the mixed-school feature, because it "would injure the great Republican party in de proachin' lection."[65]

246

Curtis also favored the civil rights bill, announcing he was "man enough to stand up to my opinion," but did not want to do anything to endanger the party in the state.[66] Jones expected a white exodus if the bill passed and predicted that African Americans in his county would vote against the bill.

The Equal Rights Association Convention

The ERA convention, assembled because white Republicans had shown a disregard for the rights of African Americans, exhibited the tendency of African Americans to remain in the party despite its ambivalent position on black rights. The conventioneers' position further revealed the reluctance of African Americans to push for integrated schools.[67] Led by Thomas Walker of Dallas County, a mere handful of African Americans demanded mixed schools.[68] One newspaper helped to inflame white rage when it recounted the story of a "Montgomery negro [who] recently sent a note to the daughter of a prominent white radical of that city requesting permission to accompany her to church."[69]

The Democratic press was quick to criticize the convention, saying it was "composed exclusively of Negroes speaking for Negroes, representing Negroes and enunciating the demands of Negroes."[70] Less than three weeks later the same organ declared the civil rights bill was "demanded by no public necessity whatsoever and animates the hostility of a large portion of the Republican party toward the white people of the South, and at the time the whole country was beginning to rejoice that these disturbing negro questions had been permanently settled."[71] To make sure its readers understood the meaning of the civil rights bill in time for the election, the *Southern Argus* defined the bill's tenets and equated its meaning with mixed schools, grave yards, hotels, and churches.[72]

White Republicans also quickly dissociated themselves from the ERA convention. Democrats had charged that the convention represented the wishes of all Republicans. Speaking through the *Daily State Journal*, white Republicans retorted that Democrats "well know that the association was composed of colored men, and that it was in no sense a Republican assembly."[73] The newspaper proceeded to support the party on separate schools for all black and white children and argued that it supported equal civil and political rights for all men. The editor further defended the party's "proud record" on the recent failure of the House to pass the civil rights bill, adding that "Republicans in the House were anxious to pass it and failed only because they lacked the four-fifths vote to take it out of the regular order."[74] For different reasons, white Democrats and Republicans failed to support the convention. Democrats saw the meeting as an opportunity to accuse the Republicans of following a black agenda. Republicans walked a tight line, affirming their support of civil rights on one side and denying black leadership on the other.[75] Neither action endeared them to their African American colleagues.

Political Disarray and the Election of 1874

In 1874 the Republican parties in Alabama and Mississippi experienced similar disarray. Alabama's two white factions became absorbed in a dispute that centered on the activities of carpetbagger Federal District Judge Richard Busteed. Controversy was nothing new to Busteed; in 1867 he had incurred the wrath of African Americans at a Republican convention and had survived an attempt to impeach him. Now the scalawag faction of his party, led by Alexander White, who had introduced articles of impeachment in Congress, hoped to succeed. Rumors circulated that White, Senator Spencer, Lewis E. Parsons, and others had conspired to ruin Busteed. The House Judiciary Committee investigated the charges, but Busteed resigned his office by December 1874, forestalling attempts at impeachment. Although Busteed vacated his post, scalawags and the Spencer faction could take little pleasure in the appointment of John Bruce, a Scottish resident of the state since 1865.[76] Yet, the Busteed affair revealed the fragility of the Republican coalition.

Black Republicans in Florida and Alabama noted with disfavor the failure of white Republicans to advance their concerns. Each group had concluded that Northern and Southern whites embraced the same ideals with regard to their rights. Capitalizing on black rejection by their party, Democrats continued to oppose the idea of black enfranchisement. Because of the declining status of the carpetbagger wing of the Republican party, especially in the case

249

of Busteed and others, Democrats viewed the upcoming statewide election as an opportunity to seize power from a divided opposition party. On the national level, Democrats received added incentive from the defeat of the civil rights bill in Congress and the death of Charles Sumner, its author and primary supporter. Democrats sought to eliminate the Blackbelt black vote and place politics again in the hands of the pre-Civil War merchant-planter class.[77] Newly elected D. J. Daniels of Russell County chastised his colleagues for their opposition to the civil rights bill:

> I, D. J. Daniels, do tender my solemn protest against the resolution that passed this House, instructing our Senators and Representatives in Congress to defeat the Sumner Civil Rights Bill.
> 1st. Because it was offered and passed by the Democratic members of this House.
> 2nd. Because I believe that the said Sumner's Civil Rights Bill embraces nothing more than what I think is right and justice.
> 3rd. Because I have taken my oath not to deprive any person of their equal, political and civil rights, &c.
> 4th. Because I believe that instructing the Senators and Representatives in Congress to defeat the Civil Rights Bill will cause them to violate their solemn oath.[78]

To oust Governor Lewis from office, Democrats chose George Smith Houston in a move designed to split the white vote of north Alabama. Houston, a Unionist, was especially appealing to Democrats; besides, it was a tactic Republicans had used to woo the votes of native Alabamians. Houston had a rich history of political service to the state; he had represented Lauderdale County in 1832 for one term; had served for 18 years in the United States House of Representatives (from 1841 to 1849 and from 1851 to

1859) as a Conservative Democrat; had sustained the bank vetoes of President John Tyler in 1841; had opposed the tariff of 1842; had advocated the annexation of Texas; had supported the presidential campaign of James K. Polk in 1844; and had favored the tariff of 1846.[79]

At the Democratic convention in Montgomery, held near the end of July, Houston, echoing the sentiments of other Democrats, proclaimed life, liberty, honor, and property as issues of paramount concern to the survival of the party. The Democrats nominated Robert Ligon of Blackbelt Macon County as lieutenant governor to appease the faction from that region.[80] Blackbelt whites had been overlooked in political affairs since the arrival of the Reconstruction epoch. This faction, in particular, wanted to control the African American vote, which usually was comprised of their former servants. Democrats decided to emphasize race as a campaign theme, following the suggestion some of its adherents had made as early as 1868. Therefore, Democrats made few overtures to African American voters in 1874 and appealed instead to the white voters of north Alabama.[81]

Aware of the times, Republicans met in Montgomery in August and renominated former Confederate officer David Peter Lewis for governor. Lewis had been one of a handful of former Confederate officers to join the Republican ranks, having done so in 1870.[82] The party also renominated Alexander McKinstry for lieutenant governor. James Thomas Rapier was renominated for Congress in the district convention, and Richard Busteed nominated political veteran Jeremiah Haralson of Dallas County for Congress to represent the First District. Republicans enhanced their chances of victory by minimizing the race issue and repudiating civil rights in areas of education and public accommodation.[83] The leadership of the party fully realized the results of the convention and concluded blacks were now wedded to the party; their votes could be taken for granted.

The campaign of 1874 was warfare for Democrats, a campaign to be won at all costs. James Lawrence Pugh of Barbour County, president of the Democratic state convention, said of the campaign, "[It] will be a contest for political power by two distinct classes of our citizens between whom there can be no comparison."[84] Pugh reasoned that whites must be the custodians of political power in Alabama.[85] Realizing the defensive position of the Republicans, Democrats raised the banner of white supremacy to bring out white voters, much as Republicans had appealed to Union sentiment to entice blacks to vote along party lines. Assuming an appeal to white supremacy would prove beneficial, Democrats also made use of a version of the "Mississippi plan," which relied on intimidation, violence, economic reprisals, murders of blacks, church burnings, and the ostracism of white Republicans.[86]

Many Democratic newspapers answered the clarion call. As early as July, the *Daily State Journal* suggested that if the Republican State Convention refuses to give countenance to the Democratic "race issue by nominating honest men for office, it will do more to exhibit the utterly malevolent spirit which inspired the race issue as a Democratic panacea, than all the arguments that could be produced."[87] The editor also considered it foolish for white Republicans to urge blacks to aspire to high political office.[88] The *Southern Argus* printed the resolutions of Democratic county conventions held that summer. On 4 July Dale County Democrats resolved to "rebuke the [Republican party] at the ballot box in November."[89]

Sanford County (renamed Lamar in February 1877) Democrats called on other Democrats to "redeem the state from radical rule and negro supremacy. This would place the government of Alabama in the hands of honest and intelligent white men."[90] Democrats in St. Clair County focused their grievances on the high salaries and fees of state officers.[91] Madison County Democrats showed more aplomb and asked African Americans to "seek security from the present and impending evils in the organization and principles of the democratic and conservative party."[92] Democratic conventions in Barbour and Shelby counties passed similar resolutions. As a climax to the spread of fear among white voters, the *Southern Argus* predicted, less than a month before the election, a white exodus if Radicals were victorious at the polls.[93] These newsorgans helped Democrats to blame Republicans for the state's financial woes.

The "race war" of the Democrats caught republicanism at its nadir, a depth from which it has never ascended. Compounding

253

Republicans' difficulties, some African American members of the party had grown weary of minor roles. The previous year Phillip Joseph of Mobile lamented, "Here, in Alabama, where the colored [people] exceed 80,000, there is not one colored man holding any state office; neither is there one in any of the departments of the State as a clerk."[94] When the Republicans held their state convention in August 1874, Joseph wanted some accommodations. Joseph argued that he was a citizen of the state and the United States and was entitled to some access to cars on railroads and, "if the Republican party cannot stand upon the platform that all men are entitled to equal rights, it ought to go down."[95] For his "decedent" stand at the convention, the party refused to nominate Joseph, even for a minor position, prompting his Mobile *Watchman* to suggest that "the Radicals, it seems, are growing tired of Negro officials as well as others [Democrats]."[96] Joseph ceased the publication of the *Watchman* one week after the election. Apparently, he was horrified at the direction of the party.

Black politician Frank H. Threatt also became disgruntled with republicanism, remarking uncompromisingly that "if the Republicans were to nominate Jesus Christ and the Democrats were to nominate the devil, I would vote for the devil."[97] Blacks themselves had divided into factions, especially in the Blackbelt, where a group led by Alexander H. Curtis supported Rapier, while a faction led by Greene Shadrack Washington Lewis supported Jeremiah Haralson. To win white support, neither faction nominated a black candidate.[98]

254

In addition, Representative Charles Smith of Bullock County was expelled from his pastorate for voting the democratic ticket in the November election.[99] The problem confronting Smith was part of a larger manifestation of black powerlessness, as black witnesses testified after the election that "colored men were threatened with loss of employment unless they voted the democratic ticket."[100] They related how planters compiled "blacklists" of men who voted the Republican ticket and planned to dismiss them.[101]

The height of Republican factionalism and troubles occurred at the Barbour County district nominating convention when Rapier, seeking reelection, pledged in writing to support the Pat Robinson-Charles Buckley faction of the party and to use his influence to defeat the impeachment of Judge Richard Busteed. J. V. McDuffie, Pat Robinson, Hershel V. Cashin, and Elijah Cook signed as witnesses to Rapier's promise. Several days later, Rapier issued a written recantation.[102] Rapier suffered defeat in the district, although he had carried the county.[103]

Republicans' plan was mild in comparison to the Democrats's use of violence and intimidation. They issued a bland position paper in which they absolved themselves of responsibility for the conditions of the state. They wrote, "In 1860 and 1870, with the same men in office and with negro votes, we made fine crops, money was plenty and property was high." Then they asked, "Did Radical rule get any credit for the state of things then? If not, why charge us with the disasters of other years?"[104] For Alabamians unable to understand political rhetoric, Republicans appealed to their baser instincts by issuing bacon. The rationale for distributing 225,167 pounds of bacon was a flood that had ravaged areas along the Tombigbee, Black Warrior, and Alabama rivers, leaving many African Americans destitute. In response, Governor Lewis appointed Holland Thompson and other party regulars to distribute the bacon, and Republicans sought a political advantage by claiming the bacon was a reward for voting the straight Republican ticket.[105]

The bacon of the Republicans apparently failed to match the chicanery of Democrats, for an unprecedented 201,052 Alabamians voted in the election of 1874. Houston was elected by a margin of 107,118 to Lewis' 93,934 votes. Black officials numbered six in the Senate and 27 in the legislature.[106] Rapier suffered defeat, while Haralson became the state's third black congressman and the last one of the period.[107] Democrats drove a death nail in the coffin of Republican politics, for after 1874 Republicans failed to offer significant competition in statewide politics. Alabamians waited 112 years before choosing another Republican governor.[108]

That intraparty strife continued among Republicans gives full meaning to their lack of understanding of the Democratic victory. They disagreed on the outcome of the election and refused initially to cooperate in the proposed constitutional convention. Most of all, Republicans refused to foster leadership within the party. Few Republicans placed party before personal considerations. The

Smith-Spencer feud was renewed over the issue of Federal patronage. One manifestation of this feud was the nomination of two state tickets in 1876. Both factions met in Montgomery, the Smith faction meeting on 14 June and nominating Thomas M. Peters of Lawrence County, after the Spencer faction had selected Judge James S. Clarke of Morgan County on 24 May. Both north Alabama candidates for governor went on to suffer decisive defeat. African American members of the party were no more unified. Rapier and the incumbent Haralson campaigned for the African American vote, and in splitting it, they made possible the election of a Democrat. The Smith faction supported Haralson, and the Spencer coalition pushed Rapier.[109]

Summary

Reconstruction ended in Alabama as it had begun--with the party split. The only surprise was that the experiment continued as long as it did. Seldom did Republicans submerge their differences for the sake of party unity. Only African American members of the party expressed a willingness to suppress individual aspirations. Unfortunately, they possessed neither the power nor the influence to dictate the outcome or the tone of party fortunes. A scrutiny of events more fully explains the declining fortunes of the party and the total disappearance of black lawmakers. The downfall of the Republican party was inevitable, given the party's propensity for intraparty strife and its ambivalence toward black suffrage. In fact, the refusal of the Unionist and carpetbagger elements to champion black suffrage hastened the decline of the party faster than the opposition of Democrats. The actions of white Republicans clearly revealed a greater desire to woo black votes than to advance their welfare.

Other forces, including factionalism, exacerbated the Republican experiment with democracy. The Republican coalition too frequently placed individual interests before partisan concerns. More specifically, the rivalry between George E. Spencer and James Thomas Rapier, on the one hand, and William Hugh Smith, Willard Warner, and Jeremiah Haralson, on the other hand, precipitated the death of the party. Assured of victory at the polls, Republicans minimized the threats of Democrats and focused prematurely on the spoils of officeholding. That no Republican occupied the governor's office for more than one hundred years shows how well Democrats had learned to retain power in Alabama.

CHAPTER 8

SECTION 1

To understand the Democrats' victory in 1874, one must come to grips with events preceding the election. Whereas Republicans focused on statewide officeholding as a key to power, Democrats perceived early on the value of a local or community power base. Although Republicans didn't unify their forces before the election, Democrats, on the other hand, fully grasped the urgency of defeating Republicans and employed every possible means to guarantee a victory at the polls. The means they employed bespeak the ruthlessness to which both parties were willing to resort to win an election, for Republicans were equally guilty of using unfair tactics, if not downright intimidation.

Democratic Challenge

As they had circumvented the intent and purpose of the Civil Rights Act of 1866 through the probate judge, Democrats again challenged Alabama's Republican party on the local level through the assistance of the sheriff, probate judge, justice of the peace, and county commissioner. Democrats already had begun to achieve a modicum of success during previous local elections. "Redemption," as Democrats called their return to power, had come to Mobile County as early as 1870. No African American officials represented Mobile County in city or state offices, though Henry J. Europe served as collector of internal revenue in 1873, and antebellum free black James Summerville served as receiver of the United States Land Office, both Federal positions. During the same year two blacks served as port collectors in Mobile and Montgomery, and one black served as collector in Eufaula.[1]

These appointments were the exceptions as William J. Haralson, judge of the Fifth Circuit Court of Alabama and a Democrat, replaced black County Commissioner I. C. Dodge of Huntsville with Unionist Nicholas Davis.[2] Democrats also removed Henry Sanders, a black county commissioner in Barbour County.[3] The startling contrast between the small number of African Americans who held local offices and state offices shows that Republicans overlooked or minimized the importance of local officeholding. If African Americans were elected to the United States Congress or to the State House, they should have been able to win local contests. African Americans in Halifax County, North Carolina, and in Alabama learned too late that the center of power was not Raleigh, Montgomery, or Washington. It was the county seat in Alabama.

260

Therefore, instead of allowing African Americans to serve as county commissioners, the white Democratic legislature discontinued popular elections and appointed magistrates for each county. These magistrates chose white county commissioners who replaced a proficient coterie of African American county commissioners.[4]

The failure of Republicans to comprehend the import of the election of 1874 and their continuing intraparty strife caused them to suffer defeat. Once it became obvious their future rested outside the political arena, African Americans, the segment of the Republican coalition with the most to lose and the least ability to salvage the Reconstruction experiment, sought political salvation through third party movements or became journalists and educators.

Democrats achieved one local victory after another during the months preceding the 14 November 1874 election. Elections held at Opelika, Talladega, Eufaula, and Tuskegee highlighted party tactics. Republicans won the Opelika election in March 1874, largely because Democrats had placed too many candidates in the running. Here, Democrats learned a valuable lesson that would guide them in the November election: choose a few good candidates. The next month, Democrats supported a few solid candidates and won the Talladega municipal election. Infuriated, Republicans charged that Democrats had bribed black voters, voted illegally, and furnished illegal returns. Democrats won the election and put Republicans on the defensive, a tactical advantage.[5]

261

Violence in Barbour County

Blacks had complained about violence since enfranchisement, but the intensity and caliber of violence that awaited them and other Republicans in Barbour County was unheard of before 1870. Realizing that black voters made the Republican party a formidable force in Alabama politics, Democratic violence attempted to weaken Republican strength by frightening off, if possible, and killing, if necessary, black voters. Eufaula, where blacks constituted 60 percent of the 3,200 residents, was an excellent barometer to measure the effectiveness of Democratic violence.[6]

Federal authorities realized as much when Federal Marshal R. W. Healy asked Attorney General George H. Williams for a company of troops to protect carpetbagger Federal District Judge Elias Keils, whose life had been threatened. Healy also sought protection to aid in the "executing process of [the] court."[7] The day before the election, Congressman Rapier gave further notice of the need for concern and asked for "a small detachment of soldiers for the area from Eufaula to Union Springs to aid the US commissioner in preserving the peace."[8]

Despite the possibility of violence, Eufaula blacks were determined to vote. Antebellum congressman and Eufaula lawyer Eli Shorter commented, "It is the hardest thing in the world to keep a negro away from the polls; that is one thing he will do, to vote."[9]

And vote they did. On the eve of the election local and county blacks, unarmed because of their determination to avoid trouble and to deter attempts by the Klan to charge them with threats of violence, camped outside the town in groups of at least 800. Mindful that local authorities had been warned of possible violence, influential area blacks such as Allen E. Williams, Edward Odum, and Methodist minister Henry Frazier cautioned blacks against carrying arms to the polls. Williams and Odum, both candidates for the legislature, held special reasons for not wanting violence to mar the election.[10] Blacks marched into Eufaula the next morning, leaving their arms at the campsite. By 9:00 most polls had opened, and the election proceeded smoothly. When Deputy Marshal James D. Williford and Democrat Shorter applauded the absence of violence, they noticed several blacks rush by. Williford went to learn more about events and overheard an argument between black Republican Silas Lawrence and Charles E. Goodwin, a local white Democrat. Goodwin had noticed that an underage African American youth was about to vote. Goodwin was willing to allow him to vote, if he favored the democracy. Lawrence noticed Goodwin escort the youth into a nearby alley. When he returned from the alley, Lawrence asked of the boy, "God damn you, are you going to vote the democratic ticket?" To this Goodwin replied, "God damn you, do you take it up?" Not intimidated, Lawrence answered, "You are taking it up for your people, and I will take it up for mine." Standing nearby, Willie Dowdy shouted, "Shoot the damned son of a bitch" and began to stab Lawrence with his Bowie knife. By this time Williford arrived and tried to restore order, but gunshots already had filled the air, and the Eufaula riot had begun. Shots felled blacks as they ran for cover. These shots came from both sides of the street, giving the appearance of organized retaliation, and African Americans heard former Confederate Brigadier General Alpheus Baker yell out, "Fall into line Company A! Fall into line Company B."[11] It was unclear which side had fired first, but when the riot had ended, eight whites had received gunshot wounds, and one hundred blacks had been killed or wounded. The tragedy of the Eufaula riot was that a detachment of Federal troops continued its daily routine and did nothing to prevent the violence.[12]

Opposition to black enfranchisement had not ended. At Spring Hill, about 18 miles from Eufaula, Judge Elias Keils supervised a peaceful election under the misapprehension that he could rely on Federal troops, who were stationed nearby. He labored under the understanding of General Orders No. 75, which limited Federal intervention in local affairs except under the most stringent conditions and not under the force of General Orders No. 57, issued by Southern commander General Irwin McDowell. This order mandated that Federal officials were to help civil authorities in the execution of court orders. General Orders No. 75 rescinded the force of General Orders No. 57. The election proceeded peacefully until local whites began to fire their weapons at about 11:00 that morning and then paraded the streets until 5:00, hoping to frighten blacks. Apparently, area whites had learned of General Orders 75, because after 4:00, Willie Keils, the judge's 16 year-old son, rushed to the office of William J. Turner, the officer in charge of monitoring the election, and asked for assistance. Having received an interpretation of General Orders No. 75 by telegram shortly after 3:00, Turner fully realized his helplessness and relayed the same to young Keils. Willie Keils relayed Turner's message to his father at 5:00 p.m., as the polls closed. With the onset of darkness, an angry mob of whites surrounded the judge and his son. Judge Keils locked the doors in the election office, but at 6:00, a Democratic election clerk opened the doors, and the angry whites rushed in, firing their pistols and wounding the younger Keils. When the whites finally called a halt to their pursuits, the judge, with the assistance of several blacks, rushed his son to a doctor. The younger Keils died two days later. Turner had sat by painfully and listened to the gunfire, unable to lend a hand because of General Orders No. 75. Keils, on the other hand, correctly assumed that local whites had intercepted the telegram and knew that Turner would not interfere.[13]

The riots in Eufaula and Spring Hill led to a congressional investigation; the majority report concluded that area whites had planned to attack blacks on election day, and the minority report absolved Democrats of any involvement. Regardless of the responsibility, Odum, Williams, and other influential African Americans who testified before the grand jury were intimidated later, and because of their testimony, they found it difficult to secure employment and protection from physical injury.[14]

A scrutiny of events in Eufaula reveals that the acrimony between Republicans and Democrats did not begin with the election of 1874. Instead, as early as 1872, according to one writer of the period, "The sign of the times pointed to the final overthrow of radical rule, and Barbour County stood almost solidly to make the issue plain."[15] Firmly entrenched in the path of Democratic resurgence in the area sat Judge Keils, whom Democrats in the area had accused of stirring up racial trouble and controlling local and county elections.[16] These whites also had long accused Keils of leniency toward black defendants.[17] As foreman of a grand jury over which Keils presided, one white resident objected to its racial composition: "I must, however, be permitted to say that putting twice as many of the former [blacks on a grand jury] as that of the latter [whites] is not only wrong but impolitic."[18]

After the election of 1874, Democrats carried out their campaign promise to rid the county of Keils. Because of articles of impeachment levelled against him, Keils resigned and left the state, the earliest Republican to resign from office because of Democratic pressure.[19] Apparently, Democrats sought to control local and county offices long before the election of 1874. Harry Philpot Owens explains that the election of 1870 was quiet in comparison, and because Eufaula was divided into wards, Democrats felt secure in their ability to maintain control of municipal government.[20]

Opposition in Macon County

Democratic opposition to black Republicans in Macon County was equally relentless. As mentioned elsewhere, Democratic opposition in Tuskegee, Macon County, already had forced African American lawmaker James Alston to flee to Montgomery. Now it was time for George Patterson and Henry St. Clair--but not A. W. Johnson, the county's other black lawmaker--to taste Democratic opposition. The wait was not a long one. According to R. J. Norrell, Democratic opposition appeared in the personage of newly elected Circuit Court Judge Edward Cobb.[21] Cobb had fought in the Civil War at Gettysburg but spent the remainder of the war in Union prisons. Upon his election in 1874, he immediately went to work against Republican officeholders. St. Clair and Patterson were charged and convicted in 1874 of adultery and grand larceny--both felonious charges. Each was sentenced to the chain gang in 1875. Thus, ending the tenure of the two Macon County Republican lawmakers. Next in line was the white Republican state senator, who escaped charges of perjury by resigning. Finally, newly reelected Probate Judge

267

Benjamin Thompson was removed from office. Cobb charged that Thompson had fixed inadequate bond for his office; he then sought the assistance of newly elected Democratic Governor George Smith Houston in choosing a replacement. They selected P. S. Holt, Thompson's Democratic challenger, to fill Thompson's vacant seat. As Norrell recounts the story, the Democratic Tuskegee *News* boasted that "for the first time since the war," all county officials had been "selected by the white people."[22] Thus, all Republican officeholding disappeared from Macon County. But, to make certain Democratic power went unchallenged, Cobb and his followers relied on the crop-lien system and the convict lease system to control county blacks. The crop-lien system bound them to the land, and the convict lease system enrolled black challengers to Democratic hegemony. A Colonel Abercrombie was known to have kept his black convicts well fed and happy.[23]

Democrats and the Color Line

By 1874 Democrats resolved that the best way to defeat other black Republican officeholders was to eliminate them from officeholding altogether; that is to rely on the color line. Initially, Democrats were divided on whether to use race as a campaign issue, and the state's leading newspapers reflected this division. The Greensboro *Beacon* determined that using race as a campaign issue was "little short of suicide."[24] The Montgomery

Daily Advertiser cautioned the party to keep the race issue to a minimum.[25] Democratic committees pondered the color line as a campaign theme, but they, too, disagreed on the race theme. Democratic committees in Lee and Shelby counties appealed to the race theme, but their peers in Perry, Limestone, Madison, Conecuh, Bibb, and Dallas counties did not. Democrats in Barbour County, in startling contrast, appealed to the black voter.[26]

Race was never considered the only campaign issue. Some party members considered the state debt as a viable issue; others wanted to emphasize Republican corruption and mismanagement in government. Initially disagreeing on the color line as a campaign theme, Democrats found it necessary to assuage the fears of small farmers of north Alabama, who agreed with the disfranchisement of black voters but held a greater fear of Blackbelt planters. To defeat Republican candidates, Democrats needed to attract these small farmers, who usually voted Republican.[27]

Democrats received assistance from an unexpected source in their efforts to identify a campaign theme. Since 1867 Charles Sumner had attempted to pass a civil rights bill in Congress. In May 1874, two months after the death of the Massachusetts senator, the Senate passed a version of his bill prohibiting racial discrimination on public transportation, in places of public accommodation, at places of public amusement, and in public schools. Southern Democrats immediately denounced the bill, claiming that Republicans sought to revive sectional animosities and allow the Federal government to interfere in Southern affairs again. Alabama Democrats charged that the civil rights bill would kill the public school system because whites would not financially support mixed schools. The passage of the bill fueled Democratic efforts to attract the north Alabama small farmer.[28] Although some white Republicans attempted to disown the civil rights bill, Democrats quickly pounced on the issue, a tactical advantage that placed Republicans on the defensive by claiming that Republicans themselves were using race as an issue. Therefore, Democrats expected their extensive measures to lead to victory at the polls and that Alabama again would have "a white man's government." Whites in Warren County, Mississippi, began the process of redemption during the same summer as they organized the Peoples, or White Man's, party along a similar white-line basis.[29]

Ensconced in office as governor on the strength of north Alabama white voters, George Smith Houston and leaders of the Democratic press immediately began to consider ways to deny offices to Republicans. Denying bond to newly elected Republicans and then awarding the vacant office to Democrats proved to be an excellent means. Employing the "Petersburg plan," named for the Virginia city in which Democrats first used it, they abolished certain local offices and instituted an appointive government. Gaining control of the government, Democrats promised to protect local communities against "wrongs."[30]

Resistance in Dallas County

Democratic opposition to black officeholding was especially vehement in Dallas County, where in 1867 African Americans began one of the richest and longest legacies of political service in the state. African Americans in Selma, for example, had been the first of their race to receive appointments as policemen.[31] Alabama journalist-turned-historian John Witherspoon DuBose charges that as early as 1868, two whites and two African Americans, who could neither read nor write, comprised the Dallas County Commission. DuBose further notes that these commissioners paid no taxes in the "great land of planters and plantations." He concludes that in the same year seven of the nine justices of the peace were African American.[32] By November 1871 nine African Americans had served as justices of the peace, and three African Americans had received appointments as constables.[33] Beginning in 1874 two African American and two white Republicans comprised the county commission. One of the black commissioners was Oscar Hunter, first elected in 1873.[34] The Democratic Montgomery *Advertiser and Mail* heartily endorsed the abolition of the court, concluding, "The courts of county commission control the finances of several counties, yet, in the blackbelt, as a rule, these courts are composed of negroes, totally unqualified for the positions, and who have been put there solely because they were Republicans."[35]

Thomas Walker, elected as clerk of the circuit court of Dallas County in November 1874, was one of the earliest African American officials to be denied his position, because Democrats discarded his votes. He complained to local authorities and later tried to get an injunction against the board of registrars, all to no avail.[36] Besides, when Benjamin S. Turner, the state's first African American congressman, was unable to post his high bond as county treasurer, the legislature declared the post vacant and named a Democrat instead. An act of the legislature made posting bond difficult by requiring that sureties on the bond reside in the same county and that property pledged exist in the same county. Republican bondsmen customarily went on vacation during the summer; therefore, Republican officeholders experienced hardships in posting bonds, while bondsmen enjoyed their vacations in the North or perhaps in Europe.[37]

Democratic opposition to black officeholding also focused on the Dallas County Criminal Court, where Roderick B. Thomas and William J. Stevens had served as judge and clerk, respectively. Twelve black jurors, who Walter Lynwood Fleming claims refused to convict a radical, had tried and acquitted Thomas of stealing cotton.[38] Judge Corbin, a white Virginian, presided over the court as its first judge. Thomas became clerk and later judge of Corbin's court, and Stevens served as Thomas' clerk.[39] On 4 February 1875 Charles E. Harris of Dallas County and 29 other lawmakers protested the abolishment of this court.[40]

Opposition to Local Patronage

Having conceived of a way to eliminate black state appointees, Democrats turned their attention to local patronage positions, hoping to destroy the final vestige of republicanism. As early as 1867, African Americans had received appointments to local patronage jobs in the fire and police departments and in construction work areas. During that year Ovide Gregory had served as a Mobile police lieutenant on the night shift.[41] General George Meade, commander of the Third Military District, and Governor William Hugh Smith had appointed the city's first black officeholders to the aldermanic board: E. D. Taylor, Henry Stewart, Freeman Smith, Constantine Perez, Gregory Laurendine, John Bryant, and Albert Gallatin. By 1869 Cleveland F. Moulton, Jacob Anderson, and other African Americans had served as city court judges and justices of the peace. During the same year, Governor Smith appointed John Carraway to the common council and 10 other African Americans--Lawrence Berry, John Bryant, Durham Davis, Albert Gallatin, Constantine Perez, C. Fernandez, E. D. Taylor, Freeman Smith, and two other African Americans identified only as Strong and Wilson--to the board of aldermen.

NEITHER CARPETBAGGERS NOR SCALAWAGS

Although African American presence in Mobile city government
ended in 1870, Smith, nevertheless, reappointed Carraway to the
council and reappointed seven other African Americans--Berry,
Davis, Gallatin, Perez, Fernandez, Smith, and Taylor--to the
aldermanic board.[42] The stultifying impact of redemption had
appeared initially in Mobile, as Democrats had rid the city of its
African American officials, and by 1874 African Americans had lost
much of their political strength in most of the other cities south
of the Tennessee Valley.

Ruse in Montgomery County

Democrats used an old ruse in Montgomery to rid the city of its
black officeholders. Black voters had declined in the capital city
from 2,779 in 1873 to 2,131 by 1875, the year Democrats ended their
seven-year hiatus from government. Again, not content solely with
a decline in the number of black voters, Democrats sought to rid
the city of black officials and black voters; they gerrymandered
district lines, thereby placing several black areas outside the
city. Gerrymandering was not novel; Governor Elbridge Gerry had
used it at the turn of the nineteenth century to give Republicans
a numerical advantage in the Massachusetts legislature, and North
Carolina Democrats had used it with success in the election of
1872.[43]

Between 1868 and 1876 Montgomery County sent 11 African Americans to the legislature: George W. Cox, Holland Thompson, Latty J. Williams, Henry Hunter Craig, Hales Ellsworth, Lawson Steele, Hershel V. Cashin, Elijah Cook, Charles Fagan, Captain Gilmer, and Charles O. Harris. Four African Americans--Holland Thompson, Alfred Billingslea, Latty J. Williams, and Henry Hunter Craig (but never more than two at a time)--served on the city council.[44] To reduce the strength of blacks, Mayor W. L. Moses, a Democrat, asked the legislature to reduce the unprofitable part of the city; that is the part that consumed a large part of city services but paid a disproportionate part of its taxes.[45]

Table 3 is a population list for Montgomery's six wards, and table 4 offers insight into the city's black-white population trends from 1850 to 1890. Beginning in 1876 the new city limits extended from the north limit of the city on the east side of the extension of Ripley Street, then to the east along Pollard Street, west to Bainbridge Street, then north along Wetumpka Road to the northern limit of the city, and then east to the point of the beginning. The act was equally descriptive in outlining other boundaries of the city.[46] These new lines encompassed the immediate area around the state capitol, thereby gerrymandering blacks outside the city. After 1877 no black officeholders graced the halls of city government, because their districts had been placed outside the city.

TABLE 3

DISTRICT POPULATION OF MONTGOMERY, 1866

	Whites			Blacks			Grand
	M	F	T	M	F	T	Total
First Ward	624	518	1,142	778	960	1,738	2,880
Second Ward	456	--	912	482	796	1,278	2,190
Third Ward	304	235	539	183	292	475	1,014
Fourth Ward	460	535	995	485	743	1,228	2,223
Fifth Ward	625	633	1,258	737	1,081	1,818	3,076
Sixth Ward	442	238	680	516	483	999	1,679
Total	2,912	2,615	5,526	3,181	4,355	7,535	13,062

Source: *The Alabama Manual and State Register for 1869*, Joseph Hodgson, ed. (Montgomery: Mail Building, 1869), 38.

The mayor emphasized to the legislature his desire to continue to serve the patrons of Swayne School. Nowhere did he cite race as a factor in his choice of the area to exclude from city services, but when it became clear the deleted areas included the fourth and fifth wards--largely black areas and foremost areas of Republican strength--his moves took on political dimensions. By gerrymandering districts lines, Democrats purged the city of its black officeholders, despite the city having a majority black population in 1880 and 1890.[47]

TABLE 4

POPULATION TRENDS IN MONTGOMERY

	1850	1860	1870	1880	1890
White	6,511	4,341	5,402	6,782	8,892
Black	2,217	4,502	5,183	9,931	12,987
% Black	25	53	49	59	59

Source: Compiled from the United States Bureau of the Census, *Ninth Census of the Unites States: 1870, Population, Schedule* 1, 81, 102, 225, 262, 280; United States Bureau of the Census, *Eleventh Census of the United States: 1890, Population, Schedule* 1, Part I, 524, 527, 546, 555, 557. Quoted in Rabinowitz, "From Reconstruction to Redemption in the Urban South," *Journal of Urban History* 2, no. 2 (February 1976): 171.

Contested Elections

Democrats further carried out their plans on the state level by contesting elections. First, they challenged the elections of African Americans who had testified against them before a congressional committee. Barbour County's three African American elected officials--Allen E. Williams, Edward Odum, and Adam Gachet--were forced from office.[48] Second, during the same year, Democrats forced from office Prince Gardner and D. J. Daniels, Russell County's black representatives. William D. Gaskin of Lowndes County fared no better than his peers from Barbour and

Russell counties. On 30 January 1875 one Jacob Pepperman charged Gaskin with bribery, and the House appointed a committee to investigate the allegation. On 2 March F. W. Baker of Clarke County introduced a resolution to suspend Gaskin, but Leroy Brewer offered a substitute resolution, which allowed Gaskin's counsel to appear. Although Brewer later withdrew his original resolution and made a substitute resolution, the House expelled Gaskin on 3 March 1875. Brewer's motion had been successful.[49]

The citizens of Lowndes County elected Hugh A. Carson to replace Gaskin.[50] The Democratic opposition immediately seized the opportunity to expel Carson as well, accusing him of being an escaped felon, producing certified copies of an earlier indictment, and concluding that the Senate should expel him. The following year--on 10 February 1876--the House recorded a memorial from the citizens of Lowndes County asking for the expulsion of Carson and black State Senator John William Jones.[51] Carson (for the second time) and Jones contested the challenge to their seats. However, the challenge was too great for Carson, for on 5 December 1878 J. F. Haigler contested Carson's recent reelection bid. The opposition successfully removed Carson in 1878, as A. A. Wiley, Carson's attorney, unsuccessfully addressed the House for his client. The House adopted the report of the Committee on Privilege and Election, which resolved that J. F. Haigler was entitled to Carson's seat. The House and Senate adopted the committee's report on 20 January 1879, and Governor Rufus Wills Cobb signed the resolution the following day, the House Committee on Privilege and Elections declaring him a felon.[52] With the stroke of his pen Governor Cobb ended the reign of the Lowndes County black lawmaker.[53]

Rapier was Alabama's first African American to challenge Democratic opposition by contesting his reelection bid. Jere N. Williams, his Democratic challenger, denied Rapier's allegations: that five-sixths of the votes at Spring Hill had been cast for Rapier; that minors had voted for Williams; that over 500 voters at Eufaula had been driven from the polls; that over 200 illegal votes had been counted for Williams at Faulk's; that 75 people had voted illegally for Williams at Atkinson; that over 75 people had voted illegally for Williams at Richard's; and that Williams had received no clear majority at Union Springs. Rapier became the first of the state's black congressmen to lose a contested election.[54]

Repeal of Legal Protection

Repealing laws of benefit to African Americans, such as House bill no. 160, which was passed on 28 December 1868 and provided for the suppressing of murder, lynching and assault and battery, was one of the initial acts of the new legislature. The House repealed the act on 14 December 1874, on the motion of Democrat J. M. Carmichael of Ozark. The legislature nullified another

Reconstruction measure--such as Act No. 160--because they no longer feared Federal intervention. The legislature then considered a constitutional convention to nullify Reconstruction legislation, since the civil rights bill had failed.[55] Governor Houston appointed Peter Hamilton to report on the desirability of holding such a convention. Pending the approval of the electorate, Hamilton's committee suggested adjusting or abolishing the state debt, the Board of Education, the judiciary, and state aid to railroads, and questioned the constitutionality of certain offices.[56] The call for a convention passed the Senate by a vote of 18 to 6 on 11 March, and five days later the House passed the measure by a vote of 52 to 32. Governor Houston signed House bill no. 24, calling for a convention to revise and amend the constitution on 19 March and set the first Monday in August 1875 as the date the electorate would decide the desirability of holding a convention. Also, they would elect candidates to the convention, which, if approved, would convene on the first Monday in September 1875.[57]

Seven years earlier Republicans had called for a convention and seemed unified, but since then factionalism had beset the Alabama Republican party. Alexander White, chairman of the state executive committee, urged all Republicans to refrain from choosing delegates to the convention. On the other hand, Datus E. Coon, an Iowa native, issued an address in which he asked his followers to vote against the convention but to choose delegates. Democrats added to Republican difficulties by claiming that the position of Republicans was designed to their advantage across the state in that White's policy benefitted the white counties of north Alabama, where few African Americans lived, and that Coon's policy worked to the advantage of the Blackbelt and its large contingent of African Americans. This ploy was intended to make certain Republicans received large numbers of votes in both regions.[58]

Democrats noted that Alexander White, former Provisional Governor Lewis E. Parsons, and Samuel F. Rice, prominent in Republican circles in 1875, were scalawags who had signed the "Address to the People" of Alabama against the Radical Constitution of 1868. Democrats charged that these Republicans for seven years had begged the people "to touch not, taste not, handle not the unclean thing," referring to the ratification of the Constitution of 1868 and suggested that the existing constitution was "not the constitution of the people of Alabama but a constitution of a minority of the whole people, and that minority, a negro minority."[59] The Montgomery *Alabama State Journal*, the Talladega *Home*, the Selma *Republican*, and other Republican organs opposed the idea of holding a convention.[60] Most of all, Republicans opposed a convention, fearing the convention would dismantle the Constitution of 1868.[61] Party leaders and a partisan press offered only feeble resistance, nonetheless.

Democrats argued that a convention would improve economic and social conditions, including the abolition of the oath of registration in the Constitution of 1868. As a prerequisite for voting, voters had to swear to support full civil and political equality of all men. Democrats further promised to reapportion the legislature to the advantage of the white counties of north Alabama, much as it had been during the antebellum period. With the threat of black Republican supremacy heightened by the passage of the Civil Rights Act of 1875, Democrats augmented their campaign with the race issue, an ingredient that worked extremely well, especially when other methods failed.[62]

Democrats were also more united in the call for a convention, and some leading Democratic newspapers led the call for the convention. John Forsyth, a leader against the adoption of the Constitution of 1868, called for a convention in his Mobile *Daily Register*. There was little opposition to the convention. Some feared the election on the call for a convention would come too soon after the November 1874 election. The Union Springs *Ledger*, Greensboro *Beacon*, Tuskegee *Weekly News*, and several other Blackbelt papers also opposed the convention. Outside the Blackbelt, the Ashville *Southern Aegis*, Birmingham *Iron Age*, and Greenville *Advocate* opposed the convention.[63] Democratic efforts to call a convention continued despite the opposition of some Democratic leaders who had accepted the idea of black suffrage and some planters who feared that a constitutional convention would repudiate large outstanding debts.[64] In the midst of Republican strife, Democrats convinced voters that Republicans were a threat to the welfare of the state. Voters responded during the August election by approving the call for a convention by a vote of 77,763 to 59,928.[65] By apportioning delegates, Democrats already had limited the chances of Republican control. The Blackbelt, for example, with a population of more than 40,000 in each county, was allotted two delegates, although the Wiregrass counties of Coffee, Dale, Geneva, and Henry, and the north Alabama counties of Blount, Morgan, and Winston were allotted five delegates to represent a population of slightly over 30,000.[66]

Eighty Democrats, 12 Republicans, and seven Independents were elected as delegates. Republican and Independent delegates were elected from the Blackbelt, the area that opposed the convention in the election.[67] Veteran black Republicans such as Alexander H. Curtis, Greene Shadrack Washington Lewis, and Hugh A. Carson attended the convention. R. A. Long of Washington County was the only African American newcomer.[68]

When the 1875 convention delegates had assembled, many influential carpetbaggers had either left the state or no longer participated in political affairs. Factionalism among African Americans hampered their effectiveness; therefore, their presence was of little concern to Democrats or to other Republicans.

283

Conversely, former Confederates, many of them leaders in the secession convention of 1861, led the Democratic party and dismantled many features of Alabama republicanism.[69] Another feature of the convention was the presence of men who dominated Alabama politics for many years after the convention. Rufus Wills Cobb, William Calvin Oates, Edward Asbury O'Neal, and William James Samford served as governors between 1878 and the turn of the century. Other delegates, such as Francis Strother Lyon and James Lawrence Pugh, served as congressmen.[70]

When the proceedings had ended, Democrats had abolished the Board of Education; denied city, county, or state aid to corporations; limited taxation; and abolished the registration oath. What they didn't abolish from the Constitution of 1868, they changed. State elections, separated from Federal elections, now occurred in August instead of November to minimize the chances of Federal intervention for the Republican party. The convention also segregated the school system. The reapportionment of the legislature, giving the counties of north Alabama a larger numerical representation; the prohibition against the introduction of local and special legislation; and the pre-1868 requirement for legislative, executive, and judicial officers, severely curtailed the power of the Republican party. Democrats didn't propose a property or educational qualification for voting, imprisonment for debt, and the submission of the constitution to the electorate for approval. When the convention closed, the provisions for manhood suffrage and popular election remained.[71] Despite the general tendency to repeal Republican measures, Democrats preserved the school system. They approved Act No. 27, which provided appropriations for public schools of the state, and Act No. 14, which established, organized, and regulated a system of public education.[72]

Partisan acrimony reached new heights during the attempts to ratify the constitution. As the Democratic party had labeled Republicans as scalawags and carpetbaggers during the campaign to ratify the Constitution of 1868, Republicans returned the favor in 1875 and called Democrats who favored the constitution Bourbons and Bourbon Repudiators. Republicans declared the new constitution was a "Bourbon Democratic Constitution and reactionary, evidence that Genuine Bourbons never learn nor forget."[73]

To Republicans, Bourbons were those in charge of political affairs from 1874 to 1901. They charged that because of the Democrats, life in Alabama was the same before and after the war. For the South this restoration was similar to the Bourbon restoration in nineteenth-century France, but those in government in Alabama after 1874 were more likely to have been old-line Whigs rather than life-long Democrats.[74]

Twenty-two months after issuing the call for a convention, Alabamians ratified the convention proceedings by a vote of 85,662 to 29,217, thus stabilizing the power of the Democratic party. Only Autauga, Dallas, Lowndes, and Montgomery counties opposed ratification of the constitution.[75] Although the election had proceeded without the violence that characterized earlier elections, Democrats, not content with their new constitution, continued to contest elections. Early in 1875 they adopted a resolution to contest the 1872 election of George E. Spencer. Although Spencer was the state's only Republican congressman, Democrats didn't unseat him.[76]

Contested Election: *Bromberg v. Haralson*

Continuing to consider black officials vulnerable, Democrats contested the election of Jeremiah Haralson, who had resigned his State Senate seat only to find his congressional election challenged by Frederick G. Bromberg. Bromberg charged that between 28 September and 27 October, within five days of the election, Republicans issued government bacon to 773 heads of families in Dallas County, 828 heads of families in Wilcox County, and 97 heads of families in Monroe County. Bromberg charged that in Wilcox County, Republicans issued bacon at a political meeting during which candidates for sheriff and clerk of the circuit court made speeches. Bromberg declared that Republicans also promised as much as one year's supply of bacon to black voters in Mobile and Clarke counties--all for casting ballots for Republican candidates.

Bromberg further alleged that he lost the election because of fraud and illegal voting. In Mobile the voter list showed the names of 6,009 qualified voters, although 8,079 had voted, he charged.[77]

According to Bromberg, the Republican Union Club instigated the fraudulent election by including on the voter list the names of persons who had died, left the state, or did not exist. In Selma minors voted, as well as persons who lived outside the district. Some voted more than once. In Wilcox County candidates for probate judge, sheriff, and clerk of the circuit court also were officers of the election, being appointed by law to count the votes. In Monroe County J. S. Perrin, a Republican candidate for the legislature, served as one of the US supervisors of the election, chairman of the county Republican executive committee, deputy United States marshal, distributor of government bacon, and commander in chief of Federal troops stationed in the county. Bromberg pointed to Perrin's many duties as a possible conflict of interest. In addition, witnesses for Bromberg affirmed that they heard Haralson harangue a crowd of African Americans in Selma that "whoever should try to get a colored man to vote the Democratic ticket and any colored man who should vote the Democratic ticket in the coming election, ought to be swung up to the limb of a tree."[78] The most serious allegation against Haralson was his earlier indictment for the theft of a bale of cotton.[79]

Haralson contested Bromberg's charges. W. J. Squire of Mobile testified as Bromberg's chief witness, and most of his testimony was unsupported by other witnesses. Bromberg alleged that the Republican Union Club, comprised of about 250 members, had caused many to vote repeatedly, but John White, attorney for Haralson, charged that Bromberg had employed Squire to contest the election and to solicit information from different counties. Squire was also the head of the Republican Union Club, according to the testimony of Constantine Perez of Mobile, who knew Squire. Perez, the black storeowner and innkeeper, was a creditable witness and had served with the elder Bromberg as a member of the Mobile city council and as an alderman for the Sixth District until 1870. The Brombergs were one of the city's most prominent families.[80]

Surprisingly, few had voted in the election. John White explained that the election had been held under the legislative guidelines of 28 November 1874, but the city election had occurred less than one month before the 22 December 1874 election, making a large voter turnout unlikely.[81] Perez's testimony that none of the Republican Union Club members were aware of the election-day scheme and that none of the witnesses could identify a member of the Republican Union Club, except those examined by the contestant, caused the House Committee on Elections to dismiss Bromberg's charges.[82] Haralson received added support from former United States Marshal George Turner, who, in a written affidavit from

288

Phelps County, Missouri, stated that he had examined W. B. Taylor of Mobile and that Taylor knew nothing detrimental about Haralson but much that was detrimental to Bromberg.   Turner's testimony suggested that Republicans had begun to patch up their differences, for Turner was a well-known Spencer supporter while Haralson was an ardent Smith adherent.[83]

Only two persons admitted having voted against their will at Monroeville. No one in Monroeville had voted Republican by "reason of bacon," and no one in Monroe County attested to the undue influence of the military. After showing that Squire arranged the evidence in Wilcox County--information that was supported by blacks who could not read nor write--the committee found Bromberg's evidence inadmissable and praised the registration efforts of John M. Tillman and Benjamin S. Turner. The committee suggested that the high-registration count undoubtedly reflected the tendency of African Americans to make certain they had registered by doing so more than once. Sumter Lea, a witness from Selma, testified that Haralson had been indicted and cleared of stealing cotton. Had the jury found Haralson guilty as charged, he would have been forced to resign his seat.[84]

The Committee on Elections announced Haralson the winner but also found cases of fraud as flagrant and abuses as violent as ever had been committed in the country: Republicans had used bacon in a district where people were prosperous to influence and control the elective franchise; Republicans had intimidated African American voters to support Haralson; and the military had relied on undue influence. Congressmen Martin Ingram Townsend of New York and John H. Caldwell of Alabama quickly accentuated these findings against the Alabama Republican party: Townsend called the testimony of witnesses for the contestee glaring and self-confuted perjury. Caldwell noted the falsehoods of the witnesses "had their origin in the brain of active, leading members of the Republican party in Alabama."[85] The committee discarded many of the Haralson votes but still found Haralson's huge majority too great to overcome and announced Haralson as the winner on 18 April 1876, one of the few instances in which a Republican emerged as the victor. Paradoxically, 10 contested elections focused on the Fourth Congressional District, the Blackbelt, and involved the efforts of Republicans to unseat Democrats.[86]

Haralson's opposition to Louis H. Mayer, Kentucky native, aide to Spencer, and collector of internal revenue at Mobile, helps to explain Republican chicanery in the November election. Senator Spencer had secured the appointment of Mayer in 1871 at the expense of scalawag John T. Foster. Spencer's action caused a sharp division in Republican circles, especially in the Smith and White camp. Haralson joined in the foray in 1875, when he asked for the removal of Mayer, charging him with employing "unworthy and unprincipled men"; using his office for scheming and corrupt cabals; having personal connections with a secret movement (the Republican Union Club) that in 1874 sought to defeat regular Republicans; voting with Democrats; giving bad advice to colored citizens and encouraging them to engage in schemes injurious to themselves; conducting himself discourteously to other Federal officials; and failing to honor personal debts.[87]

Ten days later Haralson reaffirmed his intention to remove Mayer, but on this occasion he focused on Senator Spencer, acknowledging Spencer's support of Mayer but not failing to indicate that Spencer spent very little time in the state and therefore was unaware of the conduct of many of his appointees. Haralson claimed that William Miller, collector of customs, Joshua J. Moulton, postmaster, and some of the senator's earlier appointees had defaulted on the government. Haralson emphasized his intention to use his influence to bring the Republican party to a position of respect.[88] Spencer's influence, however, stalled Haralson's efforts to remove Mayer.

Summary

Republican disunity, as revealed in the Haralson case, helped to consolidate the power of Democrats, for by 1876 they had won control of state government, state administration and its congressional delegation, and most of the local governments. They also had written a new state constitution. Besides, Democrats had won control of Mississippi on 3 November 1875, despite the state's having the best record of Republican governments in the South and far better than the national record for Republican affairs. Within two years Democrats won control of South Carolina, Florida, and Louisiana. This outcome did not come about easily, but Democrats had been prepared for the fight.

CONSTITUTIONAL CONVENTION

Montgomery Alabama, September 30th 1875.

Alabama Department of Archives and History, Montgomery

WILLIAM HOOPER COUNCILL

CHAPTER 9

Democrats were gaining strength as rapidly as Republicans were losing their hold on Alabama politics. Surely, Republicans regretted their loss of power, patronage, and prestige. Many of them relied on other professions for a livelihood, but matters were different for black members of the party. The Republican party was the black man's salvation in a land of former slaveowners and economic adversities. No one suffered more from the loss of Republican power than the party's black members.

Democratic United Front

Democrats launched a united front in 1876 and renominated George Smith Houston for governor. Initially, there was discontent toward the Houston nomination. Robert McKee and his Selma *Southern Argus* disagreed with the course Houston had taken to reverse the state's financial affairs, particularly the state debt. McKee, John Forsyth, editor of the Mobile *Daily Register*, and the editors of the Decatur *News* and the Greenville *South Alabamian* wanted an immediate repudiation of the state debt. Once it was apparent Houston would receive the nomination, the *Southern Argus* and the other newspapers originally in disagreement with the Houston nomination joined in supporting the incumbent governor. McKee, who believed whites were naturally superior and better fitted for government than African Americans, was especially pleased Houston had decided to campaign on the race issue or, as McKee expressed it, "the color line."[1]

Republican Factionalism

Democrats could have selected a campaign issue without regard for Republican opposition and still emerged victorious, largely because of intense Republican factionalism. Former Governor William Hugh Smith had helped in George E. Spencer's reelection in 1872, and Spencer had reciprocated by leaving Republican affairs to those who remained in Alabama daily. But, party strife started anew when Spencer wanted to name delegates to the Republican National Convention in return for allowing Smith to name the state candidates. Smith resented Spencer's request, and the Republican party, unable to surmount the factionalism within its ranks, split even wider. This wider political split appeared evident when the state Republican executive committee met in Montgomery and endeavored to reorganize. Thirty party regulars, including Samuel F. Rice, Benjamin F. Saffold, Smith, and John Minnis, attended the meeting, which was imperative because of the recent legislative reapportionment from six to eight districts. This redistricting gave the committee 24 members instead of 12. The meeting adjourned to reassemble on 21 December 1875.[2]

Charles Mayer, head of the state executive committee, and Spencer disagreed with the outcome of the December meeting, especially with its decision to increase membership. Mayer traveled to Montgomery from Washington, D. C., and assembled a group of five at the Exchange Hotel. They decided to meet on 24 May 1876 to nominate a slate of candidates for the upcoming election. Meanwhile, the Smith faction established a newspaper to voice its views and later assembled on 16 May 1876 to nominate officers. Despite the pleas of a group led by Jeremiah Haralson, the committee, at the insistence of Saffold and Rice, nominated a slate. Thomas M. Peters, the candidate for governor, was the best known of the lot. This committee also nominated Haralson, Rice, Smith, and Willard Warner as delegates to the Republican National Convention, scheduled to convene in Cincinnati on 14 June.[3]

The Spencer-led faction met eight days later and nominated little-known Judge James S. Clarke for governor. On 10 July Clarke resigned, and the committee replaced him with another scalawag, Charles C. Sheats. At-large delegates chosen by this faction included Spencer, Alexander White, Charles Hays, and Alexander H. Curtis, the African American state senator. The Spencer group

depended on the African American vote and included James Thomas
Rapier within its ranks. The Montgomery *Advertiser* observed that
the difference between the two groups was that the Spencer group
was "all 'nigger' and carpetbagger" and the Smith faction was
"largely scalawag and 'nigger'."[4] At the convention, however, the
National Republican Convention recognized the Smith-led faction.[5]

Republican factions compromised in time for the August state
election. Both sides withdrew their candidates, selected cotton
planter Noadiah Woodruff to head the ticket of little-known men,
and advanced a bland platform calling for support for public
schools and civil and political equality for all men. Democrats,
in turn, charged that Republicans were unworthy of public
confidence. The election not only saw Houston reelected by a
margin of 95,837 to 55,586 for Woodruff, but the number of
Republicans elected to the General Assembly--five scalawags, one
carpetbagger, and nine African Americans--was the lowest since
1868. The number of African Americans had declined proportionately
with the other members of the party. The last coterie of African
Americans to serve in the Alabama legislature included Elijah
Baldwin of Wilcox County; William J. Stevens, William H. Blevins,
and Green T. Johnston of Dallas County; Hershel V. Cashin, Charles
O. Harris, and Captain Gilmer of Montgomery County; Nicholas
Stephens and Greene Shadrack Washington Lewis of Perry County; and
Nimrod Snoddy of Greene County. These were Blackbelt counties.

Hence, the last contingent of African American politicians represented only five Blackbelt counties.[6]

One writer of the period suggests that the election of 1874 marked the death blow to the African American lawmaker, but this writer contends the election of 1878 marked his decline and disappearance. Hugh A. Carson and George English were elected in 1878, and W. P. Williams, a Greenback-Republican fusion candidate from Huntsville, served from 1882 to 1884.[7]

The newly aligned House, Senate, and congressional district lines created by the convention of 1875 offer little explanation for the decline of African American state officials. For example, the new congressional districts of Alabama, numbering eight instead of six, combined Dallas, Perry, Lowndes, Hale, and Wilcox--all located in the Blackbelt--to form the Fourth District, the only one in which blacks represented a majority. Altered district lines didn't affect black representation. Senate lines were changed also, but they didn't water down the number of African American elected officials either. Therefore, the alterations in districts lines do not explain completely the absence and decline of African American lawmakers. Instead, violence, fraud, factionalism, and economic reprisals offer a better explanation for the disappearance of African American officials.[8]

No other event in the decade after the Civil War did more to wreck the Alabama Republican party and to destroy African American solidarity than the election for the newly gerrymandered Fourth District Congressional seat in 1876. Incumbent Jeremiah Haralson had garnered the support of the Smith faction in his candidacy for a second term. This faction, while not actively soliciting the support of the black masses, rested its hopes on an appeal to old-line Whigs and disgruntled Democrats. Haralson accepted the support of the Smith faction because his antipathy for Spencer exceeded his dislike for Democrats. Rapier, in contrast, considered the Smith coalition too conservative on civil rights issues, though the Spencer faction continuously denied Federal patronage to blacks. Realizing the Spencer faction also received the support of the black masses, Rapier rented a small plantation in neighboring Hayneville in Lowndes County to qualify as a resident of the district.[9]

The debates between the two black candidates--two of the most powerful in the state--often became volatile, especially on 13 and 14 September. Haralson and Rapier maneuvered for advantage as Republican representatives met to nominate a candidate for Congress, each man trying to get his delegates seated. The Credentials Committee recognized both groups as a compromise, much to the dismay of the incumbent Haralson, who undoubtedly felt cheated. Haralson debated the seating of the Rapier delegates for nearly two hours, and when the committee remained steadfast in its decision, Haralson sped out of the meeting, declaring in his haste he would run as an Independent. Blackbelt black Representative Alexander H. Curtis then officially nominated Rapier as the committee's selection for Congress.[10]

Unlike Rapier, Haralson received additional support from Wilcox County plantation owner M. J. Candee and other vindictive Democrats who disliked Rapier because of his support of the civil rights bill. The Wilcox *Vindicator* found Haralson preferable "to that darkie Rapier, who believes a negro is as good as a white man."[11] Although some Democrats supported Haralson, he exhibited an enmity for Democratic candidate Charles Shelley, sheriff of Selma and former Confederate general. Shelley arrested Haralson on a charge of vagrancy and, during the interrogation, forced him to withdraw from the race.[12] Haralson, J. N. Perkins, L. D. Baker, black former Representative Henry A. Cochran, W. A. Brantley, and others had endorsed Shelley for sheriff in a letter to Governor Lewis. They noted that while Shelley was not a Republican, he "was a just, fair and honest man in every way."[13] These men supported Shelley, a Democrat, hoping he would reciprocate, if elected. Shelley received his appointment on 11 November 1874 and resigned on 27 February 1877, having been elected to Congress.[14]

Rapier and Haralson, running in the last Republican fortress, garnered 61 percent of the votes in a losing effort. With African Americans comprising 34,454, or 80 percent (8,759 white voters) of the population of Dallas County, black factionalism gave the Fourth

District to a Democrat.[15]   The election had become entangled in presidential politics, and on 6 December 1876 Congress resolved to investigate elections in South Carolina, Georgia, Alabama, Florida, Louisiana, and Mississippi.   Although the congressional report concluded that "the men of color and of the African race" no longer had a voice in the electoral process in Alabama, its findings were based on the intricacies of the Fourth District.[16]

Since Shelley, as sheriff of Selma, influenced voters, Haralson contested the election and charged Shelley with abuse of power and with threatening him with a cocked pistol.[17] Table 5 lists the returns, including the disputed votes from the Dallas County precinct. The county canvassing board gave these returns: Rapier, 7,236, Haralson, 8,675, and Shelley, 9,655.

TABLE 5

FOURTH DISTRICT ELECTION RETURNS

	Rapier	Haralson	Shelley
Wilcox County	664	2,922	1,506
Perry County	261	2,563	2,168
Lowndes County	3,904	163	1,312
Hale County	2,340	48	2,179
Dallas County	171	4,881	3,288
Total	7,340	10,557	10,453

Source: House of Representatives, *Committee on Elections, Contested Election: Jere Haralson v. Charles M. Shelley, 4th Congressional District of Alabama,* HR45A-F 10.4, 3, NA.

By discounting the Dallas County votes, the board returned a majority of 980 votes for Shelley. Had they included the Dallas County returns, Haralson would have won by a margin of 124. After an investigation, the House Committee on Elections unanimously accepted the returns for the Dallas County precincts except Summerfield, largely because the voting inspectors did not sign the poll-list, as required by section 40 of an act passed on 3 March 1875 and section 44 of an act passed on 6 March 1876. Section 40 required precinct inspectors, when they had ascertained the number received by each candidate, to prepare and sign a return of the election; to certify one of the poll-lists; and to seal up the returns, the poll-lists, and the registration lists. Section 44 required the county canvassers to make the county returns from precinct returns and not from poll-lists.[18]

On 17 June 1878, less than nine months before the expiration of Shelley's term in the Forty-fifth Congress, Congress authorized the parties to accept the Dallas County returns, minus the Summerfield count, giving Haralson a moot victory by a margin of 124 votes. Haralson subsequently delivered additional evidence, attesting to the veracity of the Summerfield vote by such overwhelming proof that the committee unanimously decided in his favor. They delayed their report until the expiration of the Forty-fifth Congress, and Haralson was never seated.[19] His defeat further highlighted the cancerous impact of factionalism in the Alabama Republican party,

303

only slightly less acrimonious than the feud between scalawag Franklin J. Moses and carpetbagger David Chamberlain in South Carolina.[20]

Table 6

DISPUTED ELECTION DISTRICTS

	Rapier	Haralson	Shelley
Summerfield	---	176	48
Selma, Beat 8	5	215	195
Lexington	---	283	60
Old Town	69	101	77
Portland	---	157	--
Ward 5, Selma	1	124	120
Burnsville	1	284	120
Fences	1	132	100
Vernon	26	149	22
Marion Junction	1	151	50
Boykins	---	130	6
Total	104	1,902	798

Source: House of Representatives, *Committee on Elections, Contested Election: Jere Haralson v. Charles M. Shelley, 4th Congressional District of Alabama, HR45A-F 10.4, 3, NA.*

Federal Laissez-Faire

Haralson's inability to secure a seat in Congress is outlined in table 6. His defeat was part of a larger effort by the national government to project a laissez-faire position with regard to the welfare of African Americans. Moreover, the National Republican party itself had undergone a metamorphosis: the deaths of Thaddeus Stevens, Charles Sumner, Joshua Giddings, Edwin M. Stanton, and Salmon P. Chase, coupled with the unsuccessful reelection bids of Benjamin F. Wade and George W. Julian, produced an opportunity for remaining Radicals to change direction. The new leaders--Roscoe Conkling of New York, Oliver Morton of Indiana, and Benjamin F. Butler of Massachusetts--frequently called Stalwarts, favored a return to the antebellum status quo. Another wing of the party, opprobriously called Half-breeds and led by James G. Blaine, John Sherman, John Garfield, Carl Schurz, and Horace Greeley, called themselves Liberal Republicans and advocated an end to military rule in the South. These Northern Republicans had grown weary of the complaints of Southern blacks and turned their attention toward expansion in Latin America and corruption within the party. The Stalwart wing of the party relied on the Southern black vote. Alabama blacks argued, "The half breeds and the democrats is first cousins."[21] Unfortunately for Southern blacks, the Liberal wing of the party was in the ascendancy, and nowhere was its policy of benign neglect vis-a-vis black rights better illustrated than in the election of Rutherford B. Hayes to the presidency.[22]

On 6 April, less than six months after assuming office, Hayes withdrew the remaining troops from South Carolina. The Republican party had secured what it wanted--the South's acquiescence in

Hayes' election. In return David Key, a Southern senator, was nominated postmaster general, and the Hayes administration gave its support to the Texas and Pacific railroad bill. That only one Democrat--Grover Cleveland--sat in the Oval Office between 1860 and 1912 underscores the success of the Republican party.[23] That Democrats reigned essentially unchallenged in Alabama politics--spasmodic contests with Independents, Greenbackers, and Populists, notwithstanding--highlights the amicable relationship between Southern Democrats and the National Republican party.

Some African Americans made strides within party ranks, despite the new position of Washington. For his support of Hayes during the campaign, Rapier received the nomination--and the Senate confirmed him--as collector of internal revenue in June 1878. His appointment provided a vivid picture of the increasingly close communication between Southerners and Washington. Alabama scalawags envisioned the Rapier selection as an excellent opportunity to secure a congressional seat for a white Republican. They reasoned that if Rapier were nominated to the assessor's position, Fourth District blacks would willingly vote for a white Republican. Besides, Rapier's appointment showed that Hayes, unlike his predecessor Grant, was inclined to listen to the Smith faction or the Southern wing of the party. Hayes' posture gave additional credence to the efforts of the National Republican party to abandon the carpetbagger element and to accentuate the power of local officials by listening to the scalawag element in party politics.[24]

Hayes' Southern strategy continued to gain momentum. Alabama whites and blacks applauded his nomination of Rapier. Other blacks and whites across the nation further endorsed the Hayes strategy when he appointed Frederick Douglass, the most visible and highly respected African American in the nation, as United States marshal for the District of Columbia. Republican Presidents James Garfield and Benjamin Harrison used the Hayes strategy to appease African Americans by appointing Douglass to other Federal positions, making him the first African American to hold these offices.[25] In 1879, three years after the Rapier appointment, Hayes appointed perennial black officeholder Jeremiah Haralson as collector of customs at the port of Baltimore. Haralson had supported the Smith wing of the Alabama Republican party.[26]

Hayes' election, nevertheless, further marked the declining fortunes of blacks within the Republican party. Two rulings by the national Supreme Court offered greater evidence of the declining position of African Americans. It is unclear whether the Executive Department took its cue from the Judicial Branch, or whether the reverse was true, but the impact of the two branches left Reconstruction in shambles by nullifying the protection African Americans had received. The Slaughterhouse Cases did not focus directly on the issue of black rights as citizens; yet, the court ruled the rights of individuals were derived from state citizenship and not from Federal citizenship; therefore, African Americans could not seek protection under the Fourteenth Amendment.[27] The Supreme Court had not spoken on the issue of civil rights until near the end of Reconstruction, and when the court decided to speak, it wreaked havoc on black freedom. In 1884 the Supreme Court continued to nullify legal protection for African Americans. The court sustained the position of a circuit court in its decision that the guarantee of the Fifteenth Amendment did not extend to the passage of laws for the suppression of ordinary crimes within the states.[28]

The death blow to African Americans' rights came in the decision of *United States v. Reese*, in which the court declared two provisions of the Enforcement Acts unconstitutional. The court's ruling vitiated the effectiveness of the Fifteenth Amendment. This amendment, argued the court, merely prohibited the states from discriminating based on race, color, or previous condition of servitude.[29] In 1883 the court declared the Civil Rights Act of 1875 unconstitutional.[30] These Supreme Court rulings completed the abandonment of the black man by the Executive, Legislative, and Judicial branches of government. In praise of their new-found supremacy, Democrats in Alabama proclaimed, "We thank God...that our state will hereafter be controlled by the men of our race--by the Anglo-Saxon--by the stout heart, the strong will, and the sound

308

sense of the men of our blood. We rejoice in the fact that, in almost every state, blood has asserted its supremacy."[31]

Blacks were in a position similar to slavery, since the government no longer offered protection from violence, fraud, and physical abuse. Most importantly, abandonment spelled the end of protection at the polls, which undoubtedly gave the opposition cause to rejoice. In response some blacks in Alabama formed military companies. In Clarke County a black preacher named William Mayo organized and trained a militia company in preparation for a war between Democrats and Republicans. Local officials quickly put down the Mayo effort, despite his plea that the Federal government sanctioned his movement.[32] African Americans of Prattville, Autauga County, carried their pistols to the polls.[33]

This militancy left Democrats and other whites undaunted, for in the absence of legal protection for blacks, a new kind of violence swept across Alabama, leaving fear in its tracks. One writer of the period records that as early as 1875 at least two Alabama blacks were lynched. In April Harrington Green, a local black resident, was taken from a Gadsden jail and shot. His lynching, however, was denounced because of the fear that Radicals would use it as an example of lawlessness. By July a mob had lynched a Morgan County black resident named Charles Griffin. Of his death a Huntsville paper observed, "He deserved his fate. Something swifter and more terrible than the law is needed in all such

309

cases."[34]   In 1876 black residents were lynched in Huntsville, Tuscaloosa, and Mobile.[35]   Five African Americans were lynched in 1877.   A white mob in Monroe County extricated a black resident named Adam from the local jail, riddled his body with bullets, and left him dangling from a tree.   Later that year mobs lynched blacks in Carrollton, in Pickens County; in Franklin County; Seale, in Russell County; in Clarke County; and Athens, in Limestone County. Nowhere was the plight of unprotected African Americans better illustrated than in the case of Jack Turner of Choctaw County, lynched for allegedly having planned a revolt against area whites.[36]

Lynchings occurred nationwide at an average of 67 per year during the 1880s, and an average of 116 lynchings occurred each year during the 1890s.   Years 1892 and 1894 were peak periods.   One hundred and sixty-two African Americans died by lynching in 1892, an average of one death every two days.   In 1894, 134 African Americans died because of lynching.[37]   Also, lynchings were a constant threat to African Americans in Alabama and in other Southern states for the remainder of the nineteenth century and for at least the first five decades of the twentieth century, largely because no level of government passed effective legislation.   A resolution passed by the Republican State Convention censured Governor Houston for not taking the steps necessary to end lynchings.[38]

Declining Role of Blacks

While black party regulars responded to the absence of legal protection and to lynching, its concomitant, they also sought to address their declining role in the Republican party and to offer an alternative for the masses of blacks, who had begun to vote the Democratic persuasion, especially in the Blackbelt.[39] Nowhere was the new direction of the black masses better seen than in the selection of two black delegates--John W. Allen and James A. Scott, editor of the Montgomery *Advance*--and two black alternates to the Democratic State Convention that assembled at Montgomery on 29 and 30 May 1878.[40] Black Republicans, in contrast, were divided into two factions, led by Smith and Spencer, with each group having Haralson or Rapier as its lieutenant. Black party regulars Frank H. Threatt of Marengo County and Robert Reid of Sumter County joined the Independent movement. Although Holland Thompson remained with the Rapier-led faction, Henry J. Europe, Phillip Joseph, Allen Alexander, and other prominent Mobile blacks joined the People's Democratic party. Joseph later joined the Greenback movement, with B. F. Goins of Lawrence County and William McAdory and P. B. Betts of Birmingham in Jefferson County.[41]

Making an already bad situation worse, some scalawags joined the Democrats, leaving control of the Republican party to carpetbaggers and blacks.[42] Later, some carpetbaggers left the state or retired

311

from political affairs. The Republican party also split into the black and tan factions, led by prominent black politician William J. Stevens of Selma, and the lily-whites.[43] Across the state, many prominent Republicans refused to run on a ticket with a black candidate. This phenomenon was especially true in Perry and Montgomery counties.[44] In view of mass defection, Alabama Republicans no longer offered candidates for state offices, and they nominated even fewer candidates for local and county offices. To make matters worse, Republicans lost their last newspaper when the Montgomery *Alabama State Journal* ceased publication, having realized that its chances of receiving a state printing contract were lost.[45]

Further Decline and Death of Black Officeholders

As the Reconstruction legacy ground to a close, several African American officeholders either died or left the state, no longer able to win political office. In 1872 Russell County bridgebuilder Horace King departed Phenix City for neighboring LaGrange, Georgia, where he resumed private life and, with his five sons, continued to construct homes and bridges. King died at the family home on Hill Street on 27 May 1887. He was the only African American elected official from Russell County who served without harassment.[46] The LaGrange *Reporter* observed:

> He was the benefactor of many communities in facilitating their
> social and commercial intercourse by means of the many bridges

of which he was the architect. He made much money in his calling as contractor, but saved nothing for his old age and was dependent upon his sons at the time of his death, to their honor, be it said, they have cheerfully supported their feeble parent. Horace King was one of the few persons of African descent who have risen to prominence by force of genius and character.[47]

In an article titled, "The Death of a Remarkable Negro," the Atlanta *Constitution* noted, "He [King] has always been a freeman, and had accumulated a good property, which however, he lost a few years ago in contracting. He was a freemason and possessed considerable intelligence, and was highly respected."[48]

Willis Merriwether of Prairie Bluff died in office in 1875. Fellow Blackbelt lawmaker Elijah Baldwin of Camden in Wilcox County introduced a resolution in the House in honor of Merriwether's death. Elbert C. Locke, another black lawmaker, filled the Merriwether vacancy.[49] During the same decade, two African American lawmakers died because of failing health. Hepatitis claimed the life of State Representative and Federal patronage recipient Latty J. Williams at the age of 29 in 1874.[50] Henry Hunter Craig died because of a softening of the brain on 8 August 1876 at the age of 60.[51] Both Williams and Craig had left office prior to their deaths. Montgomery County representative Hales Ellsworth died at the age of 58, three months after the death of Alexander H. Curtis, on 15 October 1878, of congestion of the brain.[52]

Two prominent African American politicians lost their lives because of accidents. Influential in religious circles and

313

promoter of the establishment of Selma University, which opened in January 1878, and the Lincoln School of Marion, which opened in July 1867, Alexander H. Curtis died from bruises sustained when he fell from his buggy during a return trip to Marion on 20 July 1878. He was buried in Perry County at the age 48.[53] Caesar Shorter, founder of the black Democratic party, was accidentally killed in a Montgomery dollar store on 4 August 1883. He was 56.[54]

Several black politicians died during the 1880s due to failing health. Joseph Drawn, who had removed to Montgomery, died of consumption on 19 February 1882 at 41 years of age.[55] James Thomas Rapier died in Montgomery on 31 May 1883 of pulmonary pneumonia at 45. He had recently accepted a position as a Federal disbursement officer for a new government office in Montgomery. His uncle, John Thomas Rapier, asked authorities to send his nephew's body to St. Louis, Missouri, where the Rapier family buried him in an unmarked grave and without ceremony.[56] Charles Smith, formerly of Bullock County, died in Montgomery of pneumonia on 31 March 1885 at the age of 40.[57] On 15 May, less than two months after Smith's death, former page Thomas Abercrombie died in Montgomery on May 15 at the age of 41 of hemorrhage of the lungs.[58] Cancer claimed the life of Holland Thompson on 31 March 1887. He was 48.[59] Thompson had lost much of his political influence by the time of his death.[60] Also, Thompson had become embroiled in personal conflicts; he was expelled from the First Colored Baptist Church, earlier the

314

cornerstone of his power, for deserting his second wife and child and for not supporting his charge of adultery.[61] Personal conflicts hastened his demise from power as rapidly as the introduction of Democratic tactics. Thomas Diggs of Barbour County had removed to Montgomery, where he died of cancer on 6 June 1887 at the age of 71.[62]

When he died at the age of 42 on 17 May 1891, former State Representative James K. Greene had removed to Montgomery, where he assumed the duties of a carpenter and later died of consumption.[63] On the other hand, Benjamin S. Turner had returned from Washington after his congressional term ended in 1873. He died on his 300-acre farm, near Selma, on 2 March 1894. Turner had saved $5,000 or $6,000 from his congressional retirement fund to purchase the farm, but a few months before his death creditors sold the farm to pay off Turner's debts. It is probable that his declining financial status, combined with a stroke that left him paralyzed for the final years of his life, caused him to grow increasingly weaker. He had been born in March 1825.[64] John Dozier retired from the legislature in 1874 and died in Uniontown in Perry County about 1892. Dozier was considered an honorable man who abstained from the use of alcohol. He was 92.[65]

Of the death of John William Jones in Montgomery at the age of 67, the Montgomery *Colored Alabamian* wrote in 1909:

NEITHER CARPETBAGGERS NOR SCALAWAGS

There passed away last Friday, 29 January, a man who was widely and favorably known throughout Alabama. Mr Jones served his state as Senator from Lowndes County. He was a delegate from Alabama to the National Republican Convention that nominated the following presidents: Grant, Garfield, McKinley, and Roosevelt. For the final 13 years of his life, he was deputy district revenue collector at Mobile and Montgomery at a salary of $900.00 and filled both positions with credit and efficiency.[66]

Self-educated, Jones operated a race track, a grocery store, and a plantation in Hayneville immediately after the war. By 1880 he had purchased large blocks of property near the High and Jackson streets area of Montgomery so his seven children could attend school during the fall and winter. He also constructed a large hall in the same area, calling it Centennial Hall. Jones actively participated in the Masonic Order, Knights of Pythias, and the Good Shepherd organizations.[67]

The praise of William H. Councill by the Birmingham *News* compares favorably with the Montgomery *Colored Alabamian*'s appraisal of Jones. Councill was one of a small number of black politicians whose fame continued to rise after his departure from the legislature. In 1875 President Grant appointed him as receiver of public lands for Huntsville. Councill also founded and became the first president of the state university in Huntsville. He died in April 1909 at the age of 61. The Birmingham *News* recounted his early life and career and said, "William H. Councill died this morning at seven o' clock. His invariable advice to the Negro was for the race to remain in the South among the people who understood

it. He started a private school in Huntsville shortly after the
Civil War, and it was adopted as a state school in 1875."[68] The
Montgomery *Advertiser* also noted Councill's death and offered a
further tribute, "The death of William Councill is a misfortune to
the Negro race. He was the greatest Negro that the race has
produced."[69]

At the time of their deaths, the Carsons (perhaps brothers) had
removed to Montgomery, having been the only African American
relatives to hold political offices during Reconstruction. William
E. Carson represented Lowndes County from 1872 to 1874, and Hugh A.
Carson served from 1875 to 1879. Hugh A. Carson became a member of
the Dexter Avenue Baptist Church and died at Hale Infirmary on 11
May 1912. Carson held a Federal position at the time of his death.
"A useful citizen has passed away," noted a local newsorgan.[70]

Charles O. Harris of Montgomery became the city's most socially
prominent resident after his departure from the legislature. By
the time of his death at his residence only blocks from the capitol
on 8 October 1913, Harris had served for 30 years as a chief in the
Montgomery post office. Considered by a local newspaper as one of
the city's leading citizens, Harris had retired from the post
office a few days before his death, largely because the job had
become taxing.[71]

Elijah Cook, having served as doorkeeper and later as a
representative in the House, became active in educational affairs

317

after his term ended in 1876; he lived near the intersection of Grove and Decatur streets and died on 2 August 1916 at the age of 75. Cook had helped to relocate the Lincoln School of Marion to Montgomery in 1887. He had served on the board of trustees of Swayne School and had been one of the founders of Selma University. He was a Mason, an Odd Fellow, and a member of the Negro Business League. More than a civic leader, Cook was one of the city's business giants. He was the city's earliest African American mortician, locating his business at 104 North Perry Street, across from City Hall. Announcing his retirement in April 1909, Cook commended Henry A. Loveless to his patrons.[72]

Jeremiah Haralson had become an itinerant worker when he died in 1916. He was employed as a clerk in the Interior Department for having supported the Chester A. Arthur administration. On 12 August 1882 he was appointed to a position in the pensions bureau in Washington but resigned on 21 August 1884 and removed to Louisiana, where he farmed, and from there to Arkansas by 1904. After a short stay in Selma in 1912, Haralson never returned to Alabama. He removed to Texas, later to Oklahoma, and finally to Colorado, where he engaged in coal mining and died of bruises sustained from an attack by wild beasts.[73]

Lloyd Leftwich was a victim of an influenza epidemic that swept across Alabama in 1918. Leftwich had held office until 1876. Senator Leftwich died at his farm, located near Forkland in Greene

County, on 19 November 1918 at the age of 86. He had donated land to build a community school and church; the Lloyd Chapel Baptist Church and the Lloyd Elementary School were named for him. Leftwich had been sold to the Gilmore family shortly before the end of the war, and he assumed the Gilmore cognomen until the end of the war, when he changed it name to Leftwich, the name of his original owner. His son, John Leftwich, was the only immediate descendent of the state's African American legislators to engage in political affairs.[74]

Methodist minister Frank H. Threatt died on 8 November 1931 at the age of 83. His parents, both former slaves and natives of Kentucky, were Archie Y. and Elizabeth Threatt.[75] Alabama's black officials died in more than one sense, for most Alabamians have forgotten these lawmakers, who left few records of their accomplishments, difficulties and, most of all, their thoughts.

Thomas Walker of Dallas County departed Alabama because he challenged the board for discarding the votes he had received for clerk of the circuit court of Dallas County--an election in which he considered himself the winner. Walker narrowly escaped death at the hands of Selma whites, learning of the plans from close white friends. He traveled incognito by train to Memphis and later to Little Rock, Arkansas, where he remained until 1881. In 1882 he accepted a patronage position as clerk in the Records and Pensions Division of the War Department, located in the Ford Building, the same building in which President Lincoln had been assassinated. Concurrent with his patronage job, Walker attended the Howard University Law School, from which he graduated in 1885. Dropped from the Federal payroll by the Grover Cleveland administration, Walker turned to real estate, but he later secured employment as a receiver of the Capitol Savings Bank. Walker financially supported Tuskegee Institute, Talladega College, and the Department of Religion and Medicine at Howard University. He continued his political interests by serving as treasurer and collecting funds for Monroe Trotter's trip to the Armistice in Paris, held after World War I. He held membership in the Association for the Study of Afro-American Life and History and for many years served as a trustee of Howard University. Walker died in Washington, D.C., on 28 May 1935 at the age of 84.[76]

Mansfield Tyler returned to his Lowndes County community after his departure from the legislature in 1872, having served a single term. A minister, Tyler built the earliest black church in Lowndesboro during the immediate postwar years. He was one of the founders of Selma University, from which he received an honorary doctoral degree at the turn of the century. Tyler served as chairman of the Selma University Board of Trustees for more than 30 years. He died at home in Lowndesboro in 1904 at the age of 75.[77]

The number of African American elected officials declined dramatically after the election of 1876, and the number of black

Federal patronage recipients showed an equal decline. George Washington served as receiver of public monies for the First District of Montgomery, beginning on 28 June 1884, but death aborted his term on 16 October 1886.[78] From 2 October 1897 to 28 February 1905, Hershel V. Cashin served as receiver of public lands in Huntsville. The Cashin family remained in the Tennessee Valley, choosing not to return to Montgomery.[79] John William Jones and Frank H. Threatt also received patronage positions. One newspaper wrote of Threatt, "Mr. F. H. Threatt of Demopolis has a Government plum in this city, we congratulate him."[80] Some black patronage recipients did not come from the ranks of black elected officials. These recipients included George Washington and Nathan Alexander of Montgomery and Allan Alexander of Mobile.[81]

Despite the rapid decline of African American officials, Democratic opposition to black officeholding continued. As stated earlier Democrats removed Lowndes County Representative Hugh A. Carson in 1878, awarding his seat to J. F. Haigler.[82] Governor Rufus W. Cobb signed the resolution in January 1879.[83] Despite the presence of Wilcox County State Representative George English, the last coterie of African American elected officials ended their careers without ceremony or an acknowledgment of what had occurred.

As Carson departed the legislature and English's term expired, African Americans continued to seek political office without success. Their only alternative was to leave politics, and as one historian of the period concludes, "They saw their votes discounted, lost or stolen, if they were even allowed to cast them. Their supposed friends, the party that claimed to be the party of emancipation, deserted them, refused to support them, withheld recognition from them, and was even considering excluding them. It is not a wonder that so many African Americans quit participating in politics but that any of them remained interested and active."[84]

The Republican party must share the responsibility for the disappearance of African American officeholders. Also, Republican factionalism defeated the party infrastructure as Democratic opposition never could have done. The dismissal of James Thomas Rapier as collector of internal revenue, the most powerful and prestigious patronage position in Alabama, highlighted the intensity of intraparty strife. High-ranking Spencer backers, such as Congressman Charles Hays, supported Rapier, claiming that "he [Rapier] was the best, most reliable, and most competent African American candidate in the state."[85] The Smith faction of the party rose, predictably, to challenge the nomination. It considered the Rapier nomination offensive to the great masses of white people in both parties. A group of north Alabama Republicans advised President Hayes against the removal of incumbent Collector D. B. Booth, alleging that "the Rapier appointment will do more to aid the opposition to your administration than any other act."[86] United States Secretary of the Treasury John Sherman remained adamant in his support of the Rapier nomination, and in July 1878 Rapier assumed his duties as collector of internal revenue, the first black Alabamian to hold that position.[87]

Rapier performed his duties with satisfaction. He canvassed the state, seizing illegal stills, confiscating tobacco, beer, and whiskey, and apprehending lawbreakers. He received the praise of his superiors, including Treasury agent A. P. Downing, who called Rapier one of the most efficient officers in the nation, and Rapier further pleased Commissioner Green B. Raum with his enforcement of revenue ordinances. Those who opposed Rapier showed little regard for his performance. J. V. McDuffie, a Smith man, blasted Rapier as immoral, devious, unreliable, and a betrayer of his constituency at the Chicago convention. Former Congressman Willard Warner considered replacing Rapier with a strong Southern man, a move that would "pretty well rid the state of the Spencer gang."[88]

Rapier assumed his alleged nonsupport of the nomination of former President Grant at the Chicago convention was the reason President Arthur sought his removal. In a lengthy letter to the president, Rapier explained his position at the convention. He recalled that he had supported Grant and had voted according to a resolution introduced by Dallas County delegate Jesse Chisholm Duke at the district convention. The Duke resolution mandated that delegates vote for Grant as long as most of the delegates thought he had a chance to win. Rapier recounted that after his departure

323

from the meeting, the remaining members "pledged to support Gen. Grant first, last, and all the time."[89] This new direction Rapier considered an afterthought, "for such a resolution had never before passed in a Republican Convention." Rapier explained that he was not opposed to Grant; he claimed to have voted for Grant in 1868, when such a vote nearly cost him his life. Continuing his letter with greater force, Rapier blamed intraparty strife for his troubles as assessor: "The same party, I am informed, is working hard to have me removed. But, at the same time he takes pain to commend a [presidential aspirant James G.] Blaine man as my successor."[90] Rapier reaffirmed, "No man in the state can serve you more effectively than I can. Certainly none is more willing I do not hesitate to say. My Republicanism has never been questioned."[91] Rapier chastised Judge J. V. McDuffie, his opponent for the job, by reminding the president that McDuffie had been ridiculed in the United States Supreme Court in 1878 for throwing out votes cast for Jeremiah Haralson; had voted for Charles Shelley (a Democrat) for Congress; and had championed the present convict system.[92]

Blacks were divided equally on the issue. With Robert Johnson serving as president and former State Representative Nicholas Stephens acting as secretary, a group of blacks met in Marion and resolved that "Rapier's political history and acts have been of such character as to bring disorganization and defeat upon the Republican party in Alabama by selling out the Montgomery

congressional district to a Democrat in 1874 and by splitting the
Republican congressional ticket in the Fourth District in 1876,
thereby causing the defeat of Jeremiah Haralson, the Republican
nominee."[93] The resolution further criticized Rapier for supporting
John Sherman instead of Grant in disregard of the wishes of his
constituency in Chicago; for giving employment to only two African
Americans out of 12 or 15 positions at his disposal; and for
tendering his services to the Queen's government to avenge Mason
and Slidell while he was a student in Canada. The group claimed
the support "of 99-100 [sic] of the 100,000 loyal black men in
Alabama" and addressed the resolution to the president of the
United States.[94]

However, Rapier was not without supporters. The charges against
Rapier astonished former Confederate A. A. Mabson, who wrote that
he knew of no other man who had more fully championed the wishes of
African American voters or who "was more universally esteemed."[95]
Not impervious to the impact of the charges, Rapier requested a
five-day leave of absence on 21 June 1882. The commissioner of
internal revenue granted his leave of absence to attend to some
business in Kansas.[96] Matters had continued to deteriorate by June,
when Rapier informed the president of a movement to remove him and
asked for his support.[97]

President Arthur suspended Rapier on 20 September 1882, causing
a furor of support for the beleaguered assessor.[98] James K. Kendall,

chairman of the Morgan County Republican Committee, informed the secretary of the treasury, "I do not believe it would be good for the service of the Republican party to have him removed."[99] Scalawag George H. Craig requested "that no changes be made in the 1st and 2nd revenue districts of Alabama pending the election for Congress as it be detrimental to my interests as the candidates of the Republican party of the 4th Ala. Dist. I must carry Lowndes and Wilcox [counties] to be elected."[100] Support for racial reasons came from Benjamin S. Turner, chairman of the Republican Executive Committee, Fourth District of Alabama, and former congressman. Turner affirmed Rapier's qualifications to hold the job in a letter to the president: "A large majority of the Republicans of the 4th Cong. Dist. of Ala., with its 20,000 majority, heard with regret the removal of the Hon. James Rapier. The removal of Rapier would be unfortunate for the Republican Party in Alabama."[101] A black congregation, in addition, advised President Arthur that Rapier's suspension "would leave us without a colored man in office in Ala."[102]

Coping with the charges levelled against him, coupled with failing health, propelled Rapier to submit his resignation, effective 30 June 1883.[103] Rapier died before the completion of the investigation and before his resignation could take effect.[104] Yet, factionalism had precipitated his premature death as much as his tuberculosis.

Pressure from Democrats continued with the arrest of former Congressman Jeremiah Haralson two years later for allegedly having removed some stolen property. He was placed in a Selma jail but later released.[105] The harassment of black elected officials and those blacks brave enough to seek office was too great. To be sure, black elected officials did not disappear with the return of the Democrats in 1874; conversely, the number of black elected officials reached an all-time high in 1874. Democrats had rid the state of its black legislators by 1884 but not its black local officials in the Tennessee Valley. In 1884 several blacks were appointed to the Huntsville school board, and four black candidates were elected as aldermen. Lucian Jones was elected as alderman in 1889. Huntsville also hired a black police officer during the same year. In addition, M. H. Banks was elected to the Decatur city council in 1884.[106] The latter group of black elected officials survived in Alabama until the arrival of the next century, when the impact of the Constitutional Convention of 1901 effectively eliminated black suffrage.

Alabama blacks turned to journalists, many of them former politicians, to champion their claims. James A. Scott echoed the aspirations of Montgomery blacks in his *Advance*.[107] Charles Hendley's Huntsville *Gazette* voiced the objections of African Americans to exclusion from jury duty, although Hendley considered it paramount that all African Americans remain in the Republican

party.[108]   Chief among these newspapermen was former assistant
engrossing clerk William H. Councill, editor of the Huntsville
Herald, who warned African Americans they were "no longer obligated
to the Republican party because it had won their freedom."[109] As
proof of his conviction, Councill claimed to have voted with the
Democrats for more than 20 years.[110]

Andrew N. Johnson, founder and editor of the Mobile Weekly
Press, was especially vociferous in his denunciation of Democrats.
Johnson's enemies chased him out of Mobile, but he held strong
reasons for his dislike of Democrats: he was a prominent Republican
who had served as chairman of the Republican Executive Committee of
Bibb County, and he claimed to have won an election to Congress,
but Democrats had discarded his votes.   Johnson served as a railway
postal clerk during the Harrison administration.[111]

Jesse Chisholm Duke intimidated Montgomery's black residents and
infuriated local whites when he described a recent lynching in his
Montgomery Herald. Whites attempted to lynch him, but Mayor Warren
S. Reese lodged him for the night and helped him to escape later to
Memphis, Tennessee.[112] These editors provided admirable leadership
as they fought for first-class citizenship for their race, but with
practically no legal protection and a slow but declining role in
political affairs, African Americans found themselves in a position
analogous to the immediate postbellum period.

Summary

White Republicans wanted only the black vote; they tolerated black officeholding, which existed in the shadows of white Republican rule. In that context, although black lawmakers belonged to the Republican party, they were neither carpetbaggers nor scalawags.

Even if the Republican coalition had strengthened with time, the party faced other obstacles. Democrats charged them with having unnecessarily increased the state's debt. Even worse, Alabama voters incorrectly assumed most of the new taxes were used to meet the needs of blacks, especially concerning education and health care. Alabama Republicans didn't show voters corruption was not unique to Alabama. Yeoman farmers, middle-class whites, and poor whites of the Democratic persuasion didn't accept increases in the state's debt and increases in taxes as a bipartisan adventure and part of an expanding capitalism. The business-planter group, the most powerful group in the South, viewed republicanism as an attack on property rights because those taxes supported persons without large personal or real property holdings. The issue of black suffrage or black inferiority loomed large in their minds, although most of them accepted black inferiority but rejected black suffrage.[113]

Nevertheless, Democrats didn't undo the Republican legacy. The largest success of Reconstruction occurred in education, where

329

black and white Alabamians realized their initial opportunity to receive a public education. Democrats enjoyed little success in dismantling universal suffrage, and they used violence and fraud and other tactics mentioned earlier to rid the state of its African Americans elected officials. The changes wrought by Republican rule in Alabama were not of exclusive benefit to African Americans; Republican programs established institutions for the blind and poor and secured rights for married women. Although they returned to power in 1874, Democrats didn't rid the state of the programs initiated by the Republican party.[114]

The reason for the failure of Reconstruction also lay with events in Washington. Despite the enactment of the Freedmen's Bureau and homestead bills and civil rights bills of 1866 and 1875, Congress never enacted legislation that benefitted Southern blacks nor one that Southern white officials seriously considered enforcing. The United States Supreme Court, in one decision after another, either diminished or nullified the impact of most of the important decisions affecting black rights.[115] As the nation emerged from the Depression of 1873, its mood changed; no longer did the welfare of African Americans in any part of the South receive adequate attention. As the nation turned its attention to expansion in the West and later in the Eastern Hemisphere, Washington abandoned African Americans. Black journalist T. Thomas Fortune observed that the black man was left to fight his battles.[116]   Journalists such as Fortune had correctly gauged the new predicament of African Americans.   Reconstruction had come to an end in Alabama.

CONCLUSION

Alabama Reconstruction shares with other Southern states the distinction of being another area where African Americans--free-born, manumitted, and emancipated--initially participated in political matters. Their participation began under a series of Congressional Reconstruction Acts and endured until 1884, when W. P. Williams of Huntsville left office. Much has been written about their role in government, but in Alabama, only a handful of these men have been studied. Suffice it is to ask, "Who were these much-maligned men?"

Most of Alabama's African American politicians were emancipated as a result of the war, and their political participation began less than two years later. Based on education and experience criteria, some were qualified for office and some were not. But these qualities make them no different from any other group. African American lawmakers shared one quality that made them the object of scorn, ridicule, and partisan and bipartisan ploys--color. Their color was the reason for the absence of a coherent plan for Reconstruction.

Black officeholders had few significant others to help them surmount the deficiencies they have been criticized for, but which were not of their making. Individual politicians or members of the American Missionary Association or the press possessed a sincere concern for blacks. Albert Griffin and Samuel S. Gardner cared for blacks, but their numbers were too few and their influence too little to direct African Americans along the road to self-reliance or in the art of electoral politics. Most post-Civil War organizations wanted black participation or membership only for selfish ends. Since they had few allies, African Americans were too fearful of going beyond making demands on the Federal government, too timid to defend themselves during riots, and too concerned with image. Even without significant others, African Americans could proudly look at men like John Carraway, James Thomas Rapier, Holland Thompson, Hershel V. Cashin, Benjamin S. Turner, and Jeremiah Haralson. Here again, the impact of color mitigated their influence.

Let us look at Republican party in general. They controlled the governor's office until 1874, when Democrats returned to power with George Smith Houston. Some Northern Republicans began their exodus soon after that, assuming their cause was lost. But, why did the Republican regime disintegrate?

Some responsibility for the failure of republicanism in Alabama rests with the attitudes of Democrats and other Southern whites, who viewed the party as intervention from the outside. White Southerners viewed Reconstruction and its emphases on black enfranchisement and funding of public education as alien to the

333

Southern scheme of things. To these people, Washington was quite a distance from Alabama. Democrats also assumed black enfranchisement meant black rule, and for that reason, black officeholders became the most conspicuous members of the Republican party and a symbol of what was wrong with Republican policies. Most white officeholders were appalled at the thought of sitting next to former servants. Democrats were well aware that when all other attempts to discredit the Republican party had failed, the call to racism would yield tremendous reward.

Despite the gerrymandering and fraud of Democrats, the violence of the Klan, the sharecropping system of planters, the racism of the white population at large, the Republican party must accept some blame for the failure of Reconstruction and its concomitant, black officeholding. The policies of the Southern wing of the party were seldom better than their Democratic neighbors, and the concerns of Northern members of the party focused too frequently on success at the polls and the patronage system. White Republicans were at odds with the concerns of their black peers; they didn't champion civil rights issues, and they disavowed any relationship with the Equal Rights Association. As the period ground to a close, white Republicans grew tired of "protecting the black man's cause." Federal protection had ended; therefore, the Klan could sleep at night because Democrats had returned to power.

Republicans lost power in Alabama because Democrats were more adept at articulating campaign issues. The Alabama electorate accepted their charge that Republicans were responsible for increases in state debt, black enfranchisement, railroad appropriations, attempts to integrate, and violence. Whites responded by electing former Confederate officers.

The African American members of the party were confronted with insurmountable obstacles and uncompromising opposition. Therefore, whatever one says or writes about them, one should note that they were men of vision. Because of these men, a semblance of leadership emerged, to be built upon later. These men helped to establish black education and helped black education to grow, although it grew slowly during the period under consideration. African American ownership, pride, businesses, and religious growth also became established, and from these roots, much later, recognition and security would come.

APPENDICES

In that biographical profiles of Alabama's Reconstruction officeholders have remained largely unresearched, I have found it quite difficult to decide who these men were. Moreover, trying to verify some of the data was equally difficult. Yet, as I persisted in my search, I began to piece together the profiles readers find within these pages.

Prewar Status: This section of the chart identifies the status of the officeholder before the Civil War ended. As outlined already, most of Alabama's officeholders were slaves; therefore, a blank space denotes an assumption of slave status. On other hand, only a handful of the state's black officeholders were free during antebellum times. The letter F indicates persons who were free-born. More of Alabama's black officeholders were manumitted than free-born. The letter M reflects those who held such status. An S indicates slave status. This space is unmarked when there was no direct evidence on status.

Office: Although they were unsuccessful in obtaining appointive positions and statewide offices, African Americans held other offices that nearly spanned the gamut of elective positions during

Alabama Reconstruction. In fact, they seldom sought statewide
offices, a testament perhaps to the political rigidity of Alabama
society. The section on offices, nevertheless, reveals the elected
and appointed positions they held during Reconstruction. Some of
these major officeholders also held minor positions. The
abbreviations follow: delegate, constitutional convention, A;
assistant secretary, AS; member, State Board of Education, B;
Congress, C; engrossing clerk, CK; assistant clerk, E; legislature,
L; page, P; senate, S; assistant engrossing clerk, ACK; assistant
sergeant at arms, ASA; enrolling clerk, EC; doorkeeper, DK;
doorkeeper, Board of Education, DKB; fireman, F; hall attendant,
HA; messenger, M; and sergeant at arms, SA. County offices listed
in the appendix include coroner, CO; circuit court clerk, CI;
county commissioner, CC; criminal court clerk, CR; criminal court
judge, CJ; sheriff, SF; tax assessor, TA; tax collector, TC; and
treasurer, T.

Date: The dates used in the chart reflect the term of office to
which the candidate was chosen to serve. In some instances, black
officeholders did not serve for the duration of their elected
terms. Several reasons account for this failure, and I have
outlined those reasons in the text. The terms of office and the
corresponding symbols are as follow: 1867, 1; 1875, 2; 1868-70, 3;
1870-72, 4; 1871-73, 5; 1872-74, 6; 1873-75, 7; 1874-76, 8; 1875-

77, 9; 1876-78, 10; 1878-80, 11; 1882-83, 12; 1874, 13; and 1877, 14.

Military Service: Although none of the Alabama's native-born black officeholders served in the military, several persons who later called Alabama home provided manpower for the military. Their military experience included the Mexican War and the Civil War. As mentioned in the text, military participation allowed these persons to travel and, in some instances, to bear arms. The war also enabled African American future officeholders to serve as role models once the war had ended. Aside from ministers, military veterans were the only persons in the black community who had traveled widely. Therefore, listed in this column is *M* for Mexican War, *C* for the Confederacy, and *U* for the Union.

Age: The age listed in the chart is based on the 1870 Population Census. Therefore, if the 1880 Population Census were used, the chart still reflects the age as of 1870.

Color Admixture: The chart shows two categories of color--black and mulatto. Although the officeholders are black, color or phenotype indicates the observable characteristics of an individual in regard to ancestry. Worth noting is that the information listed reflects what the individual related to the census taker. The letter *B* denotes a black officeholder, and the letter *M* designates a mulatto officeholder.

Occupation: A wide range of occupations was unavailable to black officeholders in Alabama. As indicated in the text, black officeholders assumed these occupations before and sometimes after their departure from public office. The list below gives corresponding number for the occupations: farmer, 1; shoemaker, 2; musician, 3; broommaker, 4; minister, 5; teacher, 6; lawyer, 7; carpenter, 8; journalist, 9; blacksmith, 10; barber, 11; dill merchant, 12; mail agent, 13; store owner, 14; postmaster, 15; tailor, 16; grocer, 17; mechanic, 18; bridgebuilder, 19; bank cashier, 20; laborer, 21; clerk in bar, 22; domestic servant, 23; college president, 24; Federal patronage recipient, 25; policeman, 26; seaman, 27; tax assessor, 28; coroner, 29; mortician, 30; carriage driver, 31; race track owner, 32; livery stable owner, 33; judge, 34; assistant clerk, 35; county commissioner, 36; solicitor, 37; court clerk, 38; deputy sheriff, 39; registrar, 40; city police, 41; constable, 42; justice of the peace, 43; commissioner of merchants, 44; city expressman, 45; inspector of customs, 46; street commissioner, 47; founder, black Democratic party, 48; and city councilman, 49.

Sources: Both primary and secondary sources proved beneficial in fleshing out biographical profiles.

Appendix A
Black Officeholders of Alabama, 1867-1884

Name	County	Prewar Status	Office Date	Nativity	Age	Color	Occupation: Prewar/Postwar	Literacy	Property: Real/Personal	Military Service	Ref.
Alexander, Benj.	Greene		A1,L3	NC	50	B	/1	N/N			3,11
Allen, G.W.	Bullock		L8	Ga	19	M	/1	Y/Y	300/		5,6
Alston, James H.	Macon	S	L3	SC	40	B	/2,3	Y/Y	500/200	M,C	3,6
Avery, Matt	Perry		L3	NC	36	B	/1,5	N/N			3
Baldwin, Elijah	Wilcox		L8,10	NC	56	M	/1	Y/Y	500/		3,5,6
Bennett, Granville	Sumter		L6,8	Ala	46	B	/1	N/N	175/		3,6
Blandon, Samuel	Lee		A1,L3	SC	24	M	/1	Y/Y	1,000/2,000		3,5,6
Blevins, William H.	Dallas		L8,10	Ala	28	M	/1,11	N/N	620/		3,5,6,8
Bliss, James	Sumter		L8	Va	50	M	/4	Y/Y			3,5
Boyd, Matthew	Perry		L8	Va	40	B	/1	N/N	135/		3,5
Braxdell, George	Talladega		L4	Ky	31	M	/11,26	Y/Y	/100		3,6
Brewington, Nathan A.	Lowndes		L3	Ala	29	M	/1	N/N	30,000/1,000		3,4
Burke, Richard	Sumter		L3	Va	63	B	/5,6	Y/Y			12
Brunson, Simeon	Pickens		L3				/1	N/N			3
Carraway, John	Mobile	M	A1,L3	NC	35	M	/7,9	Y/Y		U	3
Carson, Hugh A.	Lowndes		A2,L8,9,10,11								3,6
Carson, William E.	Lowndes		L6	NC	30	M	/1,28,29				3,32
Cashin, Hershel V.	Montgomery		L8,10	Ga	27	M	/7	Y/Y			5
Clarke, Thomas J.	Barbour		L6	SC	27	B	/1	N/N	185/		3,5,6

Name		Codes	County	State	Age	Sex	Ref	Y/N	Value	Notes
Cochran, Henry A.		L4,6	Dallas	SC	40	B	/1	N/N		3
Cook, Elijah	S	L8	Montgomery	Ala	39	B	8/5,8,30	Y/Y	700/200	3,5
Cox, George W.		L3	Montgomery	Va	36	B	/10	Y/Y	1,200/200	3
Craig, Henry Hunter		L4	Montgomery	Va	40	M	/11	Y/Y		3
Curtis, Alexander H.	S	A2, S6 / L4,6	Perry	NC	41	M	/12	Y/Y		3
Daniels, D. J.		L8	Russell			B				14,25
Diggs, Thomas	S	A1, L3, 4	Barbour	Va	55	B	/17	Y/N	300/	3,5,6
Dotson, Mentor		L6	Sumter	Ga	32	B	/6, 14	N/N		3,5
Dozier, John	M	L4, 6	Perry	SC	59	B	/6	Y/Y	1,6000/	3,4,5
Drawn, Joseph		L3	Dallas	Ga	60	B	/8	N/N		3
Ellsworth, Hales		L6	Montgomery	Ala	50	B	/1	Y/Y	500/500	3
English, George		L11	Wilcox	Ala	30	B	/1	N/N		3,5,6
Fagan, Charles		L8	Montgomery	Ala	45	B	/1	Y/N	1,100/400	3,6
Fantroy, Samuel		L6	Barbour	Ga	45	B	/5	Y/Y		3
Finley, Peyton	F	A1, B5 / L8	Montgomery	Ga	46	B	/1		/1,000	3
Gardner, Prince		L8	Russell			B				25
Gaskin, Wm. D.		L4, 8	Lowndes	Ala	23	M	/1		1,000/500	3,5
Gasket, Adam		L8	Barbour	Ga	33	M	/5	Y/Y		5
Gee, Ned		L4	Dallas	NC	64	M	/1			3
Gilmer, Captain		L8	Montgomery	Ala	50	B	/1	N/N		3
Goldsby, Joseph		L6	Dallas	Ala	19	B	/12	Y/Y	/250	5,8
Greene, James K.	S	A1,L3,4,6,8NC	Hale	Ala	47	B	/8			3
Gregory, Ovide	F	A1,L3	Mobile	Ala		M	/11,14,26,27	Y/Y		8

Name	County		Code	State	Age	B/M	Terms	Y/Y	Amount	Ref
Haralson, Jeremiah	Dallas	S	L4,S6,8,C9Ga		34	B	/5,25			13
Harris, Charles E.	Dallas		L8				/7	Y/Y		28
Harris, Charles O.	Montgomery		L10	NC	60	B	/13	N/N		3,7
Hatcher, Jordan	Dallas		A1	Ga	50	B	/15	Y/Y		3,5
Hill, D. H.	Bullock		L3	NC	42	B	/8	Y/Y	300/100	14
Houston, George	Sumter	S	L3	Ala		M	/1,16	Y/Y		3,5,6
Inge, Benjamin	Sumter		A1,L3	Va			/5	Y/Y		12
Johnson, A.W.	Macon		L8			M				19
Johnson, R.L.	Dallas		L4,6		30	B		N/N		12
Johnson, Washington	Russell		A1	Va	45	M	/1	Y/Y	350/300	3,6
Johnston, Green T.	Dallas		L10	Ala	26	B	/1,5	Y/Y		3,5
Jones, Columbus	Madison		A1, L3					N/N		12
Jones, John W.	Lowndes	S	S6,8	NC	24	M	14/17,25,32	Y/Y		3,7,22
Jones, Reuben	Madison		L6	Ala	37	M	/10	Y/Y	1,500/300	3,5
Jones, Shandy W.	Tuscaloosa	F	L3				11/5,11			24
King, Horace	Russell	M	L3,4	SC	45	M	18/19,25	Y/Y	300/	1,11,13
Lee, Samuel	Lowndes		L8	Ala	27	M	/1	Y/Y	600/500	3,4
Lee, Thomas	Perry	S	A1, L3				8/			11
Leftwich, Lloyd	Greene	S	S6,8	Va	38	B	/1	Y/Y	1,200/300	5,6
Lewis, Greene S. W.	Perry	S	L3,6,8,10,A2	NC	40	B	/1	N/N		5
Locke, Edwin C.	Wilcox		L8	Ala	15		/2	Y/Y		5
Long, R. A.	Washington		A2							15
Martin, Jacob	Dallas		L8	Ala	34	B	/1	Y/Y		3
Matthews, Perry	Bullock	M	L6,8	Ga	20	M	/6	Y/Y		5

Name	County	Code		State	Age		Ref	Y/N	$	Notes
Maul, January	Lowndes	L6		Ala	44	B	/5	N/N	200/300	3,5,8,13,22
McCalley, Jefferson	Madison	L3					5/			11
McLeod, J. Wright	Marengo	A1								11
Merriwether, Willis	Wilcox	L6,8		Ala	24	M		N/N	1,000/350	3,4
Miller, G. R.	Russell	L6							600/	4
Odum, Edward	Barbour	L8		Ala	17	B	/21			5
Patterson, George	Macon	L6,8		Ala	50	B	/1	N/N	500/	3,14
Patterson, Samuel J.	Autauga	L6		Md	46	M	/1	Y/Y	1,500/300	3,4,13
Rapier, James Thomas	Lauderdale	A1, C7	F	Ala	30	M	/1,7,9,25,28	Y/Y	500/1,100	2,3,5,6,7,10
Reese, Bristo	Hale	L6,8		SC	37	B	/1		/100	3,6,14
Reid, Robert	Sumter	L6,8		Va	47	B	/1	N/N	/300	3,6,14
Rice, H. W. W.	Talladega	L3								11
Richardson, A. G.	Wilcox	L3		Ala	30	B	/1	Y/Y		11
Robinson, Lafayette	Madison	A1	M	Ala	35	M	/20,22	Y/Y	/230	5
Rose, Edward R.	Marengo	L3		Ala	40		/1	Y/Y		3,11
Royal, Benjamin R.	Bullock	A1,S3,4,6,8	S	Ala	58	M	/1	Y/Y	6,000/600	3,4,6,11
St. Clair, Henry	Macon	L4,6		Ala	33	B	/6	Y/Y		28
Smith, Charles	Bullock	L8		Ala		B	/1	N/N		5
Snoddy, Nimrod	Greene	L10		SC	47	B	/1	N/N	1,800/500	3,4,6,11
Speed, Lawrence S.	Bullock	L3,4,6		Ga	42	M	/1	Y/Y	/700	5,6,11
Steele, Lawson	Montgomery	L6		Ala	50	B	/1	Y/Y	5,836/200	3,4
Stephens, Nicholas	Perry	L10					/25	Y/Y		30
Stevens, William J.	Dallas	L10		Ala	25	B	/21			3,9,13
Stokes, Henry	Dallas	A1		SC	45		/1	Y/Y		3

Taylor, W. L.	Chambers		L3	Ga	50	B		Y/Y	157/	3,13
Taylor, William	Sumter		L6							14
Thomas, B. R.	Marengo	S	L6				/25	N/N	500/200	10,14,21
Thompson, Holland	Montgomery		L3,4	Ala	30	B	/9,14,17	Y/Y		3,5,7,11
Threatt, Frank H.	Marengo		L6	Ala	21	M	/5,22	Y/Y		3,16
Treadwell, J. R.	Russell		L6	Va	40	B	/1	N/N		5
Turner, Benjamin S.	Dallas	S	C5	NC	45	B	33/33	Y/Y	2,150/10,000	3,9,20
Turner, Wm. V.	Elmore		L3	Va	48		/6,9	Y/Y		3,21
Tyler, Mansfield	Lowndes	S	L4	Ga	40	M	5/5	Y/Y	300/300	3,13,23
Walker, Thomas	Dallas	S	L6	Ala	21	M	21/38			3,13
Weaver, Spencer	Dallas		L3	Va	60	M	/1			3,11
Wells, Levie	Marengo		L4							13
Williams, A. E.	Barbour		L6,8		26		/6	N/N		28
Williams, Latty J.	Montgomery		L3,4,6	Ga				N/N		28
Williams, W. P.	Madison		L12							33
Witherspoon, J. R.	Greene		L8	NC	40	B	/1			5,14
Wynne, Manly	Hale		L8	Ala	35	B	/1		200/	3
Young, Henry	Lowndes		L3	SC	42	M	/1	Y/Y	600/325	3,4,13

Appendix B

Black Minor Officeholders of Alabama, 1867-1884

Name	County	Prewar Office		Nativity	Age	Color	Occupation: Prewar/Postwar	Literacy	Property: Real/Personal	Military Service	Ref.
		Status	Date								
Abercrombie, Nicholas	Tallapoosa										15
Abercrombie, Thom	Montgomery		P6,M6	Ala	32	M	/8	N/N			3
Alexander, Nathan	Montgomery					M	/25,28				7
Allen, James	Mobile			Ala	51	B	/26				3
Alston, James H.	Macon			SC		B	/40				15
Anderson, Jacob	Mobile			SC	65	B	/34,43		1,500/		3,8
Ash, Simon	Mobile			NC	50	M	/44		8,000/3,000		3
Avery, Moses Brown	Mobile	M	AS1	Fla		M	/5,9,40	Y/Y		U	16
Banks, Edward	Mobile			Ala	28	M	/26		400/		3
Bardwell, Ben	Sumter						/37				15
Bates, Wm.	Mobile			Ala	34	B	/42		1,000/800		3
Belser, John	Montgomery			Ala	29	B	/26				3
Berry, Lawrence S.	Mobile		SA3				/49				8
Billingsley, Alfred	Montgomery						/49				31
Billingsley, John	Perry				15		/16				16
Blevins, William H.	Dallas				26						3,9,20
Boyd, Wilborne	Mobile			Ala	45	M	/26		200/		3
Boyd, A.	Dallas		TA13								30
Braggs, James	Mobile			NC	44	M	/40,47		4,000/1,000		3,15
Brown, Abrom	Mobile			Ala	35	B	/26				3

Name	County	Code	State	Age	Race	Ref	Y/N	Value	Notes
Bryant, John	Mobile								8
Burkely, Joseph	Mobile		SC	40	B	/42		200/100	3
Burt, Edwin	Perry		Ala	25	B	/26			3
Bussey, R. H.	Wilcox	TC13				/39			30
Bynum, Sandy	Lawrence		Ala			/40			15
Cain, Sam	Elmore					/36			21
Carson, William E.	Lowndes	TA14							30
Carter, Anderson	Mobile		Ga	40	B	/26		/150	3
Carter, Samuel	Jackson					/40			15
Carwell, Warren	Mobile		Ala	45	M	/42			3
Cashin, Hershel V.	Madison	ACK6	Ga		M	/25			7,36
Castick, Robert	Mobile		Ala	35	M	/42			3
Chapman, Henry	Mobile		Va	60	M	/26			3
Cherry, Lisbon	Chambers					/40			15
Coleman, James	Mobile		Ala	23	M	/26			3
Cook, Elijah	Montgomery	DKB6							30
Cook, Robert	Montgomery	P6			B		N/N		3,36
Councill, Wm. H.	Madison	ACK6,EC6	NC	22	M	/6,7,9,24	Y/Y	100/50	3,36
Cox, George W.	Tuscaloosa		Va		B	/40			15
Craig, Henry Hunter	Barbour	DK3	Va		M	/40			15,34
Curtis, Alexander H.	Perry	CC13							30
Darden, Thomas	Montgomery		Md	47	B	/26			3
Dean, James	Blount, St. Clair					/40			15
Dennis, Edward	Mobile		Ala	24	M	/26			3

Name	Place	Code	State	Age	Race		
Dodge, I. C.	Madison					/36	27
Dozier, John	Bibb, Shelby		SC		B	/40	15
Drawn, Joseph	Dallas		Ga		B	/40	15
Ellsworth, Hales	Montgomery	DK3, CO13					30,34
Fiers, George J.	Mobile		Ga	29	B	/26	3
Files, Richo	Mobile		Ala	30	M	/26	3
Finley, Peyton	Clark, Monroe		Ga		B	/40	15
Floyd, Levi	Montgomery	ACK4,6					36
Foman, A.	Dallas	CO13					30
Ford, Henry	Mobile		SC	45	M	/26	3
Gallatin, Albert	Mobile					/42	8
Garth, George	Limestone, Morgan					/40	15
Goins, Aaron	Dale, Henry, Montgomery	HA6	Ala	23	M	/23,40	3,15,36
Hagen, G. W.	Wilcox					/40	15
Harris, Chester	Montgomery		Ga	35	B	/26	3
Harris, C. O.	Montgomery	ACK4,6					36
Harris, Lewis	Montgomery		Ala	32	M	/26	3
Henly, Gabriel	Covington, Coffee					/40	15
Henry, Benjamin	Marshall, Blaine					/40	15
Hill, Henderson	Madison					/40	15
Houston, George	Sumter		Ala		M	/40	15
Hunter, Oscar	Dallas					/36	26
James, Newton	Mobile		Ala	30	B	/26	3

Name	County		Code	State	Age					
Johnson, Abram	Montgomery			NC	42	B	/26		600/200	3
Johnson, Daniel	Montgomery			Ga	36	M	/26			3
Johnson, Richard	Montgomery			Va	42	B	/39			3
Johnston, Albert	Mobile			Ala	27	B	/45		/200	3
Jordan, Daniel	Jefferson						/40			15
Joseph, Phillip	Mobile	F	CK6	Fla		M	/9	Y/Y		2,8,36
King, Henry	Mobile			Md	36	B	/26			3
King, Horace	Lee, Russell			SC	45	M	/40			15
King, Thaddeus	Dallas							26		20
Laundrax, George	Mobile			La	33	B	/38		/500	3
Laurendine, Gregory	Mobile									8
Lawdine, Paul	Mobile			Ala	24	M	/26			3
Lloyd, James	Lowndes						/40			15
Lucas, L. K. P.	Lowndes		Cl13							30
Malone, William	Calhoun, Cleburne						/40			15
Mayberry, Joseph L.	Coosa						/40			15
Mays, Pleasants	Mobile			Ky	26	M	/26			3
McCall, Bruce	Lowndes		T14							30
McGee, Alexander	Mobile			Ala	29	M	/26		/150	3
Miller, J.	Marengo						/40			15
Mitchell, Noah	Mobile			SC	38	B	/46		150/150	3
Mitchell, Washington	Dallas			Ky	36	B	/26		500/	3,20
Moon, J. L.	Wilcox		T13							30
Moore, Allen	Dallas						/26			9

Name	County	Code	State	Age				Notes
Morgan, Henderson	Montgomery		Ala	35	M	/26	/300	3
Moulton, Cleveland	Mobile		NY	41	B	/34	400/5,000	3,10
Nettles, James	Montgomery		Ala	55	M	/26		3
Nunn, James	Clay, Randolph					/40		15
Oliver, Martin	Montgomery		Ala	27	B	/26		3
Osborne, Sandy	Colbert, Franklin					/40		15
Parker, Benjamin	Mobile		MD	48	M	/26		3
Patterson, Lewis	Mobile		Ala	35	M	/26		3
Perez, Constantine	Mobile		Fla		M	/42		8
Pickett, Thomas	Dallas		MD	32	B	/26		3
Portis, Isaac	Dallas		Ala	42	M	/26	500/	3,20
Rapier, John	Lauderdale					/40	4,000/3,400	1,2,15
Roberts, Lewis	Mobile		Fla	37	M	/26		3
Robinson, Dick	Mobile		Ala	27	M	/26		3
Robinson, Henry	Dallas		Va	36	B	/26	500/	3,20
Ross, Henry	Mobile		Ark	30	B	/26		3
Royal, Benjamin F.	Bullock, Pike		Ala		M	/40		15
Russell, Stephen	Montgomery	P6	NC		B		N/N	3,36
Saton, David	Mobile		Tenn	40	B	/26		3
Saywer, Thomas	Mobile		SC	43	M	/44	1,000/1,000	3
Sharp, John	Mobile		Md	28	M	/26		3
Shorter, Ceasar	Montgomery		Tenn	41	B	/48	200/	5,7
Shortridge, Wm.	Pickens					/40		15
Simpson, J. B.	Autauga	TA13,SF14						30

Name	County	Code	State	Age	Race		$	No.
Sims, Yancy	Talladega							15
Smith, Addison	Dallas		Ala	40	B	/40		3,20
Smith, Freeman	Mobile					/26		8
Spiers, Johnson	Mobile		NC	43	B	/42	400/	3
Starks, Frank	Mobile		SC	53	M	/26	1,200/	3
Stevens, William J.	Dallas	CR13				/41		30
Stewart, Henry	Mobile					/42		8
Summerville, James	Mobile					/25		29
Taylor, E. D.	Mobile					/42		8
Taylor, Spencer	Montgomery		SC	38	M	/26		3
Thomas, Alfred	Choctaw, Washington					/40		15
Thomas, Nathan	Mobile		Ga	35	B	/26		3
Thomas, Roderick B.	Dallas	CJ13	Tenn	24	B	/38		3,30
Todd, Tom	Dallas					/26		20
Turner, Benjamin S.	Dallas	T13						30
Turner, Wm. V.	Elmore, Autauga	E6	Va			/40		15,36
Walden, Jeff	Dallas					/39		9
Williams, Ed.	Montgomery		Ala	28	M	/26		3
Williams, Latty J.	Montgomery		Ga	26		/40		15
Willis, Hilliard	Montgomery		Ala	29	M	/26		3
Willis, Isaac	Butler, Crenshaw					/40		15
Wilson, Samuel	Mobile		Ala	29	M	/26	/150	3
Wright, Wade	Baldwin, Conecuh					/40		15
Young, Isaac	Montgomery		Va	59	B	/26	2,500/250	3

Sources

1. US Bureau of the Census, *Seventh Census of the United States: 1850. Schedule 1, Alabama.*

2. _____. *Eighth Census of the United States: 1860, Schedule 1. Alabama.*

3. _____. *Ninth Census of the United States: 1870, Schedule 1. Alabama.*

4. _____. *Ninth Census of the United States: 1870, Schedule 2. Alabama.*

5. _____. *Tenth Census of the United States: 1880, Schedule, 1. Alabama.*

6. _____. *Tenth Census of the United States: 1880, Schedule 2. Alabama.*

7. *City Directory, 1883-1884*, Montgomery.

8. *City Directory, 1869*, Mobile.

9. *City Directory, 1880-1881*, Selma.

10. *State and Judicial Officers, 1868-1911.*

11. Secretary of State Files.

12. Ibid., 1869.

13. Ibid., 1870-72.

14. Election Returns for Miscellaneous Officers.

15. Mobile *Nationalist*, 30 May 1867.

16. Montgomery *Daily State Sentinel*, 3 December 1867.

17. Selma *Southern Argus*, 27 March 1874.

18. Ibid., 24 November 1874.

19. Tuskegee *News*, 3 March 1875.

20. John Hardy, *Selma: Her Institutions and Her Men* (Selma: Time Book and Job Office, 1879), 90-100.

21. Thomas McAdory Owen, *History of Alabama and Dictionary of Alabama Biography* (Chicago: S. J. Clark Publishing Co., 1921) 4: 1.

22. William Warren Rogers and Ruth Pruitt, *Stephen Renfro, Alabama's Outlaw Sheriff* (Tallahassee: Sentry Press, 1970), 21.

23. Mildred Brewer Russell, *Lowndes County Courthouse: A Chronicle of Hayneville, An Alabama Black Belt Village, 1820-1900* (Montgomery: Paragon Press, 1951), 46.

24. *Journal of the Session of 1869-70 of the House of Representatives of the State of Alabama, Held in the City of Montgomery, Commencing on the Third Monday in November, 1869* (Montgomery: John G. Stokes and Co, 1870).

25. *Journal of the House of Representatives, of the State of Alabama, Session of 1874-75, Held in the City of Montgomery, Commencing November 16, 1874* (Montgomery: W. W. Screws, 1875).

26. Montgomery *Alabama State Journal*, 1 January 1874.

27. Greenville *Advocate*, 28 August 1873.

28. John William Beverly, *History of Alabama for Use in Schools and for General Reading* (Montgomery: Press of the Alabama Printing Company, 1901), 202-6.

29. Peter Kolchin, *First Freedom: The Responses of Alabama's Blacks to Emancipation and Freedom* (Westport, Conn.: Greenwood Press, Inc., 1972), 141.

30. Gerald Lee Rouse, "Aftermath of Reconstruction, Race, Violence, and Politics in Alabama, 1874-1884" (Master's thesis, Auburn University, 1973), 362-64, 389.

31. Morris Boucher, "The Free Negro in Alabama Prior to 1860" (Ph.D. diss., The State University of Iowa, 1950), 21-25, 175-77.

32. *Journal of the House of Representatives of the State of Alabama, Session 1872-73* (Montgomery: Arthur Bingham, 1874); Sarah Woolfolk Wiggins, *The Scalawag in Alabama Politics, 1865-1881* (University, Ala.: The University of Alabama Press, 1977), 150.

33. *Journal of the House of Representatives of the State of*

Alabama, Session of 1882-83, Held in the City of Montgomery, Commencing Tuesday, November 14th, 1882 (Montgomery: W. D. Brown and Co., 1883).

34. William H. Smith, "Message of William H. Smith, Governor of Alabama to the General Assembly, November 15, 1869" (Montgomery: J. G. Stokes & Co., 1870), 87.

35. Robert B. Lindsay, "Message of Robert B. Lindsay, Governor of Alabama to the General Assembly, Nov. 21, 1871" (Montgomery: W. W. Screws, 1871), 57.

36. "Report of the Treasurer of the State of Alabama for the Fiscal Year Ending Sept. 30th, 1873, to the Governor" (Montgomery: Arthur Bingham, 1873), 16-17.

37. "Report of the State Auditor of Alabama for the Fiscal Year Ending 30th September, 1873, to the Governor" (Montgomery: Arthur Bingham, 1873), 31-33.

NOTES

Introduction

1. Robert Reid, "Changing Interpretations of the Reconstruction Period in Alabama History," *The Alabama Review* 27, no. 4 (October 1974): 265; Fletcher M. Green, "Walter Lynwood Fleming: Historian of Reconstruction," *Journal of Southern History* 2 (November 1936): 499-500; Walter Lynwood Fleming, *Civil War and Reconstruction in Alabama* (New York: Columbia University Press, 1905; Spartanburg, S.C.: The Reprint Company Publishers, 1978), iii-viii.

2. Reid, "Changing Interpretations," 266-68.

3. Ibid., 269-71.

Notes

Chapter 1

1. Elizabeth Bethel, "The Freedmen's Bureau in Alabama," *Journal of Southern History* 19 (February 1948): 49; John B. Myers, "Reaction and Adjustment: The Struggle of Alabama Freedmen in Post-Bellum Alabama, 1865-1867," *The Alabama Historical Quarterly* 32, nos. 1 and 2 (Spring and Summer 1970): 5; Richard L. Hume, "The Freedmen's Bureau and the Freedmen's Vote in the Reconstruction of Southern Alabama: An Account by Agent Samuel S. Gardner," *The Alabama Historical Quarterly* 37, no. 3 (Fall 1975): 217; Robert C. Alston, "Reconstruction in Alabama" (paper presented for the Symposium, Atlanta, Ga., November 1931), 7.

2. Peter Kolchin, *First Freedom: The Responses of Alabama Freedmen to Emancipation and Reconstruction* (Westport, Conn.: Greenwood Press, 1972), 3; Montgomery *Weekly Mail*, 16 July 1860; Bethel, 49; Myers, 5; Hume, 217.

3. Kolchin, 6-7, 10; Mobile *Nationalist*, 31 December 1866, 1.

4. Myers, 7.

5. Ibid., 7-8. The Dallas County black population increased from 25,840 in 1860 to 29,601 in 1866; Mobile County's black population

increased from 12,571 to 16,684; Montgomery County, 23,780 to 30,762. The combined increase for Dallas, Mobile, and Montgomery counties was more than 14,000.

6. Thomas McAdory Owen, *History of Alabama and Dictionary of Alabama Biography* (Chicago: S. J. Clark Publishing Co., 1921), 1: 629; Horace Mann Bond, "Social and Economic Forces in Alabama Reconstruction," *Journal of Negro History* 23, no. 3 (July 1938): 301-2; Kenneth B. White, "The Alabama Freedmen and Black Education: The Myth of Opportunity," *The Alabama Review* 34, no. 2 (April 1981): 108.

7. Montgomery *Daily Advertiser*, 21 October 1865, 1.

8. Ibid.

9. Ibid.

10. Ibid.

11. Ibid., 24 October 1865, 3.

12. Ibid., 18 October 1865, 4; Myers, 8.

13. "Anticipated Famine in Alabama," found in Montgomery *Daily Advertiser*, 9 January 1866, 1.

14. Ibid., 10 November 1865, 2.

15. John B. Myers, "The Alabama Freedmen and Economic Adjustments During Presidential Reconstruction, 1865-1867," *The Alabama Review* 26 (October 1973): 253-54. Most of the whites who received rations were children. Of a total of 166,589 whites who received rations, 112,208, or 67 percent, were listed as children; of the 72,115

blacks who received rations, 39,187, or 54 percent, were listed as children. The number of black and white recipients declined to 166,127, or by 34 percent (slightly less than the total number of whites recipients for the previous period), for December 1866 to August 1867. Again, more white children than adults received rations. For this period, 40,341 white adults and 86,906 children (68 percent of total) received rations, as compared to a total of 41,591 black recipients. Of this total, 25,134 black children (60 percent) received rations. The number of black children receiving rations showed a significant increase, suggesting a continued decline in the economic condition of blacks in general. The Bureau was not alone in its support of the destitute in Alabama; on the contrary, the National Freedmen's Relief Association, the Southern Famine Relief Committee of New York, and the American Union Commission sought to improve economic conditions in Alabama. The Bureau, nonetheless, provided the bulk of the assistance. In contrast to the findings of Myers, Elizabeth Bethel argues that Bureau rations were more abundant. She suggests that rations intended for adult refugees and freedmen consisted of "ten ounces of pork or bacon or sixteen ounces of fresh beef daily, sixteen ounces of corn meal, five times a week, sixteen ounces of flour or soft bread or twelve ounces of hard bread twice a week, and to every one hundred rations, ten pounds of beans, peas or hominy, eight pounds of sugar, two quarts of vinegar, two pounds of salt and two ounces of pepper." "Children under fourteen," she continues, "were allowed half rations." She paints a more optimistic picture of the amount of Bureau rations. See Bethel, 59-60.

16. "The Poor of North Alabama," Montgomery *Daily Advertiser*, 25 November 1865, 2.

17. Ibid., 10 November 1865, 2.

18. Gail S. Hasson, "The Health and Welfare of Freedmen in Reconstruction Alabama," *The Alabama Review* 35, no. 2 (April 1982): 96-97. Hasson maintains that historians have overlooked Bureau health and welfare services. She further notes that while historians have investigated the medical activities of Bureau work in Louisiana, Kentucky, and Mississippi, they have overlooked Bureau services in Alabama. She notices that the obviously less than harmonious relationship between state and Bureau officials hampered the work of the Bureau on behalf of needy freedmen. Hasson defines home colonies as "farms used as places of transit where freedmen could be kept and employed until work was found for them, but they [home colonies] also were used as reception centers for the aged and infirmed who had nowhere else to go." See also Bethel, 60. Myers claims that in an old abandoned plantation in Huntsville freedmen were growing 400 acres of cotton and corn. His statement points out that some of the colonies may have been partially self-supporting. See Myers, "Alabama Freedmen and Economic Adjustments," 255.

19. Montgomery *Daily Advertiser*, 10 November 1865.

20. Ibid., n.d., probably 20 October 1865.

21. Charles J. Lipp to Wager Swayne, 25 October 1868. Report of the Assistant Commissioner for the State of Alabama, Bureau of Refugees, Freedmen, and Abandoned Lands, 1865-70, Bureau of Refugees, Freedmen, and Abandoned Lands Papers, National Archives, Washington, D. C. (hereafter referred to as BRFAL, NA).

22. Ibid.

23. Montgomery *Daily Advertiser*, 20 October 1865, 2.

24. C. W. Buckley to Brig. Gen. W. Swayne, 5 January 1866, BFRAL, NA.

25. John B. Myers, "The Freedmen and the Labor Supply: The Economic Adjustments in Post-Bellum Alabama, 1865-1867," *The Alabama Historical Quarterly* 32, nos. 3 and 4 (Fall and Winter 1970): 158-62.

26. Kenneth B. White, "Wager Swayne: Racist or Realist?" *The Alabama Review* 31, no. 2 (April 1978): 98-101.

27. "The Freedmen," Montgomery *Daily Advertiser*, 10 January 1866, 4.

28. Ibid., 2 January 1866. For details of the observance of the signing of the Emancipation Proclamation, see "Celebration of Freedmen of Montgomery," Montgomery *Daily Advertiser*, 31 December 1865. Chapter 5 offers details.

29. "Furnishing Negro Labor in Every Department," Montgomery *Daily Advertiser*, 31 December 1865, 4. Many blacks were unfit for work, mainly due to physical limitations, BFRAL, NA.

30. Myers, "Freedmen and the Labor Supply," 159.

31. Bethel, 55.

32. Ibid.

33. E. M. Portis Papers, Alabama Department of Archives and History, Montgomery (hereafter referred to as ADAH).

34. Myers, "Reaction and Readjustment," 11.

35. Ibid., 10-11.

36. Myers, "Freedmen and the Labor Supply," 157.

37. Brvt. Col. C. Cadle, Jr., Office of the Assistant Commissioner, Bureau Freedman, Refugees, and Abandoned Lands, BRFAL, NA.

38. Bethel, 55; Myers, "Freedmen and the Labor Supply," 161.

39. Bethel, 55-56, 71.

40. Myers, "Freedmen and the Labor Supply," 161. Myers suggests that the lack of capital made the use of the sharecrop system necessary. Therefore, the weaknesses of the system did not lie with its theory; instead, the shortcoming resulted from the application of the theory. The Freedmen's Bureau lacked sufficient personnel to enforce labor contracts. Bethel lists three types of contracts: (1) the black laborer received one-fourth of the crop and the employer provided him with provisions and the means of planting the crop; (2) one-third of the crop and furnished his own

means of provisions but the employer provided him with the means to plant the crop; and (3) one-half of the crop and provided his own provisions and one-half of the expenses of cultivation. See Bethel, 55-56; J. Wayne Flynt, "Spindle, Mine and Mule: The Poor White Experience in Post-Civil War Alabama," *The Alabama Review* 34, no. 4 (October 1981): 246.

41. Myers, "Freedmen and Economic Adjustment," 261-62; Kolchin, 40-43; Bethel, 55-56.

42. Bethel, 57; Myers, "Freedmen and the Labor Supply," 164; Kolchin, 43.

43. Kolchin, 41-42.

44. Ibid., 45-47; August Meier and Elliot Rudwick, *From Plantation to Ghetto* (New York: Hill and Wang, 1966), 172-73; Bethel, 55, 57-58, 66-67.

45. Joe Gray Taylor, "Louisiana: An Impossible Task," in *Reconstruction and Redemption in the South*, ed. Otto H. Olsen (Baton Rouge: Louisiana State University Press, 1980), 215-16.

46. White, "Alabama Freedmen and Black Education," 107-8; Donald G. Nieman, "Andrew Johnson, the Freedmen's Bureau, and the Problem of Equal Rights, 1865-1866," *Journal of Southern History* 44, no. 3 (August 1978): 409.

47. Report of John Alvord, Freedmen's Bureau General Superintendent of Education for Alabama, 1 January 1866 to 10 October 1867, BRFAL, NA; Bethel, 61.

48. White, "Alabama Freedmen and Black Education," 109-10; Myers, "Reaction and Adjustment," 20; Bethel, 61. The only Bureau schools established outside of the Tennessee Valley in 1865 were located in Montgomery and Mobile. The Northwestern Freedmen's Aid Society of Chicago provided the teachers for these schools. The school in Montgomery was the initial educational opportunity afforded slaves and free blacks in the Blackbelt town. See Edward Marven Kramer, "Alabama Negroes, 1861-1865" (Master's thesis, Auburn University, 1965), 63. Mobile's free black population had enjoyed educational privileges much earlier, in accordance with the provisions of the Louisiana Treaty Purchase. See Horace Mann Bond, *Negro Education in Alabama: A Study in Cotton and Steel* (Washington, D.C.: Associated Publishers, Inc., 1939), 15; Kolchin, 82. The best-known of the aid societies was the American Missionary Association. See Bethel, 70; Loren Schweninger, "The American Missionary Association and Northern Philanthropy in Reconstruction Alabama," *The Alabama Historical Quarterly* 32, nos. 3 and 4 (Fall and Winter 1970): 135-38.

49. Minnie Rhodes Darden, "History of Marion, Alabama, 1817-1940" (Master's thesis, Auburn University, 1941), 40-41; Joe M. Richardson, *Christian Reconstruction, The American Missionary Association and Southern Blacks, 1861-1890* (Athens: The University of Georgia Press, 1986), 229.

50. White, "Alabama Freedmen and Black Education," 108, 115-16.

51. Bethel, 11-62; White, "Alabama Freedmen and Black Education," 117; Kolchin, 92-94. Joseph A. Mills maintains that teachers came south either because of religious motivation, a deep sympathy for the blacks, or financial reasons. Other teachers traveled to the south for their health. See Joseph A. Mills, "The Motives and Behaviors of Northern Teachers in the South during Reconstruction," *Negro History Bulletin* 34 (March 1979): 9; Walter Lynwood Fleming, *Civil War and Reconstruction in Alabama* (New York: Columbia University Press, 1905), 463-66.

52. Taylor, 213.

53. White, "Alabama Freedmen and Black Education," 117.

54. Such reports were based on the observations of Northern travelers who investigated the willingness of Southern whites to cooperate with Bureau officials. See White, "Alabama Freedmen and Black Education," 117-18; William C. Harris, "Republican Factionalism and Mismanagement," in Olsen, 83.

55. Bethel, 70; White, "Alabama Freedmen and Black Education," 110, 112; Kenneth B. White, "Black Lives, Red Tape: The Alabama Freedmen's Bureau," *The Alabama Historical Quarterly* 43, no. 4 (Winter 1981): 242-47.

56. Kolchin, 82-84.

57. Ibid., 85.

58. Sarah Woolfolk Wiggins, *The Scalawag in Alabama Politics, 1865-1881* (University, Ala.: The University of Alabama Press, 1977), 10.

59. *The Constitution, and Ordinances, Adopted by the State Convention of Alabama, Which Assembled at Montgomery, on the Twelfth Day of September, A. D. 1865* (Montgomery: Gibson and Whitfield, 1865), 45; Wiggins, 10; John B. Myers, "The Freedmen and the Law in Post-Bellum Alabama, 1865-1867," *The Alabama Review* 23, no. 1 (January 1970): 56-57.

60. Myers, "Freedmen and the Law," 57; Wiggins, 12.

61. *Journal of the Constitutional Convention of 1865*, 15, 27; Myers, "Freedmen and the Law," 58; Wiggins, 12-14.

62. Wiggins, 8.

63. Fleming, 374.

64. Otto H. Olsen, "An Incongruous Presence," in Olsen, 162.

65. *Journal of the Constitutional Convention of 1865*, 20, 27, 42, 57, 63, 65; Wiggins, 13; Myers, "Freedmen and the Law," 59; Sarah Woolfolk Wiggins, "Unionist Efforts to Control Reconstruction Alabama," *The Alabama Historical Quarterly* 30, no. 1 (Spring 1968): 56-57.

66. Wiggins, *Scalawag*, 13; Myers, "Freedmen and the Law," 59.

67. Wiggins, *Scalawag*, 13; Myers, "Freedmen and the Law," 60; Jon L. Wakelyn, ed., *Biographical Sketches of the Confederacy* (Westport, Conn.: Greenwood Press, 1977), 394-95; Owen, 3: 253.

68. Wiggins, *Scalawag*, 14; Myers, "Freedmen and the Law," 61; Wiggins, "Unionist and Reconstruction Alabama," 57.

69. Wiggins, *Scalawag*, 14-15.

70. Ibid., 14-16; Myers, "Freedmen and the Law," 61; Wiggins, "Unionist and Reconstruction Alabama," 58; Bethel, 57.

71. Myers, "Freedmen and the Law," 61-62.

72. Ibid., 62; Bethel, 58.

73. Myers, "Freedmen and the Law," 61-63; Bethel, 58.

74. Myers, "Freedmen and the Law," 63-64.

75. Ibid., 63-66.

76. Ibid., 67.

77. Ibid., 67-68.

78. Wiggins, *Scalawag*, 15; Fleming, 288.

79. Wiggins, "Unionist and Reconstruction Alabama," 58; Fleming, 388.

80. Michael Martin and Leonard Gelber, *Dictionary of American History* (Totowa, N.J.: Littlefield, Adams and Co., 1978), 119; Bethel, 65-66; Myers, "Freedmen and the Law," 68; Nieman, 409, 417-19.

81. Wiggins, *Scalawag*, 16; *The American Annual Cyclopedia of Important Events of the Year 1870; Embracing Political, Civil, Military, and Social Affairs; Public Documents, Biography, Statistics, Commerce, Finance, Literature, Science, Agriculture, and Mechanical Industry* (New York: Appleton and Company, 1873), 3: 9.

82. A. B. Moore, "Railroad Building in Alabama During the Reconstruction Period," *Journal of Southern History* 1, no. 4 (November 1935): 421-22; Carter Goodrich, "Public Aid To Railroads

in the Reconstruction South," *Political Science Quarterly* 71 (September 1956): 422; Mark Summers, *Railroads, Reconstruction, and the Gospel of Prosperity: Aid under the Radical Republicans, 1865-1877* (Princeton, N.J.: Princeton University Press, 1984), 214.

83. Moore, 423.

84. Ibid., 423-24; Goodrich, 422-23.

85. Summers, 214; Wiggins, *Scalawag*, 16-17.

86. Martin and Gelber, 532; Bethel, 72-73. To pass the oath of loyalty to the United States oath takers had to swear never to have been disfranchised for participation in the rebellion and never to have been a state or Federal official who had taken an oath of loyalty to the United States and later engaged in the rebellion against the United States. The basic tenet of this oath was incorporated in the Fourteenth Amendment to the U. S. Constitution. See, *Constitution of the State of Alabama As Amended by the Convention Assembled at Montgomery on the Fifth Day of November, A. D. 1867* (Montgomery: Barret and Brown, 1867), 10; Malcolm Cook McMillan, *Constitutional Development in Alabama, 1798-1901: A Study in Politics, the Negro, and Sectionalism*, "The James Sprunt Studies in History and Political Science," no. 37 (Chapel Hill: The University of North Carolina Press, 1955), 110-11.

87. Wiggins, "Unionist and Reconstruction Alabama," 58-60; Wiggins, *Scalawag*, 19-20; Myers, "Freedmen and the Law," 69.

88. August Meier, *Negro Thought in America, 1880-1915: Racial Ideologies in the Age of Booker T. Washington* (Ann Arbor: The University of Michigan Press, 1963), 3-5; Kolchin, 153; *The National Freedman* 2, no. 2, 15 December 1865, 365.

89. *The National Freedman* 2, no. 2, 15 December 1865, 365.

90. Edmund L. Drago, *Black Politicians and Reconstruction in Georgia: A Splendid Failure* (Baton Rouge: Louisiana State University Press, 1982), 27-29; Thomas Holt, *Black Over White: Negro Political Leadership in South Carolina during Reconstruction* (Urbana: The University of Illinois Press, 1977), 16-18.

91. Fleming, 364.

92. Wiggins, *Scalawag*, 8-9.

93. Fleming, 364; Marjorie Howell Cook, "Restoration and Innovation: Alabamians Adjust to Defeat, 1865-1867" (Ph.D. diss., University of Alabama, 1968), 211; Wiggins, *Scalawag*, 12-20.

94. Walter Lynwood Fleming, "The Formation of the Union League in Alabama," *The Gulf States Historical Magazine* 2, no. 2 (September 1903): 73-76.

95. Ibid.

96. Wiggins, *Scalawag*, 19.

97. Ibid., 19-20; Wiggins, "Unionist and Reconstruction Alabama," 58-59.

98. Mobile *Nationalist*, 28 March 1867, 2.

99. Kolchin, 115; Wiggins, *Scalawag*, 21.

100. Mobile *Nationalist*, 28 March 1867, 2; 9 May 1867, 1-2; 23 May 1867, 1.

101. Mobile *Nationalist*, 23 May 1867, 1; Kolchin, 157-58; Wiggins, *Scalawag*, 21.

102. Quoted in Mobile *Nationalist*, 28 March 1867, 2.

Notes

Chapter 2

1. Holt, 27; Kenneth M. Stampp, *The Era of Reconstruction, 1865-1877* (New York: Vintage Books, 1965), 156; Robert Cruden, *The Negro in Reconstruction* (Englewood Cliffs, N.J.: Prentice-Hall, Inc., 1969), 133; John Hope Franklin, *Reconstruction After the Civil War* (Chicago: The University of Chicago Press, 1961), 123-25; Fleming, "Union League," 75. Free blacks had voted in the antebellum South in some counties of North Carolina and Tennessee before 1835 and in one Louisiana parish--all prior to the Reconstruction Acts. See Roger Wallace Shugg, "Negro Voting in the Ante-Bellum South," *Journal of Negro History* 21, no. 4 (October 1936): 357-59.

2. Bond, "Social and Economic Forces," 329; Fleming, "Union League," 74, 79-80.

3. Fleming, "Union League," 77, 80-81.

4. Mobile *Nationalist*, 24 January 1867; Montgomery *Advertiser*, 25 July 1867.

5. Fleming, "Union League," 85-86.

6. Stampp, 204; Mobile *Nationalist*, 16 January 1868.

7. Fleming, "Union League," 86; Stampp, 156.

8. On the controversy surrounding the establishment of registration districts, see Fleming, *Civil War and Reconstruction*, 488, 488n. Fleming suggests that Pope's 44 election districts gerrymandered Alabama so that large black majorities would overcome white majorities in the 10 counties to which they were joined. In contrast to Fleming, Robert H. Rhodes maintains that the majority of the 10 counties so combined had been legislated into existence in 1866 and were not fully organized by 1867. Thus, according to Rhodes, these counties were combined with older "mother" counties simply to aid the process of voter registration. See Robert H. Rhodes, "The Registration of Voters and the Election of Delegates to the Reconstruction Convention in Alabama," *The Alabama Review* 8, no. 2 (April 1955): 124-25n; Lucille Griffith, *Alabama, A Documentary History to 1900* (University, Ala.: The University of Alabama Press, 1972), 447.

9. Loren Schweninger, "Alabama Blacks and the Reconstruction Acts of 1867," *The Alabama Review* 31, no. 3 (July 1978): 182-83.

10. Ibid., 186-96; Mobile *Nationalist*, 25 April 1867, 1.

11. Schweninger incorrectly identifies Carraway as a fugitive slave, an Alabama native, and the state's first black lawyer. Carraway was not a fugitive slave, an Alabama native, nor the state's first black attorney. Appearing in the Montgomery *Alabama State Journal* on 15 January 1872, the following article shows the North Carolina native was not the state's first black attorney:

On 4 January, Moore was admitted to practice in the Supreme
Court of Alabama. He graduated from law Department of Howard
University and was a practicioner to the Supreme Court of the
District of Columbia. A few weeks ago he was admitted to
practice in the circuit court of Mobile County. After a
thorough and exhaustive examination by leading members of the
bar of Mobile. This is the first instance in the history of
Alabama, of a Negro man being presented to the Supreme Court
of the state as a candidate for admission to practice in the
court. Moses W. Moore is a true type of the colored man, being
full blooded and comes well recommended and endorsed as a man
of learning and ability. This is the age of progress. Ten
years ago there was not one of our citizens who could have
believed that a Negro man would ever become a member of the
bar of the Supreme Court of the state. We do not know of
another colored lawyer in the state at this time. Carraway of
Mobile was, we believe, admitted to practice in our city
court. A dispute, however, afterward arose about Carraway's
examination and it was generally agreed that he did not
exhibit any marked abilities. Also see Schweninger,
"Reconstruction Acts," 189.

12. Wiggins, *Scalawag*, 24.

13. Ibid.; Kolchin, 160.

14. Kolchin, 161.

15. Ibid., 160.

16. Ibid., 161.

17. Schweninger, "Reconstruction Acts," 195; R. Blair, Office of
Registration, to Superintendent of Registration, Montgomery, 25
June 1867, ADAH.

18. Kolchin, 161.

19. R. Blair to William Hugh Smith, 29 June 1867, ADAH.

20. Schweninger, "Reconstruction Acts," 191.

21. Sarah Woolfolk Wiggins, "The 'Pig Iron' Kelly Riot in Mobile,
May 14, 1867," *The Alabama Review* 23, no. 1 (January 1970): 45-49;
The Montgomery *Daily State Journal* praised Cox and said, "Everybody

should read the address delivered by George W. Cox, a colored man, at Tuscaloosa on the evening of the 13th. This speech exhibits the best proof of the capability of the colored men to improved." Montgomery *Daily State Journal*, 24 June 1867; Kolchin, 162; Opelika *Times*, 19 October 1883; Owen, 1: 655-56. Smith was later appointed as registrar for Jefferson County. The black registrars included: First District; City of Mobile, Moses Brown Avery; Second District, County of Mobile, James Braggs; Third District, Baldwin and Conecuh counties, Wade Wright; Fourth District, Covington and Coffee counties, Gabriel Henley; Fifth District, Dale and Henry counties, Aaron Goins; Sixth District, Barbour County, Henry Hunter Craig; Seventh District, Bullock and Pike counties, Benjamin F. Royal; Eighth District, Crenshaw and Butler counties, Isaac Willis; Ninth District, Clarke and Monroe counties, Peyton Finley; Tenth District, Washington and Choctaw counties, Alfred Thomas; Eleventh District, Marengo County, J. Miller; Twelfth District, Wilcox County, G. W. Hagen; Thirteenth District, Dallas County, Joseph Drawn; Fourteenth District, Lowndes, James Lloyd; Fifteenth District, Montgomery County, L. J. Williams; Sixteenth District, Macon County, James H. Alston; Seventeenth District, Russell and Lee counties, Horace King; Eighteenth District, Elmore and Autauga counties, William V. Turner; Nineteenth District, Hale and Greene counties, Alexander Webb; Twentieth District, Perry County, Albert J. Webb; Twenty-First District, Sumter County, George Houston;

Twenty-Second District, Pickens County, William Shortridge; Twenty-Third District, Tuscaloosa County, George W. Cox; Twenty-Fourth District, Bibb and Shelby counties, John Dozier; Twenty-Fifth District, Coosa County, Joseph Mayberry; Twenty-Sixth District, Tallapoosa County, Nicholas Abercrombie; Twenty-Seventh District, Chambers County, Lisbon Cherry; Twenty-Eighth District, Randolph and Clay counties, James Nunn; Twenty-Ninth District, Talladega County, Yancey Sims; Thirteenth District, Jefferson County, Daniel Jordan; Thirty-First District, Walker and Winston counties, Albert Smith; Thirty-Second District, Jones and Fayette counties, Allen A. Williams; Thirty-Third District, Blount and St. Clair counties, James Dean; Thirty-Fourth District, Marshall and Blaine counties, Benjamin Henry; Thirty-Fifth District, Calhoun and Cleburne counties, William Malone; Thirty-Seventh District, Jackson County, Samuel Carter; Thirty-Eighth District, Madison County, Henderson Hill; Thirty-Ninth District, Morgan and Limestone counties, George Garth; Fortieth District, Lauderdale County, John Rapier; Forty-First District, Lawrence County, Sandy Bynum; and Forty-Second District, Franklin and Colbert counties, Sandy Osborne. See Mobile *Nationalist*, 30 May 1867, 3.

22. Wiggins, *Scalawag*, 25.

23. Registration accelerated when a supplemental Reconstruction Act, the Reconstruction Act of July 1867, provided for revisions of the registration lists and the number of enrollees increased. Wiggins, *Scalawag*, 25; idem, "Democratic Bulldozing and Republican

Folly," in Olsen, 51. Registered voters determined the numbers of delegates for each election district. The election was a victory for the Blackbelt, the region of Lowndes County Representative John L. Brooks, who pushed for black suffrage as early as January 1866. It was to the disadvantage of white lawmakers of the Blackbelt that by the time of the convention, November 1867, they had all but acquiesced the black vote to the influence of the Northerners. See McMillan, 113; Schweninger, "Reconstruction Acts," 196-97; Owen, 3: 327.

24. Kolchin, 163, 167; Wiggins, *Scalawag*, 23; idem, "Bulldozing," 51. Sources differed on the number of total delegates to the convention. See Franklin, 102; W. E. B. DuBois, *Black Reconstruction in America: An Essay Toward a History of the Part Which Black Folk Played in the attempt to Reconstruct Democracy in America* (New York: Harcourt, Brace and Company, 1935), 490. Sources also differ on the total number of black delegates. See Franklin, 102; DuBois, 490; Fleming, *Civil War and Reconstruction*, 517-18; Thomas McAdory Owen, *Alabama Official and Statistical Register* (Montgomery: Brown Printing Company, 1903), 125-26; Stampp, 169n; John William Beverly, *History of Alabama for Use in Schools and for General Reading* (Montgomery: Press of the Alabama Printing Company, 1901), 208; Richard L. Hume, "The 'Black and Tan' Conventions of 1867-1869 in Ten Former Confederate States: A Study of Their Membership" (Ph.D. diss., University of Washington, 1969). These

authors conclude that the Constitutional Convention of 186?
included 18 black members. Bethel lists only 14 black members.
See Bethel, 75; Kolchin, 163; Monroe N. Work, "Some Negro Members
of Reconstruction Conventions and Legislatures and of Congress,"
Journal of Negro History 5 (January 1920): 64, lists 17 black
members. James D. Thomas and Wiggins list 19 delegates. See James
D. Thomas, "The Alabama Constitutional Convention of 1867"
(Master's thesis, Auburn University, 1974), 46, 46n; Wiggins
Scalawag, 151-52.

25. Kolchin, 167; Wiggins, *Scalawag*, 26; Stampp, 156; McMillan
114; Loren Schweninger, "Black Citizenship and the Republican Party
in Reconstruction Alabama," *The Alabama Review* 29, no. 2 (April
1976): 84; Bond, "Social and Economic Forces," 290; Allan G. Bogue
"Historians and Radical Republicans: A Meaning for Today," *Journal
of American History* 70, no. 1 (June 1983): 13. For an assessment
of Alabama Reconstruction historiography, see Reid, "Changing
Interpretations of the Reconstruction Period in Alabama," 63-81
Olsen, 166.

26. For deaths see Secretary of State Files, 15 November 1869
Montgomery *Alabama State Journal*, 25 February 1871.

27. These delegates included James Thomas Rapier, who was elected
to the Forty-Third Congress; James K. Greene, who was elected to
the legislature and the State Senate; and Benjamin Royal, who
served with Greene in the State Senate. Thomas J. Davis suggest
that turnovers were characteristic of Alabama's congressional

delegation. See Thomas J. Davis, "Alabama's Reconstruction Representatives in the U. S. Congress, 1868-1878: A Profile," *The Alabama Historical Quarterly* 44, nos. 2 and 3 (Spring and Summer 1982): 36-37; *Journal of the Constitutional Convention of 1867*, 3-5.

28. Hume, "'Black and Tan' Conventions," 83-84; DuBois, 490-91; McMillan, 117n; Loren Schweninger, *James T. Rapier* (Chicago: The University of Chicago Press, 1978) is a full-length biography of Rapier.

29. Montgomery *Daily State Sentinel*, 22 November 1867, 3; Mobile *Nationalist*, 13 June 1867; Hume, "'Black and Tan' Conventions," 82; Thomas, "Alabama Constitutional Convention," 31; DuBois, 490; Owen, *Official Register*, 125; McMillan, 117n; Fleming, Civil War and Reconstruction, 518n.

30. Hume, "'Black and Tan' Conventions," 81; Thomas, "Alabama Constitutional Convention," 36; DuBois, 490; Fleming, *Civil War and Reconstruction*, 488n, 518n, 532, 617, 617n; McMillan, 118n; Owen, *History of Alabama*, 1: 125.

31. Hume, "'Black and Tan' Conventions," 80; Thomas, "Alabama Constitutional Convention," 30-31; DuBois, 490; Owen, *Official Register*, 125; McMillan, 117n-18n; Fleming, *Civil War and Reconstruction*, 518n, 532; Mobile *Nationalist*, 12 September 1867; Montgomery *Daily State Sentinel*, 27 November 1867.

32. Hume, "'Black and Tan' Conventions," 83; Thomas, "Alabama Constitutional Convention," 38; Fleming, *Civil War and Reconstruction*, 519n; Owen, *Official Register*, 126; Beverly, 203.

33. Morris Boucher, "The Free Negro in Alabama Prior to 1860" (Ph.D. diss., The State University of Iowa, 1950), 21-22; Hume "'Black and Tan' Conventions," 84; Beverly, 203; Fleming, *Civil War and Reconstruction*, 519n; McMillan, 118n; Owen, *Official Register* 126; Ira Berlin, *Slaves Without Masters, The Free Negro in the Antebellum South* (New York: Random House, 1974), 140-41.

34. McMillan, 116-17.

35. Hume, "'Black and Tan' Conventions," 81; Thomas, "Alabama Constitutional Convention," 40; Owen, *Official Register*, 126 Fleming, *Civil War and Reconstruction*, 518n, 532; McMillan, 118n Beverly, 203-5; DuBois, 490.

36. Hume, "'Black and Tan' Conventions," 83; Thomas, "Alabama Constitutional Convention," 39; Beverly, 203; Fleming, *Civil War and Reconstruction*, 519n, 532; DuBois, 490; Owen, *Official Register*, 126; McMillan, 118n.

37. John Hope Franklin, *From Slavery to Freedom: A History of Negro Americans*, 4th ed. (New York: Alfred A. Knopf, 1974), 81; For information on antebellum education, see Henry Allen Bullock, *A History of Negro Education in the South* (Cambridge: Harvard University Press, 1967), 6-10.

38. Holt, 37.

39. Hume, "'Black and Tan' Conventions," 79; Thomas, "Alabama Constitutional Convention," 40; Fleming, *Civil War and Reconstruction*, 518n, 532; DuBois, 490; Beverly, 203; McMillan, 118n; Owen, *Official Register*, 126.

40. Hume, "'Black and Tan' Conventions," 80; Thomas, "Alabama Constitutional Convention," 38; DuBois, 490; McMillan, 118n; Fleming, *Civil War and Reconstruction*, 519n; Beverly, 203.

41. Hume, "'Black and Tan' Conventions," 82; Thomas, "Alabama Constitutional Convention," 37; Fleming, *Civil War and Reconstruction*, 518n; Beverly, 203; McMillan, 118n.

42. Hume, "'Black and Tan' Conventions," 84; Fleming, *Civil War and Reconstruction*, 519n; Beverly, 203.

43. Hume, "'Black and Tan' Conventions," 82; Fleming, *Civil War and Reconstruction*, 518n, 519n; Beverly, 203; McMillan, 118n; Owen, *Official Register*, 125.

44. Hume, "'Black and Tan' Conventions," 82; Thomas, "Alabama Constitutional Convention," 38; DuBois, 490; Fleming, *Civil War and Reconstruction*, 532; Owen, *Official Register*, 126.

45. Hume, "'Black and Tan' Conventions," 83; Fleming, *Civil War and Reconstruction*, 532; Beverly, 203; Owen, *Official Register*, 126.

46. Hume, "'Black and Tan' Conventions," 79; Thomas, "Alabama Constitutional Convention," 38; Owen, *Official Register*, 126.

47. Hume, "'Black and Tan' Conventions," 81; Thomas, "Alabama Constitutional Convention," 32; Beverly, 203-4; DuBois, 490; Owen,

Official Register, 125; Fleming, *Civil War and Reconstruction*, 532.

48. Hume, "'Black and Tan' Conventions," 84; Thomas, "Alabama Constitutional Convention," 32; Fleming, *Civil War and Reconstruction*, 519n; Beverly, 203-5.

49. Franklin, *From Slavery to Freedom*, 256.

50. Holt, 37; Charles Vincent, *Black Legislators in Louisiana during Reconstruction* (Baton Rouge: Louisiana State University Press, 1976), 48; Taylor, 204-5.

51. The local press classified Unionists as "Pale faces" and did not use "scalawag" until July 1867. By February 1868, however, scalawag was in vogue. See Wiggins, *Scalawag*, 22; idem, "Unionist and Reconstruction Alabama," 51; Sarah Van Woolfolk, "Carpetbaggers in Alabama: Tradition Versus Truth," *The Alabama Review* 15, no. 4 (April 1962): 133-44; idem; "George E. Spencer: A Carpetbagger in Alabama," *The Alabama Review* 19, no. 1 (January 1966): 41-52; idem, "Five Men Called Scalawags," *The Alabama Review* 17, no. 1 (January 1964): 45-55.

52. Wiggins, *Scalawag*, 26; McMillan, 123.

53. McMillan, 119.

54. Ibid., 119-20; Hume, "The Freedmen's Bureau," 219-20.

55. McMillan, 123.

56. Wiggins, *Scalawag*, 27.

57. McMillan, 124-25.

58. Michael Perman, *The Road to Redemption: Southern Politics, 1869-1879* (Chapel Hill: The University of North Carolina Press, 1984), 37.

59. Found in ibid., 36.

60. McMillan, 129.

61. Ibid., 126.

62. Ibid., 128.

63. Ibid., 127.

64. Ibid.

65. Ibid., 126.

66. Ibid., 129

67. Ibid.

68. *Journal of the Constitutional Convention of 1867*, 97; McMillan, 129; William A. Russ, Jr. "The Negro and White Disfranchisement During Radical Reconstruction," *Journal of Negro History* 19, no. 2 (April 1934): 171.

69. Schweninger, "Black Citizenship," 87.

70. Ibid.

71. McMillan, 135-36; William McKinley Cash writes that "the Republicans were faced with a choice between building a party upon a Unionist foundation or utilizing fully the black vote at the risk of keeping the white membership small. The failure of Republicans to reach a consensus on either one of these choices led to a permanent schism that hastened the demise of the Republicans as a

viable party." See William McKinley Cash, "Alabama Republicans During Reconstruction: Personal Characteristics, Motivations, and Political Activity of Party Activists, 1867-1880" (Ph.D. diss., University of Alabama, 1973), 380.

72. Cash, 380; McMillan, 135; Schweninger, "Black Citizenship," 88

73. *Journal of the Constitutional Convention of 1867*, 217-18; McMillan, 139-40.

74. McMillan, 140-42.

75. Bond, "Social and Economic Forces," 315; Kolchin, 79.

76. *Journal of the Constitutional Convention of 1867*, 12-13; McMillan, 143-44.

77. Fleming, *Civil War and Reconstruction*, 623; McMillan, 153-54. Local editors were powerful and influential during most of the nineteenth century, and political concerns were a major topic of discussion. As an opponent of black suffrage, for example, John Forsyth wrote that "we [blacks and whites] could not live together sixty days." He accused the Radicals of making a special case of the treatment of blacks since blacks in the North and West were not treated as the Radicals desired and they (Radicals) made no complaints. He later endorsed black suffrage. See John Kent Folmar, "Reaction to Reconstruction: John Forsyth and the Mobile *Register*, 1865-1867," *The Alabama Historical Quarterly* 37, no. 4 (Winter 1975): 251-51n.

78. *Journal of the Constitutional Convention of 1867*, 152-54; McMillan, 145; Perman, 31.

79. McMillan, 145-46.

80. Ibid., 147-48, 150; Wiggins, *Scalawag*, 28.

81. McMillan, 151-52.

82. Ibid., 157; Perman, 15-16; Wiggins, *Scalawag*, 35-36.

83. McMillan, 152, 161; Wiggins, *Scalawag*, 35.

84. McMillan, 156.

85. Ibid., 168.

86. Ibid., 169; Wiggins, *Scalawag*, 36.

87. McMillan, 169; Wiggins, *Scalawag*, 36.

88. McMillan, 169-70.

89. Ibid., 170-71

90. Wiggins, *Scalawag*, 37-38; Schweninger, "Black Citizenship," 88-89.

91. McMillan, 174.

92. United States Army, Third Military District, Atlanta, Georgia, *Orders #101*, 14 July 1868, W. S. Hoole Special Collection, UA.

93. McMillan, 174.

94. Schweninger, "Black Citizenship," 87-88.

95. Ibid., 88.

96. Ibid.

97. Wiggins, *Scalawag*, 39.

Notes

Chapter 3

1. James B. Sellers, "Free Negroes of Tuscaloosa County Before the Thirteenth Amendment," *The Alabama Review* 23, no. 4 (April 1970): 110-11.

2. Leon Litwack, *Slaves Without Masters* (New York: Vintage Books, 1974), 131; Boucher, 22-24.

3. Boucher, 101; Vincent, 16.

4. Boucher, 97; Kolchin, 121.

5. Boucher, 167; Hume, "'Black and Tan' Conventions," 81.

6. Kolchin, 79.

7. Ibid.

8. Boucher, 105-17.

9. Ibid., 217.

10. Eugene Feldman, "James T. Rapier, Negro Congressman from Alabama," Feldman Files, ADAH; Griffith, 174; Owen, *History of Alabama*, 3: 152.

11. Boucher, 46. Schweninger contends that Rapier's father was John H. Rapier, Sr. See, Schweninger, *Rapier*, 15.

12. James Thomas Rapier to George L. White, AMA Papers, ADAH.

13. Boucher, 8.

14. James Bogle, "Horace King, Master Covered Bridge Builder, 1807-1887," Reprinted from *Georgia Life*, Spring 1980, 3.

15. Ibid.

16. Tom and Dess Sangster, *Alabama's Covered Bridges* (Montgomery: Coffeetable Publications, 1980), 40; Owen, *History of Alabama*, 1: 656; Mark Clark, "Horace King, Posthumous Dream Come True," Montgomery *Advertiser*, 1 May 1979; Opelika *Times*, 19 October 1883; Fleming, *Civil War and Reconstruction*, 209.

17. Bogle, 3.

18. Fleming, *Civil War and Reconstruction*, 208.

19. Boucher, 21-25, 175-77.

20. Charles Octavia Boothe, *Cyclopedia of Colored Baptists in Alabama* (Birmingham: Alabama Publishing Company, 1895), 138-39; Charles A. Brown, "John Dozier: A Member of the General Assembly of Alabama, 1872-1873 and 1873-1874," *Negro History Bulletin* 26 (December 1962): 113, 128.

21. Boucher, 15.

22. Mobile *Nationalist*, 12 September 1867; Montgomery *Daily State Sentinel*, 22 November 1867, 1; McMillan, 117-18.

23. Boothe, 132.

24. E. Delorus Preston, Jr., "Thomas Walker and His Times," *Journal of Negro History* 21 (1936): 275-77.

25. Maurine Christopher, *America's Black Congressmen* (New York: Thomas Crowell, 1971), 124-25; Turner File, ADAH.

26. Turner File; Christopher, 124-25.

27. *Biographical Directory of the American Congress, 1774-1971* (Washington, D.C.: Government Printing Office, 1971), 185.

28. Tuscumbia *American Star*, 5 September 1905.

29. House, *Testimony Taken by the Joint Select Committee to Inquire into the Condition of Affairs in the Late Insurrectionary States* (Washington, D.C.: Government Printing Office, 1872), 2, Ser. 3, 1537 (hereafter referred to as *Klan Testimony*); Bullock, 6-10; Bond, *Negro Education in Alabama*, 15.

30. Thomas, "Alabama Constitutional Convention," 36.

31. Montgomery *Herald*, 25 September 1886; Charles A. Brown, "Reconstruction Legislators in Alabama," *Negro History Bulletin* 26 (March 1963): 198.

32. Howard N. Rabinowitz, "Holland Thompson and Black Political Participation in Montgomery, Alabama," in *Southern Black Leaders of the Reconstruction Era*, ed. Howard N. Rabinowitz (Chicago: The University of Illinois Press, 1982), 249; Kolchin, 110.

33. Senate, *Testimony of James K. Greene, Testimony Taken by the Joint Select Committee to Inquire into the Condition of Affairs Between Labor and Capital* (Washington, D.C.: Government Printing Office, 1872), 9: 451-52.

34. Ibid.

35. United States Census Office, *Tenth Census of the United States: 1880, Agricultural*, 4, Forkland Beat, ADAH.

36. Charles A. Brown, "Lloyd Leftwich, Alabama State Senator," *Negro History Bulletin* 26 (February 1963): 161-62.

37. Brown, "Reconstruction Legislators," 199-200.

38. *Biographical Dictionary of American Congress, 1774-1971* (Washington, D.C.: US Printing Office, 1971), 1066.

39. 21 January 1875, AMA Papers, ADAH.

40. Marion *Commonwealth*, 15 January 1874, 2.

41. Council Family Files, ADAH.

42. *Testimony of James H. Alston, Klan Testimony*, 9: 1018-20.

43. *Compiled Military Records*, RG 94, NA.

44. Ibid.

45. Ibid.; Franklin, *From Slavery to Freedom*, 228; Hume, "'Black and Tan' Conventions," 80.

46. Montgomery *Daily State Sentinel*, 3 December 1867.

47. C. Peter Ripley, *Slaves and Freedmen in Civil War Louisiana* (Baton Rouge: Louisiana State University Press, 1976), 102; Vincent, 2. Vincent explains that, in Louisiana, blacks armed themselves at their own expense and served in the Confederacy to protect personal property. This scenario was especially true when the Native Guards refused to engage in combat outside the city boundaries. Also especially interesting is that the invitation to enlist free blacks in this area came in April 1861, two months after the firing on Fort Sumter.

48. John Gill Shorter to J. F. Bozeman, 6 December 1862, *Patriotism of Negroes Folder*, Manuscripts and Maps Division, ADAH.

49. J. F. Bozeman to Gov. Shorter, 29 December 1862, ADAH.

50. Columbus, (Georgia) *Ledger*, 17 May 1979, 2; Maxine Turner, "Naval Operations on the Apalachicola-Chattahoochee Rivers, 1861-1865," *The Alabama Historical Quarterly* 36, nos. 3 and 4 (Fall and Winter 1974): 189, 191-92.

51. Montgomery *Alabama State Journal*, 4 April 1873.

52. Livingston *Journal*, 18 October 1872.

53. Governor's Letter File shows no such pardon for Joseph. See Governor's Letter File, ADAH.

54. Ripley, 113-25.

55. Bogle, 4.

56. Schweninger, *Rapier*, 119.

57. It is clear that Rapier was a bachelor but not so conclusive that he was fatherless. See, *Tenth Census of the United States: 1880, Population*, White Hall, Beat 19, 8.

58. Schweninger, *Rapier*, 178.

59. Montgomery *Colored Alabamian*, 1 April 1913, 1; 11 October 1913.

60. Montgomery *Alabama Journal*, 19 October 1982, 13.

61. Montgomery-Tuskegee *Times*, 30 September-6 October 1982.

62. Montgomery *Advertiser*, 3 March 1873.

63. United States Census Office, *Ninth Census of the United States: 1870, Agricultural*.

64. Ibid., *Ninth Census of the United States: 1870, Population*.

65. Ibid.

66. Ibid.

67. Ibid.

68. Ibid.

69. Ibid.

70. Drago, Appendix; Janice Carol Hood, "Brotherly Hate: A Quantitative Study of Southern Reconstruction Congressmen, 1867-1877" (Ph.D. diss., Washington State University, 1874), 63.

Notes

Chapter 4

1. War Department, 26 November 1866, BRFAL Papers, NA.

2. Kolchin, 85.

3. Ibid.

4. Ibid.

5. Ibid., 87-89.

6. Ibid., 87.

7. January 1870, BRFAL Papers, NA.

8. Montgomery *Alabama State Journal*, 6 March 1873.

9. Montgomery *Daily State Sentinel*, 1 June 1867.

10. Montgomery *Daily State Journal*, 11 June 1867.

11. Montgomery *Advertiser*, 17 August 1867; Union Springs *Times*, 25 September 1867.

12. *Klan Testimony*, 9, Ser. 15, 1016-72; Allen W. Trelease, *White Terror: The Ku Klux Klan Conspiracy and Southern Reconstruction* (New York: Harper and Row, 1971), 270-71.

13. *Klan Testimony*, 9, Ser. 15, 1016-72; Trelease, 270-71.

14. *Klan Testimony*, 2, Ser. 15, 1537.

15. Ibid., 1956.

16. Trelease, 248; William Warren Rogers and Ruth Pruitt, *Stephen Renfroe* (Tallahassee: Sentry Press, 1972), 32-33; Montgomery *Daily State Journal*, 12 August 1874.

17. H. Ellsworth, 3 October 1871, AMA Papers, ADAH; 5 September 1873, AMA Papers, ADAH; Holland Thompson to Mr. Smith, 30 September 1868, AMA Papers, ADAH; J. Silsby to Chaplain C. W. Buckley, 14 February 1866. AMA Papers, ADAH.

18. Schweninger, "American Missionary Association," 130-33.

19. Ibid., 129-31.

20. Bond, "Social and Economic Forces," 301.

21. The Reverend William Fiske to the Reverend George Whipple, 14 March 1866, AMA Papers, ADAH.

22. John Silsby to George Whipple, 23 March 1866, AMA Papers, ADAH.

23. The Reverend William Fiske to the Reverend George Whipple, 23 February 1866, AMA Papers, ADAH.

24. White, "Alabama Freedmen," 115, 119.

25. Schweninger, "American Missionary Association," 139.

26. Ibid., 145.

27. G. L. Putnam to the Reverend E. P. Smith, 9 November 1868, AMA Papers, ADAH.

28. J. W. Alvord to the Reverend R. D. Harper, 19 August 1868, FBP.

29. Owen, *History of Alabama*, 1: 531; Schweninger, "American Missionary Association," 146.

30. Richardson, 128.

31. Ibid.

32. Ibid.

33. Ibid.

34. Kolchin, 90.

35. Richardson, 128.

36. 18 July 1867, AMA Papers, ADAH.

37. B. S. Williams, 10 September 1868, AMA Papers, ADAH.

38. Schweninger, "American Missionary Association," 138.

39. Hume, "'Black and Tan' Conventions," 83; Charles Brown, "A. H. Curtis: An Alabama Legislator, 1870-1876 with Glimpses into Reconstruction," *Negro History Bulletin* 25 (February 1962): 99-101.

40. T. C. Steward to the Reverend E. M. Cravath, 17 June 1872, AMA Papers, ADAH.

41. Helen M. Leonard to Mr Cravath, 18 September 1872, AMA Papers, ADAH.

42. Ibid., 14 September 1872, AMA Papers, ADAH.

43. Ibid., 18 September 1872, AMA Papers, ADAH.

44. Ibid., 11 November 1872, AMA Papers, ADAH.

45. Ibid., 8 April 1873, AMA Papers, ADAH.

46. N. E. Willis to the Reverend E. M. Cravath, 26 May 1873, AMA Papers, ADAH.

47. Ibid., to the Reverend E. M. Cravath, 30 June 1873, AMA Papers, ADAH.

48. Ibid., to Cravath, 25 August 1873, AMA Papers, ADAH.

49. Boothe, 138; Owen, *History of Alabama*, 2: 1269.

50. *Acts of the Sessions of the 1869-70 of the General Assembly of Alabama, Held in the City of Montgomery, Commencing on the Second Monday in November, 1869* (Montgomery: John G. Stokes and Company, 1870), act no. 76; *Acts of the Sessions of 1870-71 of the General Assembly, Held in the City of Montgomery, Commencing November 21st, 1870* (Montgomery: W. W. Screws, 1871), act no. 189; *Acts of the Session of 1873, of the General Assembly of Alabama and of the Board of Education, Held in the City of Montgomery, Commencing November 17th 1873* (Montgomery: Arthur Bingham, 1874), act nos. 15, 16, 17, and 18.

51. *State and Judicial Officers, 1868-1911*, 5.

52. John Silsby to the Reverend E. M. Cravath, 29 December 1874, AMA Papers, ADAH.

53. Rabinowitz, 252.

54. Boothe, 37.

55. C. W. Buckley to the Reverend G. O. Whipple, 13 March 1866. AMA Papers, ADAH.

56. C. W. Buckley to the Reverend E. M. Cravath, 15 August 1867, BRFAL, NA.

57. Schweninger, "American Missionary Association," 137.

58. Montgomery *Colored Alabamian*, 8 April 1916, 2-3. This school originally was operated in a building called the Franklin Academy and later was transferred to the "colored methodist church." The Franklin Academy school was opened on 31 July 1865 and was operated by J. Silsby, who later worked for the Freedmen's Bureau. A Mr.

James operated a school in Montgomery a few weeks before 21 July, but he became ill, abandoned the school, and "forgot" to refund his pupils' tuition. This action on the part of Mr. James caused many blacks in the area to oppose schooling for their children, but their attitudes soon changed when the school affiliated with a religious body, and Landy Franklin, Solomon Derry, and Solomon Terry were hired as teachers. See Mobile *Nationalist*, 14 December 1865, 2.

59. Rabinowitz, 256.

60. Fleming had argued that the Union League had given black leaders the greatest opportunity for leadership. See Fleming, *Civil War and Reconstruction*, 557.

61. See for example, *Acts of the General Assembly, 1869-70*, act no. 76; *Acts of the General Assembly, 1870-71*, no. 189; *Acts of the General Assembly, 1873*, nos. 15, 17. See also, letters of Helen M. Leonard to Mr Cravath, 14 September 1872, AMA Papers, ADAH; T. C. Steward to the Reverend E. M. Cravath, 17 June 1872; AMA Papers, ADAH; A. A. Saffold to the Reverend E. M. Cravath, 25 January 1872.

62. Kolchin, 108-14.

63. Ibid., 115; Mobile *Southern Watchman*, 6 January 1900, 3.

64. Wiggins, *Scalawag*, 148-51.

65. Schweninger, "American Missionary Association," 150.

66. Davis, 32-46.

67. Ibid.

68. For an extended listing of blacks who excelled during this battle, see E. Jay Ritter, "Congressional Medal of Honor Winners," *Negro History Bulletin* 23 (1960): 135.

69. *Compiled Military Records*, Record Group 94. NA.

70. For a full-length biography of Delaney, see Victor Ullman, *Martin R. Delaney: The Beginning of Black Nationalism* (Boston: Beacon Press, 1971). For a general evaluation of blacks in the Union army, see Dudley Taylor, *The Sable Arms: Negro Troops in the Union Army, 1861-65* (New York: W. W. Norton, 1966).

71. Montgomery *Daily State Sentinel*, 3 December 1867.

72. C. R. Gibbs, "Blacks in the Union Navy," *Negro History Bulletin* 36, no. 6 (October 1973): 138.

73. Christopher, 124-25.

74. B. S. Turner to William Smith, 10 August 1869, Governor's Letter File, ADAH.

75. Christopher, 126.

76. Ibid., 125.

77. Turner File, nd, np, ADAH; Alrutheus A. Taylor, "Negro Congressmen A Generation After," *Journal of Negro History* 7 (April 1922): 131.

78. *Military and Civil Register of Appointments Made by Governor, 1867-1868; State and Judicial Officers*, 4 (1868-1911), 9.

79. *Military and Civil Register of Appointments Made by Governor, 1867-1868*.

80. Montgomery *Daily State Sentinel*, 25 November, 3 December 1867; Schweninger, *Rapier*, 38-40.

81. Schweninger, *Rapier*, 37.

82. Ibid., 38-40, 41; Rapier File, ADAH; Taylor, "Negro Congressmen A Generation After," 134; Loren Schweninger, "James Rapier and the Negro Labor Movement, 1869-1872," *The Alabama Review* 28, no. 3 (July 1975): 185.

83. *Civil Register, County Officers* 63, no. 1 (1868-1882), 3.

84. Ibid., 58, no. 23 (1868-1882), 1.

85. *Commissioners, Perry County* 50, no. 34 (1868-1883), 1.

86. Ibid., 50, no. 68 (1868-1883), 2.

87. *Civil Register* 10, (1880-1888), 91.

88. Ibid., 138.

89. *Commissions, Dallas County* 23 (1868-1882).

90. *Commissions, Madison County* 43, no. 21 (1868-1882), 10.

91. Taylor, "Louisiana," 203.

92. Olsen, 166.

1. William Warren Rogers, *The One-Gallused Rebellion, Agrarianism in Alabama, 1865-1896* (Baton Rouge: Louisiana State University Press, 1970), 4.

2. W. E. B. DuBois, *The Negro American Family, The Atlanta University Publications, no. 13* (Atlanta: Atlanta University Press, 1908), 21, found in Kolchin, 56.

3. Ibid., 57.

4. Ibid.; Herbert G. Gutman, *The Black Family in Slavery and Freedom 1750-1925* (New York: Vintage Books, 1976), 159-60.

5. Kolchin, 59.

6. Mobile *Nationalist*, 24 December 1865.

7. Ripley, 147.

8. *Journal of the Constitutional Convention of 1865*, 63.

9. Ripley, 147; Kolchin, 60; Gutman, 418; *Journal of the Constitutional Convention of 1867*, 262-63.

10. Gutman, 418.

11. Rabinowitz, 249.

12. Thomas, "Alabama Constitutional Convention of 1867," 94.

13. Mobile *Nationalist*, 22 January 1866, 2.

14. Ibid.

15. Ibid.

16. Ibid.

17. Ibid.

18. Ibid.

19. Schweninger, "Reconstruction Acts," 183.

20. Schweninger, "Rapier and Negro Labor," 185.

21. Ibid.

22. Meier, *Negro Thought*, 4-6.

23. *Testimony of James K. Greene*, 9: 451-52.

24. Ibid.

25. Mobile *Nationalist*, 24 December 1865.

26. Ibid., 26 July 1866, 1.

27. Kolchin, 63; Henry E. Cobb, "Negroes in Alabama During Reconstruction, 1868-1875" (Ed.D. diss., Temple University, 1952), 181.

28. Richard Irwin Lester, "Greensboro, Alabama, 1861-1874" (Master's thesis, Auburn University, 1956), 70.

29. Ibid.

30. Kolchin, 64.

31. Ibid.

32. Mobile *Nationalist*, 8 March 1866.

33. For a brief evaluation of the Alabama penal system, see David Ward and William Warren Rogers, "Racial Inferiority and Modern

Medicine: A Note on the Coalburg Affair," *The Alabama Historical Quarterly* 44, nos. 3 and 4 (Fall and Winter 1982): 203-12.

34. Kolchin, 64.

35. Ibid., 91.

36. Ibid., 93; Lester, 71.

37. Kolchin, 95.

38. Fleming, *Civil War and Reconstruction*, 456.

39. Schweninger, "Rapier and Negro Labor," 188-89.

40. Owen, *History of Alabama*, 1: 94.

41. Meier, *Negro Thought*, 8

42. Montgomery *Advertiser and Mail*, 28 March 1874.

43. Kolchin, 10.

44. Ibid.; Rogers, *Rebellion*, 7; Perman, 31.

45. Mobile *Nationalist*, n.d.

46. Ibid., 2 February 1866, 22 February 1866, and 30 August 1866; Kolchin, 135-36.

47. Mobile *Nationalist*, 22 February 1866; Meier, *Negro Thought*, 11.

48. Kolchin, 135.

49. Ibid., 41.

50. *Journal of the House of Representatives of the State of Alabama, Session 1876-7* (Montgomery: Barret and Brown, 1877), 729.

51. Fleming, *Civil War and Reconstruction*, 452. *The New National Era* listed John Watson Alvord, a Yale graduate, as the founder of

the Freedmen's Savings and Trust Company. During the autumn of 1864, Alvord proposed to a friend in New York the idea of a financial institution for freedmen. During the winter of 1864-65 the two men secured the cooperation of Charles Sumner and other members of the House of Representatives in passing an act that chartered the Freedmen's Savings and Trust Company. President Lincoln signed the bill as one of his final actions. The incorporators met on 4 April 1865 and elected William A. Booth as its president. They chose Alvord as its corresponding secretary and directed him to establish branches throughout the Southern states. Alvord had established fifteen branches by March 1865, with the Norfolk, Virginia, branch having the distinction of being the first branch. The incorporators located their first office in New York City, but in 1867 the board of trustees decided to transfer its offices to Washington, D.C., locating the offices on Pennsylvania Avenue. Beginning on 12 March 1868 Alvord assumed the presidency of the organization and held that position until the demise of the bank in 1873. See "Origin of the Freedmen's Savings and Trust Company, and Sketch of Its Founders," *The New National Era*, 22 March 1868, Howard University Archives, Washington, D.C. 52. Fleming, *Civil War and Reconstruction*, 453. To enhance the confidence of blacks for the Augusta, Georgia, branch, *The New National Era* urged blacks to make deposits for the following reasons:

a. That it has one of the strongest vaults in the state.
b. That deposits of five cents and upwards are received

from any person.
c. That deposits in the sums of fifty dollars and upwards
will always draw interest from date of deposit. If it
remains in the Bank thirty days or longer, and such sums,
if not in time for five per cent interest, will receive
four per cent.
d. That deposits can always be withdrawn without notice.
e. That if a depositor dies, leaving money in this bank, it
is paid to the family or legal representative. See *The New
National Era*, nd.

53. William Fiske to the Reverend George Whipple, 23 February 1866,

AMA Papers, ADAH.

54. *The New National Era*, 9 June 1870.

55. Fleming, *Civil War and Reconstruction*, 453.

56. Ibid., 455. At its evening session, the National Negro Labor
Union endorsed the Reverend Sella Martin's resolution to make the
National Freedmen's Savings Bank as a place of deposit. *The New
National Era*, 13 January 1870, 1.

57. Fleming, *Civil War and Reconstruction*, 454-55. At the
convention of the National Negro Labor Union, George Downing
reported that 30 branches of the bank were in operation, with a
surplus of over $2.5 million. *The New National Era*, 19 January
1871, 1.

58. Fleming, *Civil War and Reconstruction*, 455.

59. Robinson explained his difficulty in obtaining a branch of the
bank in Huntsville. He wrote, "As you cannot furnish me room for
the Freedmen's Savings and Trust Bank in your office-I will have to
call on you to give me some direction [as to] what I shall do
[about] the above." See Lafayette Robinson to Col D. C. Rugg, Sub.

Assistant, Bureau of Refugee, Freedmen, and Abandoned Lands. January-December 1866, BRFAL, NA.

60. Meier records that "after the failure of the Freedmen's Savings Bank in the Panic of 1873, the next two black banks were the True Reformers [Bank] of Richmond, Virginia, and the Capital Savings Banks of Washington, D.C., both founded in 1888." See Meier, *Negro Thought*, 143.

61. Schweninger, "Rapier and Negro Labor," 193, 197-98;

62. Ibid., 191, 193; Schweninger, *Rapier*, 107-8; L. C. Andrews to the Reverend M. E. Strieby, 20 July 1878, AMA Papers, NA; Montgomery *Alabama State Journal*, 9 February 1877; Samuel J. Patterson also urged immigration. See Montgomery *Advertiser* Files, ADAH.

63. Meier, *Negro thought*, 4.

64. Meier claims that despite the passage of these amendments and civil rights legislation such as the Civil Rights Act of 1866, blacks had continued to hold their conventions and toward the end of the war, they had met in Washington, D. C., as part of the National Equal Rights League. See Meier, *Negro Thought*, 4-8.

65. Schweninger, "Rapier and Negro Labor," 186.

66. Ibid., 189.

67. Vincent, 34-35.

68. Taylor, "Louisiana," 215.

69. In 1867 the Carpenters and Joiners Union No. 1 of Boston stood as the only union to admit blacks. At its convention in 1868, the

National Labor Union ignored the issue of admitting blacks. See Philip S. Foner, *Organized Labor and the Black Worker, 1619-1973* (New York: International Publishers, 1974), 21.

70. *The New National Era*, 2 June 1870.

71. Schweninger, "Rapier and Negro Labor," 190. The convention of 203 delegates grew out of an earlier meeting held in Baltimore, with Myers presiding. The delegates elected Rapier as one of the several vice presidents and passed several resolutions that called for the establishment of a cooperative workshop, land, building, and loan association, as a remedy against their exclusion from their worksites on account of color; prohibition on intoxicating liquors; improvements in education; and offered thanks to Major General O. O. Howard, the Reverend J. W. Alvord, and John Mercer Langston. *The New National Era*, 13 January 1870, 1. *The New National Era* printed the constitution of the National Negro Labor Union. See *The New National Era*, 28 May 1870.

72. Schweninger, "Rapier and Negro Labor," 190. The labor convention fully outlined its intent:

> The one question is, 'How can the workingmen best improve his conditions? It should be the aim of every man to become a capitalist; that is, every man should try and receive an exchange for his labor, which, by proper economy and investment, will, in the future, place him in the position of those on whom he is now dependent for a living. *The New National Era*, nd.

The statement adequately illustrates the changing tone and direction of African American concerns, for by 1870 they certainly had begun to concentrate on economic matters.

73. Schweninger, "Rapier and Negro Labor," 190.

74. Meier, *Negro Thought*, 8.

75. Schweninger, "Rapier and Negro Labor," 190.

76. Ibid., 191.

77. Ibid., 191-92.

78. Ibid., 192. This was not the first occasion for a visit by blacks to the White House, nor the first time that they had received similar promises. George Downing and Frederick Douglass had visited President Andrew Johnson on 7 February 1866 and asked for his assistance in improving the conditions of former slaves. Johnson promised:

> Now it is always best to talk about things practically and in a common sense way. Yes, I have said, and I repeat here, that if the colored people of the United States could find no other Moses, or any Moses that would be more able and efficient than myself, I would be his Moses to lead him from bondage to freedom; that I would pass him from a land where he had lived in slavery to a land (if it were within our reach) of freedom. Yes, I would be willing to pass with him through the Red Sea to the land of Promise, to the land of liberty. See "Negroes Demand a Political

Role," in *The Black American: A Documentary History*, Third Edition, Leslie Fishel and Benjamin Quarles, eds. (Dallas: Scott, Forseman and Company, 1976), 276. Still, *The New National Era* painted a bright picture of the economic plight of blacks and stated, "Last year the price of common labor averaged $1.50 per day. Admitting that the laborer who received $1.50 a day, and if required the whole of that sum to support his family, nevertheless, we contend

404

that the laborer was worth, in cash to his family, the sum of $7,989." See *The New National Era*, 2 June 1870.

79. Schweninger, "Rapier and Negro Labor," 192; Feldman, "Negro Congressman," 419.

80. The Montgomery *Alabama State Journal* recorded, "We believe this movement, conducted in the proper spirit and proper principals a good one...it is for the utmost importance, not only to the colored, but to the white race, and to the very existence of the government itself, that citizens of the colored as well as all the other races, should be protected, improved, and elevated...we hope to see the colored race looking to their elevation as laborers and as citizens." Quoted in Feldman, "Rapier," 19.

81. Ibid., 18; Schweninger, "Rapier and Negro Labor," 88.

82. Feldman, "Negro Congressman," 420.

83. Schweninger, "Rapier and Negro Labor," 193.

84. Ibid.

85. Montgomery *Weekly Advertiser*, 31 July 1872; Cobb, 266.

86. Schweninger, "Rapier and Negro Labor," 194.

87. Ibid., 193-94; Feldman, "Rapier," 18.

88. Feldman, "Rapier," 20; Feldman, "Negro Congressman," 420.

89. Schweninger, "Rapier and Negro Labor," 194. Former slaves in Georgia also considered emigration. In a convention held on 1 January 1873, the delegates exclaimed, "The people of the South desire to live in peaceful relation to the whites, but do not wish to purchase peace at the expense of their advancement,

405

educationally and politically." *The New National Era*, 27 December 1872. Both Henry McNeil Turner and Martin R. Delaney, the nation's most prominent emigrationalists, did not live in Alabama. Each man served with the Freedmen's Bureau after the war, and unlike Delaney in South Carolina, Turner served in the Georgia legislature. On Turner see Drago, 24, 26-28; On Delaney see Holt, 75-76, 112.

90. Schweninger, "Rapier and Negro Labor," 195.

91. Ibid., 195-96.

92. Ibid., 197.

93. Montgomery *Alabama State Journal*, 14 November 1873; *The New National Era*, 27 December 1872.

94. Schweninger, "Rapier and Negro Labor," 200.

95. Mobile *Nationalist*, 13 December 1866, 1.

96. Robert Arthur Gilmour, "The Other Emancipation: Studies in the Society and Economy of Alabama Whites During Reconstruction" (Ph.D. diss., The Johns Hopkins University, 1972), 116.

97. Quoted in the Montgomery *Advertiser*, 11 November 1867.

98. *Acts of the General Assembly of Alabama, Sessions of 1876-7, Held in the City of Montgomery, Commencing the Third Monday in November, 1876* (Montgomery: Barret and Brown, 1877), 30 January 1877, 225.

99. L. C. Andrews to the Reverend M. E. Strieby, 20 July 1878, AMA Papers, ADAH.

100. William H. Ash to the Reverend M. E. Strieby, 15 September 1878, AMA Papers, ADAH.

101. Montgomery *Alabama Republican*, 18 September 1880, 3.

102. Montgomery *Daily State Journal*, 9 February 1877.

103. Senate, *Report of the Minority, Committee to Investigate the Causes Which Have Led to the Emigration of Negroes from the Southern to the Northern States*, 46th Cong, 1st sess., xiii, NA.

Notes

Chapter 6

1. Perman, 22.

2. *Memorial Record of Alabama: A Concise Account of the State's Political, Military, Professional and Industrial Progress, Together With The Personal Memorials of Its People* 1 (Spartanburg, S.C.: The Reprint Company, 1976), 88.

3. Found in Cobb, 249.

4. Ibid., 247-48; Perman, 61.

5. Wiggins *Scalawag*, 41.

6. Montgomery *Mail*, 1 August 1868. Quoted in Cobb, 266.

7. Ibid.

8. Ibid.

9. Wiggins, *Scalawag*, 50-51.

10. Ibid., 51-52.

11. Ibid., 51-54; Cobb, 263-64; Perman, 9-15.

12. Wiggins, *Scalawag*, 42-44; Summers, 214.

13. Moore, 428.

14. Ibid., 429; Summers, 215.

15. Summers, 216; Moore, 429.

16. Summers, 216.

17. Ibid.

18. Moore, 423, 431.

19. Summers, 218-19.

20. Cobb, 260.

21. Ibid., 261.

22. Wiggins, *Scalawag*, 39.

23. John Z. Sloan, "The Ku Klux Klan and the Election of 1872," *The Alabama Review* 18, no. 2 (April 1965): 114.

24. Trelease, 273.

25. Sloan, 113-14.

26. Melinda M. Hennessey, "Political Terrorism in the Black Belt: The Eutaw Riot," *The Alabama Review* 33, no. 1 (January 1980): 41-42.

27. Wiggins, *Scalawag*, 61.

28. Ibid., 57.

29. Ibid.; Sloan, 117.

30. Wiggins, *Scalawag*, 59.

31. Ibid.

32. Trelease, 246, 264-65.

33. Ibid., 132-33.

34. Ibid., 265.

35. Ibid.

36. *Annual Cyclopedia* 10: 15.

37. Wiggins, *Scalawag*, 63.

38. Ibid., 62; *Annual Cyclopedia* 10: 15.

39. *Annual Cyclopedia* 10: 15.

40. Ibid., 10: 10; Moore, 431.

41. Wiggins, *Scalawag*, 61.

42. Ibid.

43. *Annual Cyclopedia* 10: 15.

44. Cobb, 252; Wiggins, *Scalawag*, 64.

45. *Annual Cyclopedia* 10: 15.

46. Wiggins, *Scalawag*, 64.

47. Schweninger, *Rapier*, 74.

48. Ibid., 75.

49. Ibid.

50. Ibid.

51. Ibid., 76.

52. Summers, 215-16; Moore, 429; Goodrich, 423.

53. Schweninger, *Rapier*, 77-78.

54. Ibid., 76.

55. Ibid.

56. Ibid.

57. Ibid., 79.

58. Ibid.

59. Ray Granade, "Violence: An Instrument of Policy in Reconstruction Alabama," *The Alabama Historical Quarterly* 30, nos. 3 and 4 (Fall and Winter 1968): 179-81.

60. Green Shadrack Washington Lewis to Governor William Hugh Smith, 8 April 1870, Governor William Hugh Smith Papers, ADAH.

61. Ibid.

62. Ibid., 28 April 1870.

63. Trelease, 252.

64. Ibid.; Hennessey, 36.

65. Montgomery *Alabama State Journal*, 21 November 1874.

66. *Klan Testimony*, 334-35, 1579, 1581, 1587, 1607, 1647, 1686, 1774-75; Livingston *Journal*, 26 August 1870; Livingston *West Alabamian*, 7 September 1870; Trelease, 251-52; Kolchin, 121; James Taylor, "History of the Ku Klux Klan in Alabama, 1865-1874" (Master's thesis, Auburn University, 1957), 85.

67. Trelease, 253.

68. Hood, 361.

69. Schweninger, *Rapier*, 80.

70. Trelease, 252.

71. Schweninger, 80.

72. Trelease, 303.

73. Ibid.; Selma *Southern Argus*, 2 November 1870, 2; Trelease, 303, 313.

74. Sloan, 120.

75. Wiggins, *Scalawag*, 68-69.

76. Ibid., 69.

77. Montgomery *Mail*, 28 October 1874.

78. Sloan, 121.

79. Trelease, 273.

80. Ibid.

81. Schweninger, *Rapier*, 81-83.

82. Cobb, 252.

83. *National Cyclopedia of American Biography* (Clifton, N.J.: J. T. White, 1893), 10: 435.

84. Ibid.; Cobb, 263; Sloan, 119; Wiggins, *Scalawag*, 67-68.

85. Cobb, 263.

86. Wiggins, *Scalawag*, 73.

87. Moore, 434.

88. Summers, 220.

89. Ibid., 223.

90. Ibid., 223-25.

91. Moore, 434.

92. Summers, 235.

93. Wiggins, *Scalawag*, 75; Moore, 429.

94. Summers, 90.

95. Ibid.; Moore, 422, 425-26, 429, 431; John C. Jay, "General N. B. Forrest As A Railroad Builder in Alabama," *The Alabama Historical Quarterly* 24, no. 1 (Spring 1962): 16-21; David Maldwyn Ellis, "The Forfeiture of Railroads Land Grants, 1867-1894," *Mississippi Valley Historical Review* 33 (June 1946): 36.

Notes

Chapter 7

1. Wiggins, *Scalawag*, 77.

2. Ibid., 77-78.

3. Schweninger, *Rapier*, 96.

4. Ibid., 97.

5. Ibid., 98.

6. Charles W. Buckley, Charles Hays, and George Spencer to the President, 7 March 1871, Rapier File, NA.

7. Ibid.

8. Charles Hays to George Boutwell, 14 March 1871, NA.

9. Montgomery Advertiser, 20 April 1871. Quoted in Schweninger, *Rapier*, 94-95.

10. Ibid., 95.

11. Ibid., 95-99.

12. Ibid., 99-100.

13. Eugene Cory to Rapier, 3 November 1871, Rapier File, RG 56, NA.

14. James Thomas Rapier to J. D. Douglass, 7 November 1871, Rapier File, RG 56, NA.

15. Schweninger, *Rapier*, 103.

16. Rapier to Douglass, 18 February 1873, RG 56, NA.

17. Trelease, 302.

18. Ibid.

19. Schweninger, *Rapier*, 104.

20. John A. Minnis to George H. Williams, 1 April 1872, Department of Justice, Source Chronological File, RG 60, NA.

21. Ibid.

22. Ibid., 27 August 1872, Box 125.

23. George Spencer to George H. Williams, 14 September 1872, RG 60, NA; Everette Swinney, "Suppressing the Ku Klux Klan: The Enforcement of the Reconstruction Amendments, 1870-1874" (Ph.D. diss., University of Texas, 1966), 298-302.

24. Perman, 20.

25. Wiggins, *Scalawag*, 75; Owen, *History of Alabama* 3: 327; Perman, 78-85; Cobb, 264-65.

26. Cobb, 265.

27. Schweninger, "Black Citizenship," 95; Wiggins, *Scalawag*, 79-80.

28. Cobb, 265-67.

29. Montgomery *Weekly Advertiser*, 31 July 1872.

30. Montgomery *State Journal*, 3 August 1872.

31. Cobb, 266-67.

32. Wiggins, *Scalawag*, 80-81.

33. Christopher, 126.

34. Schweninger, *Rapier*, 107.

35. Schweninger, "Black Citizenship," 97.

414

36. Schweninger, *Rapier*, 112.

37. Ibid., 111.

38. Ibid., 113.

39. Wiggins, *Scalawag*, 83.

40. Schweninger, *Rapier*, 114.

41. Wiggins, *Scalawag*, 83-84; Cobb, 264.

42. Schweninger, "Black Citizenship," 98.

43. Ibid.

44. Wiggins, *Scalawag*, 89; Schweninger, "Black Citizenship," 93-98; Schweninger, *Rapier*, 117, 158-59; James Thomas Rapier, 22 April 1873, RG 56, NA.

45. Arthur Williams, "The Participation of Negroes in the Government of Alabama, 1867-1874" (Master's thesis, Atlanta University, 1946), 49.

46. Selma *Southern Argus*, 11 September 1872.

47. Wiggins, *Scalawag*, 86-87.

48. Ibid., 87; Montgomery *Advertiser and Mail*, 6 March 1873.

49. Montgomery *Advertiser and Mail*, 6 March 1873.

50. Greenville *Advocate*, 20 March 1872; Montgomery *Advertiser and Mail*, 13 March 1873.

51. Selma *Southern Argus*, 20 March 1873; Montgomery *Daily Advertiser and Mail*, 26 February 1873.

52. Selma *Southern Argus*, 20 March 1873; Montgomery *Daily Advertiser and Mail*, 26 February 1873.

53. Selma *Southern Argus*, 20 March 1873; Montgomery *Daily Advertiser and Mail*, 26 February 1873.

54. Wiggins, *Scalawag*, 87.

55. Montgomery *Advertiser*, 19 August 1874.

56. Cobb, 269.

57. Selma *Southern Argus*, 20 March 1873.

58. Cobb, 268.

59. Wiggins, *Scalawag*, 88.

60. Perman, 38-39.

61. Montgomery *Alabama State Journal*, 26 June 1874; Montgomery *Advertiser*, 30 June 1874; Montgomery *Daily State Journal*, 21 August 1874, 2.

62. Gerald Lee Roush, "Aftermath of Reconstruction: Race Violence and Politics in Alabama, 1874-1884" (Master's thesis, Auburn University, 1973), 25; Jimmy Frank Gross, "Alabama Politics and the Negro, 1874-1901" (Master's thesis, University of Georgia, 1970), 28-29.

63. Cobb, 259, 270; R. J. Norrell, "Perfect Quiet, Peace, and Harmony: Another Look At The Founding of Tuskegee Institute," *The Alabama Review* 36, no. 2 (April 1983): 110-29.

64. Montgomery *Advertiser and Mail*, 23 October 1874.

65. Ibid.

66. Cobb, 270-72.

67. Schweninger, *Rapier*, 134.

68. Selma *Southern Argus*, 24 July 1874.

69. Ibid., 17 July 1874.

70. Ibid.,

71. Ibid., 7 August 1874.

72. Selma *Southern Argus*, 28 August 1874; John Tyler Morgan Papers on Social Equality, ADAH.

73. Montgomery *Daily State Journal*, 4 July 1874.

74. Ibid.

75. Wiggins, *Scalawag*, 90; Harris, "Republican Factionalism," 102.

76. Jerrell H. Shofner, "A Failure of Moderate Republicanism," in Olsen, 42.

77. George Smith Houston Papers, ADAH.

78. *Journal of the House of Representatives, Session of 1874-5, Held in the City of Montgomery, Commencing November 16, 1874* (Montgomery: W. W. Screws, 1875), 85.

79. Edward Williamson, "The Alabama Election of 1874," *The Alabama Review* 17, no. 3 (July 1964): 213; Wiggins, *Scalawag*, 92-93.

80. Williamson, 211-12.

81. Ibid., 214.

82. Wiggins, *Scalawag*, 94-95.

83. Ibid.

84. Selma *Southern Argus*, 7 August 1874.

85. Wiggins, *Scalawag*, 95-96.

86. Ibid., 95.

87. Montgomery *Daily State Journal*, 14 July 1874, 2.

88. Selma *Southern Argus*, 24 July 1874.

89. Ibid.

90. Ibid.

91. Ibid.

92. Ibid., 30 October 1874.

93. Montgomery *Alabama State Journal*, 12 September 1873.

94. Montgomery *Advertiser and Mail*, 23 August 1874.

95. Quoting the Mobile *Register*, 19 November 1874.

96. Ibid.

97. Montgomery *Daily Advertiser*, 16 October 1874.

98. Roush, 184.

99. Selma *Southern Argus*, 27 November 1874.

100. *House Select Committee on Affairs in Alabama, The Special Committee Appointed to Investigate Political Affairs in the State of Alabama*, 43d Cong., 2d sess., 23 February 1875, H. Rept. no. 262, vi, xvi, NA.

101. Ibid.

102. Selma *Southern Argus*, 28 August 1874, 18 September 1874.

103. Harry Philpot Owens, "History of Eufaula, 1832-1882" (Master's thesis, Auburn University, 1963), 115.

104. Montgomery *Alabama State Journal*, 30 June 1874.

105. Roush, 50; Wiggins, *Scalawag*, 96-97.

106. Wiggins, *Scalawag*, 98; Fleming, *Civil War and Reconstruction*, 784-85.

107. Schweninger, *Rapier*, 146; Wiggins, *Scalawag*, 139.

108. Guy Hunt, a Republican from Holly Pond, defeated Bill Baxley to become the state's first Republican governor in 112 years. See, Montgomery *Advertiser*, 5 November 1986, 1.

109. Wiggins, *Scalawag*, 115.

1. Montgomery *Alabama State Journal*, 21 May, 12 September 1873.

2. Greenville *Advocate*, 28 August 1873.

3. Montgomery *Alabama State Journal*, 21 May 1873.

4. Peyton McCrary, "The Political Dynamics of Black Reconstruction," *Reviews in American History* 12, no. 1 (March 1984): 53-54.

5. Roush, 12-13.

6. Melinda M. Hennessey, "Reconstruction Politics and the Military: The Eufaula Riot of 1874," *The Alabama Historical Quarterly* 38, no. 2 (Summer 1976): 113.

7. Federal Marshal R. W. Healy to Attorney General George W. Williams, 17 September 1874, RG 60, NA.

8. James Thomas Rapier to George H. Williams, nd, RG 60, Box 125, NA.

9. Hennessey, "The Eufaula Riot," 116.

10. Ibid.

11. Ibid., 118.

12. Schweninger, *Rapier*, 145.

13. "Affairs in Alabama," xvi; Hennessey, "The Eufaula Riot," 121.

14. Hennessey, "The Eufaula Riot," 123-24.

15. Anne Kendrick Walker, Backtracking in Barbour County: A Narrative of the Last Alabama Frontier (Richmond, Va.: The Deitz Pres, 1941), 254.

16. Mattie Thomas Thompson, History of Barbour County, Alabama (Eufaula, Ala., 1939), 182.

17. Roush, 13-14.

18. City Court, State Minutes, Book A, 105; Bluff City Times, 30 June 1870, 2; Quoting Owens, 87.

19. Hennessey, "The Eufaula Riot," 124-25.

20. Owens, 85.

21. Norrell, 117.

22. Tuskegee News, 3, 17 June 1875. Quoting Norrell, 117.

23. Ibid.

24. Found in Roush, 19.

25. Ibid.

26. Ibid., 21.

27. Ibid., 16-17.

28. Ibid., 23.

29. Ibid., 30-31.

30. Ibid., 18.

31. Kolchin, 158-59.

32. John Witherspoon DuBose, Alabama's Tragic Decade: Ten Years After, 1865-1874, ed. James K. Greer (Birmingham: Webb Book Company, 1940), 268-69.

33. Hilary A. Herbert, et. al., *Why the Solid South? or Reconstruction and Its Results* (Baltimore: R. H. Woodward and Company, 1890), 54.

34. Montgomery *Alabama State Journal*, 8 January 1874; Herbert, 53-54; DuBose, 268.

35. Montgomery *Advertiser and Mail*, 9 December 1874.

36. Preston, 289-90.

37. Roush, 90-94.

38. Fleming, *Civil War and Reconstruction*, 745-46.

39. *State and Judicial Officers, 1868-1911*, 15; Herbert, 60-61; Fleming, *Civil War and Reconstruction*, 745-46.

40. The House *Journal* recorded the protest as follows:

> We, the undersigned members of the General assembly, hereby solemnly protest against the act of the majority of this General assembly in abolishing the criminal court of Dallas County.
> First. Because we believe that said act is in violation of both the letter and spirit of the constitution of our State.
> Second. Because we believe that the only reasons for the abolition of said court, are the color and political connection of the judge.
> Third. Because the judge of said court was elected by the people, and to legislate men out of offices to which they have been elected by the free choice of the people, is subversive of the principle of popular government, substitutes the will of the minority for that of the majority, and tends towards revolution and anarchy.
> Fourth. Because we believe that the will of the people, as expressed at the ballot-box, cannot be defeated by the Legislature without danger to the liberties to the people.
> Fifth. Because we believe any interference of the Legislature with the judicial department of a State, makes the judiciary dependent on the political complexion of the Legislature.
> (Signed) Chas. E. Harris, Perry Mathews, B. W. Reese, A. W. Johnston, M. Wynne, Chas. Smith, W. Merriwether, Elijah Baldwin, D. J. Daniels, G. Bennett, John A. J. Sims, G. W. Allen, D. E. Coon, J. R. Witherspoon, W. H. Blevins, Elijah

Cook, Robert Reid, Gilmer of Montgomery, Chas. Fagan, G. S. W. Lewis, W. G. Brantley, Prince Gardner, J. T. Harris, W. .D Gaskin, E. R. Mitchell, Charles S. Wood. See House *Journal, 1874-5*, 327-28.

41. Mobile *Register*, 8 August 1868.

42. *Containing the Names of the Citizens of Mobile, A Business Directory* (Mobile: Henry Farrow and Company, 1869), 113-14; Robertha Steele, "Some Aspects of Reconstruction in Mobile" (Master's thesis, Auburn University, 1937), 45, 55, 65, 75.

43. Martin and Gelber, 253.

44. Beverly, 65-69; Rabinowitz, 261, 265, 279.

45. Howard N. Rabinowitz, "From Reconstruction To Redemption in the Urban South," *Journal of Urban History* 2, no. 2 (February 1976): 184.

46. *Acts of the General Assembly, 1876-7*, 8 February 1877, 254-57.

47. Ibid., 256-57.

48. House *Journal, 1874-5*, 744.

49. Roush, 94-96. Pepperman charged:

> On the 16th of January, William Gaskin, a colored representative in the legislature from Lowndes county, offered an amendment to a bill to consolidate the offices of sheriff and tax assessor of Hale county, whereby it was proposed to include the county of Lowndes in said bill. I have good reason to believe that Gaskin did this by way of retaliation. Some time since I refused to employ him as my assistant. He knows as well as I do that the people of Lowndes do not desire the consolidation of these offices, and as he must have had some motive I am at a loss to imagine any other than revenge. Yesterday, for instance, he sent me a message by a gentleman that he would withdraw the amendment if I would pay one hundred and twenty-five dollars! And if so, how can it benefit the people of

Lowndes for him to receive and use the money? Perhaps Gaskin, who thinks that one hundred and twenty-five dollars will check the progress of this bill (which is now before the committee on ways and means,) rates the members by his own standard. He thinks, perhaps, that they can be bought as cheaply as he. If so, he will find himself wofully [sic] mistaken, for all the money in Alabama can not corrupt them. If the "honorable gentleman" (?) desires to raise a question of privilege on this subject, I am ready to go before a committee of investigation. See House *Journal, 1874-5*, 289.

50. House *Journal, 1874-5*, 45, 68.

51. The motion to oust Carson had been postponed, but C. B. St. John of Marshall County made a successful motion to reconsider that motion. Hershel V. Cashin of Montgomery County sought to lay St. John's motion on the table. Cashin's motion failed, thus the road to Carson's removal was clear. See, *Journal of the House of Representatives, Session of 1875-6, Held in the City of Montgomery, Commencing on Tuesday, December 28, 1875* (Montgomery: W. W. Screws, 1876), 74, 709.

52. Ibid., 347.

53. *Journal of the House of Representatives of the State of Alabama, Session of 1878-9, Held in the City of Montgomery, Commencing November 12th, 1878* (Montgomery: Barret and Brown, 1879), 219-20, 820.

54. "Answer of Jere N. Williams to Notice of James T. Rapier on Matter of Contest for Seat in 44th Congress, 2nd Congressional District of Alabama," 31 December 1874, NA.

55. Roush, 104.

56. McMillan, 175-77.

57. Ibid.; *Acts of the Sessions of 1874-75 of the General Assembly of Alabama, Held in the City of Montgomery, Commencing November 16, 1874* (Montgomery: W. W. Screws, 1874), 109-112; Roush, 104.

58. McMillan, 178.

59. Ibid.

60 Ibid., 178-79.

61. Roush, 103.

62. Ibid., 106-7.

63. McMillan, 175-77.

64. Tuskegee *Weekly News*, 12 December 1874, 21 January 1875, 4 February 1875; Montgomery *Daily Advertiser*, 24 January, 31 March 1875; Birmingham *Iron Age*, 18 February 1875; Quoting Roush, 102-3.

65. McMillan, 187.

66. Roush, 105.

67. McMillan, 188.

68. Wiggins, *Scalawag*, 153.

69. McMillan, 190; Donald B. Dodd, *Historical Atlas of Alabama* (University, Ala.: The University of Alabama Press, 1974), 64-66.

70. McMillan, 190-91.

71. Ibid., 209-10.

72. *Acts of the Sessions of 1875-76 of the General Assembly, Held in the City of Montgomery, Commencing December 28th 1876* (Montgomery: W. W. Screws, 1877), 98, 115.

73. McMillan, 212.

74. Griffith, 496-97; Dewey Grantham, "The Southern Bourbons Revisited," *The Bobbs-Merrill Reprint Series in History*, Reprinted from *The South Atlantic Quarterly* 60, no. 3 (Summer 1961): 286-95.

75. McMillan, 216.

76. Roush, 122.

77. Ibid.

78. Ibid., 123.

79. *Frederick G. Bromberg v. Jeremiah Haralson, Contest for Seat in 44th Congress from the First Congressional District of Alabama, Brief for Contestant*, NA, 1-31.

80. *Mobile City Directory*, 1-31; Margaret Davidson Sizemore, "Frederick G. Bromberg of Mobile: An Illustrious Character, 1837-1928," *The Alabama Review* 29, no. 2 (April 1976): 104-8.

81. *Haralson v. Bromberg*, 10.

82. Ibid., 5.

83. George Turner to Henry S. S. Skatts, 18 October 1875, Collector of Internal Revenue File, RG 56, NA.

84. *Haralson v. Bromberg*, 1-20.

85. *Congressional Record*, 18 March 1876, 2553.

86. McMillan, 218-19.

87. Jeremiah Haralson to D. D. Pratt, 8 September 1875, RG 56, NA. Haralson's attempt to remove Mayer was a clear indication of his understanding of the politics of the times. His efforts also indicated that African American politicians were indeed key players during Reconstruction.

88. Ibid, 18 September 1875.

1. Roush, 129-30.

2. Wiggins, *Scalawag*, 108-9.

3. Ibid., 112.

4. Found in Roush, 134-35.

5. Wiggins, *Scalawag*, 112-13; Roush, 134.

6. *Journal of the House of Representatives, 1876-7*, 1-8.

7. Wiggins, *Scalawag*, 151; Roush, 302.

8. *Code of Alabama, 1876*, 192-93; *Alabama Congressional and Legislative Representation, 1819-1960*, "The Alabama State Department of Archives and History Historic and Patriotic Series Number 17" (Montgomery: Walker Printing Company, nd), np.

9. Schweninger, *Rapier*, 153.

10. Montgomery *Advertiser and Mail*, 16 September 1876; Schweninger, *Rapier*, 154; Roush, 133.

11. Schweninger, *Rapier*, 156.

12. Ibid.

13. Jeremiah Haralson, J. N. Perkins, Henry A. Cochran, W. A. Brantley, L. D. Barker, and John White to David Peter Lewis, 20 November 1874, *Dallas County Commissions, 1868-1882* 7, ADAH.

14. Ibid.

15. Selma *Southern Argus*, 10 November 1876, 2; House, *Committee on Elections, Contested Election: Jere Haralson V. Charles M. Shelley,* 4th Congressional District of Alabama, 45A-F 10.4, 2, NA. .

16. Roush, 164-65.

17. Ibid., 167.

18. House, *Contested Election: Jere Haralson V. Charles M. Shelley,* 2, NA.

19. Ibid., 3.

20. Stampp, 192.

21. Montgomery *Colored Alabamian*, 12 September 1884, 1.

22. Stampp, 190-92.

23. Franklin, *Reconstruction*, 213-15.

24. Charles Pelham to John Sherman, 15 May 1878, Collector of Internal Revenue File, RG 56, NA; Roush, 177.

25. Ibid.; Edgar Toppin, *A Biographical History of Blacks in America Since 1528* (New York: David McKay, Inc., 1969), 282-83.

26. Wiggins, *Scalawag*, 122-24.

27. *Great Issues in American History: From Reconstruction to the Present Day, 1864-1969*, ed. Richard Hofstadter (New York: Vintage Books, 1958), 47-50.

28. Ibid.

29. Franklin, *Reconstruction*, 207-9.

30. Toppin, 143.

31. Roush, 147.

32. Ibid., 165.

33. Ibid., 162.

34. Quoting Roush, 168.

35. Ibid., 168-69.

36. William Warren Rogers and David Ward, *August Reckoning: Jack Turner and Post Racism in Post-Civil War Alabama* (Baton Rouge: Louisiana State University Press, 1973), 148.

37. Toppin, 144.

38. Roush, 193-95.

39. Ibid., 150.

40. Ibid., 195.

41. Rabinowitz, "Holland Thompson," 264; Roush, 186, 210.

42. Stampp, 198.

43. Roush, 99-102.

44. Ibid., 109.

45. Ibid.

46. Bogle, 3-6.

47. LaGrange *Reporter*, 4 June 1885. The date of King's death is listed as 28 May 1885.

48. "The Death of a Remarkable Negro," Atlanta *Constitution*, 30 May 1885. Here again, the date of King's death is listed as May 1885.

49. House *Journal, 1875-6*, 29-30.

50. *Oakwood Cemetery Records of Interment, ca 1880-1920* (Montgomery: Platt Book and Index).

51. *Oakwood Cemetery Records of Interment, 1876-1896*, 163, ADAH.

52. *Records of Interments, 1876-1896*, 128.

53. Brown, "A. H. Curtis," 101; Boothe, 132.

54. *Records of Interments, 1876-1896*, 387.

55. Ibid., 109.

56. Schweninger, *Rapier*, 173.

57. *Records of Interments, 1876-1896*, np.

58. Ibid., 90.

59. Ibid., 427.

60. Rabinowitz, "Holland Thompson," 264-66.

61. The Reverend J. A. Foster to Mr. L. J. Bryan, 30 January 1882, Treasury Dept., NA.

62. *Records of Interments, 1876-1896*, np.

63. Ibid.

64. *Biographical Directory of the American Congress*, 1835; Selma *Times*, 29 March 1894.

65. Brown, "John Dozier," 113, 128.

66. Montgomery *Colored Alabamian*, 6 February 1909, 1. See also, Montgomery *Herald*, 25 September 1886, 3; Mobile *Southern Watchman*, 6 January 1900, 3.

67. Brown, "Reconstruction Legislators," 198.

68. Birmingham *News*, 19 April 1909; Owen, *History of Alabama*, 2: 846-47; *The Cyclopedia of the Colored Race*, Clement Richardson, ed. (Montgomery: National Publishing Co. Inc., 1919), 1: 460.

69. Quoting the Montgomery *Colored Alabamian*, 24 April 1909, 1-2.

70. Ibid., 4 February 1911, 3; Wiggins, *Scalawag*, 150.

71. Montgomery *Colored Alabamian*, 23 November 1907; 24 May 1913, 2; 11 October 1913; 11 November 1917, 3.

72. Ibid., 26 October 1907, 5; 28 December 1907, 1; 27 March 1909, 2; 17 April 1909, 3; 8 April 1916, 2-3; Beverly, 65; *Records of Interments, 1876-1896*, np.

73. *Biographical Directory*, 1006.

74. Brown, "Lloyd Leftwich," 161-62.

75. Alabama Bureau of Vital Statistics, 1930, Montgomery.

76. Preston, 275-92.

77. Montgomery *Colored Alabamian*, 20 December 1902, 1.

78. Montgomery *Weekly Citizen*, 28 June 1884, 4; Montgomery *Herald*, 16 October 1886, 3.

79. Owen, *History of Alabama*, 2: 846-47; Montgomery *Colored Alabamian*, 18 April 1908, 2; 4 January 1913, 1.

80. Mobile *Southern Watchman*, 6 January 1900, 3.

81. Montgomery *Colored Alabamian*, 13 June 1908, 4 October 1915; Charles A. Brown, "William Hooper Councill: Alabama Legislator, Editor, and Lawyer," *Negro History Bulletin* 26 (February 1963): 171-72.

82. House *Journal, 1874-5*, 45-68; House *Journal, 1875-6*, 374.

83. House *Journal, 1878*, 219-20, 820.

84. Roush, 356-57.

85. Schweninger, *Rapier*, 158.

86. Joseph Bradley, John C. Thomas, J. M. Hambrick to R. B. Hayes, 21 May 1878, Treasury Dept., RG 56, NA.

87. Schweninger, *Rapier*, 159.

88. Ibid., 175.

89. James Thomas Rapier to the President, 31 May 1882, Treasury Dept., RG 56, NA.

90. Ibid.

91. Ibid.

92. Ibid.

93. Robert Johnson to the President of the U.S., 31 January 1882, RG 56, NA.

94. Ibid.

95. A. A. Mabson to Secretary of the Treasury, 13 February 1882, Treasury Dept. RG 56, NA.

96. James Thomas Rapier to Honorable Commissioner, RG 56, NA.

97. James Thomas Rapier, Rapier File, ADAH.

98. James Thomas Rapier to Executive Mansion, 5 June 1882, Rapier File, ADAH.

99. James K. Kendall to Secretary of the Treasury, 23 September 1882, Treasury Department, RG 56, NA.

100. George Scott to Mr. President, 6 October 1882, RG 56, NA.

101. Benjamin S. Turner to President, 25 October 1882, RG 56, NA.

102. Thomas Biddell to President Arthur, 28 December 1882, RG 56, NA.

103. James Thomas Rapier to the President, 3 March 1883, Treasury Department, RG 56, NA.

104. Schweninger, *Rapier*, 178. Rapier's life was as illustrious as James P. Thomas, his cousin; yet, their funerals were in startling contrast. See Loren Schweninger, "Thriving Within The Lowest Caste: The Financial Activities of James P. Thomas In The Nineteenth-Century South," *Journal of Negro History Journal* 63, no. 4 (Fall 1978): 353-64.

105. Montgomery *Advertiser*, 11 November 1885.

106. Gross, 102-6.

107. Ibid., 94.

108. Roush, 304; Gross, 91.

109. Gross, 98.

110. Ibid.

111. Mobile *Southern Watchman*, 11 May 1901, 1.

112. Allen W. Jones, "The Black Press in the 'New South': Jesse C. Duke's Struggle for Justice and Equality," *Journal of Negro History* 64, no. 3 (Summer 1979): 215-22.

113. T. Harry Williams, "An Analysis of Some Reconstruction Attitudes," *Journal of Negro History* 12, no. 4 (November 1946): 469-86; Armstead L. Robinson, "Beyond the Realm of Social Consensus: New Meanings of Reconstruction for American History," *Journal of American History* 48, no. 2 (September 1981): 276-97; Bogue, 7-34.

114. McMillan, 210.

115. Rayford Logan, *The Betrayal of the Negro: From Rutherford B. Hayes to Woodrow Wilson*, new enlarged edition (New York: Collier Books, 1954), 104-24.

116. Ibid., 19-56.

BIBLIOGRAPHY

I. Primary Sources

 A. Manuscripts

  Alabama Department of Archives and History, Montgomery.

   Acts of the Sessions of 1870-71 of the General Assembly, Held in the City of Montgomery, Commencing November 21st, 1870. Montgomery: W. W. Screws, 1870.

   Acts of the Sessions of 1875-76 of the General Assembly, Held in the City of Montgomery, Commencing December 28th 1876. Montgomery: W. W. Screws, 1877.

   Acts of the Sessions of 1874-75 of the General Assembly of Alabama, Held in the City of Montgomery, Commencing November 16, 1874. Montgomery: W. W. Screws, 1874.

   Acts of the General Assembly of Alabama, Session of 1876-7, Held in the City of Montgomery, Commencing the Third Monday in November, 1876. Montgomery: Barret and Brown, 1877.

   Acts of the Session of 1873, of the General Assembly of Alabama and of the Board of Education, Held in the City of Montgomery, Commencing November 17th 1873. Montgomery: Arthur Bingham, 1874.

Acts of the Sessions of the 1869-70 of the General Assembly of Alabama, Held in the City of Montgomery, Commencing on the Second Monday in November, 1869. Montgomery: John G. Stokes and Company, 1870.

Alabama Congressional and Legislative Representation, 1819-1960, "The Alabama State Department of Archives and History Historic and Patriotic Series Number 17." Montgomery: Walker Printing Company, nd.

The Alabama Manual and State Register for 1869. Joseph Hodgson, ed. Montgomery: Mail Building, 1869.

Matthew P. Blue Papers.

Bureau of Vital Statistics, 1930.

City Court, State Minutes Book, A.

City Directory, Mobile 1869.

City Directory, Montgomery, 1883-1884.

City Directory, Selma, 1880-1881.

Civil Register, County Officers, Vols. 3, 10, 58, 63.

Code of Alabama, 1876. Montgomery: Barret and Brown, 1877.

Confederate Military Records.

The Constitution, and Ordinances, Adopted by the State Convention of Alabama, Which Assembled at Montgomery, on the Twelfth Day of September, A. D. 1865. Montgomery: Gibson and Whitfield, 1865.

Constitution of the State of Alabama As Amended by the Convention Assembled at Montgomery on the Fifth Day of November, A. D. 1867. Montgomery: Barret and Brown, 1867.

William H. Councill Family Files.

County Commissioner Reports.

Election Returns for Miscellaneous County Officers.

Eugene Feldman File.

Governor Letter File.

Governor George Smith Houston Papers.

Jabez Lamar Monroe Curry Papers.

Journal of the House of Representatives of the State of Alabama, Session of 1882-83, Held in the City of Montgomery, Commencing Tuesday, November 14th, 1882. Montgomery: W. D. Brown and Co., 1883.

Journal of the House of Representatives of the State of Alabama, Session of 1878-9, Held in the City of Montgomery, Commencing November 12th, 1878. Montgomery: Barret and Brown, 1879.

Journal of the House of Representatives, Session of 1875-6, Held in the City of Montgomery, Commencing on Tuesday, December 28, 1875. Montgomery: W. W. Screws, 1876.

Journal of the House of Representatives, Session of 1874-5, Held in the City of Montgomery, Commencing November 16, 1874. Montgomery: W. W. Screws, 1875.

Journal of the House of Representatives, Session of 1871-2, Held in the City of Montgomery, Commencing on the Third Monday in November, 1871. Montgomery: W. W. Screws, 1872.

Journal of the House of Representatives of the State of Alabama, Session 1876-7. Montgomery: Barret and Brown, 1877.

Journal of the House of Representatives of the State of Alabama, Session 1873. Montgomery: Arthur Bingham, 1874.

Journal of the House of Representatives of the State of Alabama, Session 1872-73. Montgomery: Arthur Bingham, 1873.

Journal of the Session of 1869-70, of the House of Representatives of the State of Alabama, Held in the City of Montgomery, Commencing on the Third Monday in November, 1869. Montgomery: John G. Stokes and Company, 1870.

David P. Lewis Governor Letter File.

Lindsay, Robert B. "Message of Robert B. Lindsay, Governor of Alabama to the General Assembly, Nov. 21, 1871." Montgomery: W. W. Screws, 1871.

Military and Civil Register of Appointments, 1867-1868.

John Tyler Morgan Papers.

Office of Registration, 25 June 1867.

E. M. Portis Papers.

James T. Rapier File.

Records of the Negroes Folder.

"Report of the State Auditor of Alabama for the Fiscal Year Ending 30th September, 1873, to the Governor." Montgomery: Arthur Bingham, 1873.

"Report of the Treasurer of the State of Alabama for the Fiscal Year Ending Sept. 30th, 1873, to the Governor." Montgomery: Arthur Bingham, 1873.

Secretary of State Files, 1868, 1869, 1870-1872.

Governor John Gill Shorter Papers.

Smith, William H. "Message of William H. Smith, Governor of Alabama to the General Assembly, November 15, 1869." Montgomery: J. G. Stokes & Co. 1870.

Governor William Hugh Smith Papers.

State and Judicial Officers, 1868-1911.

Benjamin Sterling Turner Files.

United States Bureau of Census, *Seventh Census of the United States, 1850, Population.*

_____. *Ninth Census of the United States, 1870, Agriculture.*

_____. *Ninth Census of the United States, 1870, Population.*

_____. *Tenth Census of the United States, 1880, Agriculture.*

_____. *Tenth Census of the United States, 1880, Population.*

Auburn University, Montgomery

  Proceedings of the Constitutional Convention of 1865.

Dillard University Library, New Orleans

  American Missionary Association Papers.

Howard University Library, Washington, D.C.

  James T. Rapier Papers.

National Archives, Washington, D.C.

  Applications for Collectors of Customs, Alabama, Records of
  the Department of the Treasury, Record Group 56.

  Applications for Collectors of Internal Revenue, Alabama,
  Records of the Department of Justice, Record Group 60.

  Applications of Customs, Records of the Department of
  Treasury, Record Group 56.

  Bureau of Freedmen, Refugees, and Abandoned Lands Papers.

  Congressional Record. 18 March 1876.

  Records of the Adjutant General's Office, Record Group 94.

  Records of the Bureau of Refugees, Freedmen, and Abandoned
  Lands, Record Group 105.

  US Congress. House. *Committee on Elections, Contested
  Election: Jere Haralson V. Charles M. Shelley, 4th
  Congressional District of Alabama.* HR45A-F 10.4.

  _____. *Frederick G. Bromberg v. Jeremiah
  Haralson, Contest for Seat in 44th Congress from the First
  Congressional District of Alabama, Brief for Contestant.*

  _____. *Testimony Taken by the Joint Select Committee*

to *Inquire into the Condition of Affairs in the Late Insurrectionary States*. Washington, D.C.: Government Printing Office, 1872.

_____. *The Special Committee Appointed to Investigate Political Affairs in the State of Alabama*. 43d Cong., 2d sess, H. Rept. no. 262, 23 February 1875.

US Congress. Senate. *Report of the Committee of the Senate upon the Relations Between Labor and Capital*. Washington, D.C.: Government Printing Office, 1885.

_____. *Report of the Minority, Committee to Investigate the Causes Which Have Led to the Emigration of Negroes from Southern to the Northern States*. 46th Cong., 1st sess. Source Chronological Files. Alabama. Records of the Department of Justice. Record Group 60.

_____. *Papers Pertaining to Presidential Nominations to Civil and Military positions in the U.S. Government*. Record Group 56.

University of Alabama, Hoole Special Collections

Alston, Robert C. "Reconstruction in Alabama for the Symposium." Atlanta, Georgia. November 1931.

US Army. 3rd Military District, Atlanta. General Orders no. 101. Atlanta, Georgia, 14 July 1868.

B. Newspapers

Atlanta *Constitution*, 1885.

Birmingham *Iron Age*, 1875.

Birmingham *News*, 1872-1873.

Birmingham *Post-Herald*, 1969.

Columbus (Georgia) *Ledger*, 1979.

Greenville *Advocate*, 1872-1873.

Huntsville *Weekly Democrat*, 1876.

LaGrange (Georgia) *Reporter*, 1885.

Livingston *Journal*, 1870.

Livingston *West Alabamian*, 1870.

Marion *Commonwealth*, 1871-1874.

Mobile *Advertiser and Register*, 1865-1868.

Mobile *Daily Register*, 1871-1877.

Mobile *Nationalist*, 1865-1869.

Mobile *Southern Watchman*, 1870, 1875, 1901.

Montgomery *Advertiser and Mail*, 1873, 1874.

Montgomery *Advertiser*, 1871.

Montgomery *Alabama Republican*, 1880.

Montgomery *Alabama Journal*, 1982.

Montgomery *Alabama State Journal*, 1867, 1872-1874.

Montgomery *Colored Alabamian*, 1884, 1902, 1907-1909, 1911, 1913, 1915-1916.

Montgomery *Daily Advertiser*, 1865, 1866, 1867, 1875.

Montgomery *Daily State Journal*, 1867, 1874.

Montgomery *Daily State Sentinel*, 1867.

Montgomery *Herald*, 1886.

Montgomery *Mail*, 1868, 1874.

Montgomery-Tuskegee *Times*, 1982.

Montgomery *Weekly Advertiser*, 1872.

Montgomery *Weekly Citizen*, 1884.

Montgomery *Weekly Mail*, 1860.

Opelika *Times*, 1883.

Selma *Southern Argus*, 1870, 1872-1874, 1876.

Talladega *Democratic Watchtower*, 1866.

Tuscumbia *American Star*, 1905.

Tuskegee *Weekly News*, 1874-1875.

Union Springs *Times*, 1867.

Howard University, Washington, D.C.

The New National Era, 1870-1871.

The New National Freedmen, 1865.

II. Secondary Sources

A. Articles, Monographs, and Special Studies

The American Annual Cyclopedia of Important Events of the Year 1870: Embracing Political, Civil, Military, and Social Affairs; Public Documents, Biography, Statistics, Commerce, Finance, Literature, Science, Agriculture, and Mechanical Industry. 10. New York: D. Appleton and Company, 1873.

Berlin, Ira. *Slaves Without Masters: The Free Negro in the Antebellum South.* New York: Random House, 1974.

Bethel, Elizabeth. "The Freedmen's Bureau in Alabama."
   Journal of Southern History 14 (1948): 49-92.

Beverly, John William. *A History of Alabama for Use in
   Schools and for the General Reader*. Montgomery: Press
   of the Alabama Printing Co., 1901.

Biographical Dictionary of American Congress, 1774-1971.
   Washington: U.S. Printing Office, 1971.

Bogle, James. "Horace King, Master Covered Bridge Builder,
   1807-1887." Reprinted from *Georgia Life*, Spring 1980, 3-
   6.

Bogue, Allan. "Historians and the Radical Republicans: A
   Meaning for Today." *Journal of American History* 70,
   no. 1 (June 1983): 7-34.

Bond, Horace Mann. *Negro Education in Alabama: A Study
   in Cotton and Steel*. Washington, D.C.: Associated
   Publishers, 1939.

_____. "Social and Economic Forces in Alabama
   Reconstruction." *Journal of Negro History* 33, no. 3
   (July 1938): 290-348.

Boothe, Charles Octavia. *Cyclopedia of Colored Baptists
   in Alabama*. Birmingham: Alabama Publishing Company,
   1895.

Boucher, Morris, "The Free Negro in Alabama." Ph.D.
   diss., The State University of Iowa, 1950.

Brown, Charles A. "A. H. Curtis: An Alabama Legislator, 1870-1876 with Glimpses into Reconstruction." *Negro History Bulletin* 25 (Feb 1962): 99-101.

_____. "John Dozier: Member of the General Assembly of Alabama, 1872-1873 and 1873-1874." *Negro History Bulletin* 26 (Dec 1962): 113, 128.

_____. "Lloyd Leftwich: Alabama State Senator." *Negro History Bulletin* 26 (Feb 1963): 161-62.

_____. "Reconstruction Legislators in Alabama." *Negro History Bulletin* 26 (Mar 1963): 198-200.

_____. "William Hooper Councill, Alabama Legislator, Editor, and Lawyer." *Negro History Bulletin* 26 (Feb 1963): 171-72.

Bullock, Henry Allen. *A History of Negro Education in the South*. Cambridge: Harvard University Press, 1967.

Cash, William McKinley. "Alabama Republicans During Reconstruction: Personal Characteristics, Motivations, and Political Activity of Party Activists, 1867-1880." Ph.D. diss., University of Alabama, 1973.

Christopher, Maurine. *America's Black Congressmen*. New York: Thomas Crowell. 1971.

Clark, Mark. "Horace King, Posthumous Dream Come True." Montgomery *Advertiser*, 1 May 1979.

Cobb, Henry E. "Negroes in Alabama During Reconstruction, 1868-1875." Ed.D. diss., Temple University, 1952.

Containing the Names of the Citizens of Mobile, A Business Directory. Mobile: Henry Farrow and Company, 1869.

Cook, Marjorie Howell, "Restoration and Innovation: Alabamians Adjust to Defeat, 1865-1867." Ph.D. diss., University of Alabama, 1968.

Cruden, Robert. *The Negro in Reconstruction*. Englewood Cliffs, N.J.: Prentice-Hall, 1969.

Darden, Minnie Rhodes, "History of Marion, Alabama, 1817-1940." Master's thesis, Auburn University, 1941.

Davis, Thomas J. "Alabama's Reconstruction Representatives in the U. S. Congress, 1868-1878: A Profile." *The Alabama Historical Quarterly* 44, nos. 1 and 2 (Spring and Summer 1982): 32-64.

Dodd, Donald B. *Historical Atlas of Alabama*. University, Ala.: The University of Alabama Press, 1974.

Drago, Edmund L. *Black Politicians and Reconstruction in Georgia: A Splendid Failure*. Baton Rouge: Louisiana State University, 1982.

DuBois, William Edward Burghardt. *Black Reconstruction in America: An Essay Toward a History of the Part Which Black Folk Played in the attempt to Reconstruct Democracy in America*. New York: Harcourt, Brace and Company, 1935.

DuBose, John Witherspoon. *Alabama's Tragic Decade: Ten Years After, 1865-1874*. Edited by James K. Greer. Birmingham: Webb Book Company, 1940.

Ellis, David Maldwyn. "The Forfeiture of Railroad Land Grants, 1867-1894." *Mississippi Valley Historical Review* 33 (June 1946): 27-60.

Fishel, Leslie H., and Benjamin Quarles, eds. *The Black American: A Documentary History*. Dallas: Scott, Foresman and Company, 1976.

Fleming, Walter Lynwood. *Civil War and Reconstruction in Alabama*. New York: Columbia University Press, 1905.

_____. *Civil War and Reconstruction in Alabama*. 1905. Reprint. Spartanburg, S.C.: The Reprint Company, 1978.

_____. "The Formation of the Union League in Alabama." *Gulf States Historical Magazine* 2, no. 2 (September 1903): 73-90.

Flynt, Wayne J. "Spindle, Mine and Mule: The Poor White Experience in Post-Civil War Alabama." *The Alabama Review* 34, no. 4 (October 1981): 243-86.

Folmar, John Kent. "Reaction to Reconstruction: John Forsyth and the Mobile *Register*, 1865-1867." *The Alabama Historical Quarterly* 37, no. 4 (Winter 1975): 251-51n.

Foner, Philip S. *Organized Labor and the Black Worker, 1619-1973*. New York: International Publishers, 1974.

Franklin, John Hope. *From Slavery to Freedom: A History of Negro Americans*. 4th Edition. New York: Alfred A. Knopf, 1974.

_____. *Reconstruction After the Civil War*. Chicago: The University of Chicago Press, 1961.

Gibbs, C. R. "Blacks in the Union Navy." *Negro History Bulletin* 36, no. 6 (October 1973): 137-39.

Gilmour, Robert Arthur. "The Other Emancipation: Studies in the Society and Economy of Alabama Whites During Reconstruction." Ph.D., diss., The Johns Hopkins University, 1972.

Goodrich, Carter. "Public Aid to Railroads in the Reconstruction South." *Political Science Quarterly* 71 (September 1956): 407-42.

Granade, Ray. "Violence: An Instrument of Policy in Reconstruction Alabama." *The Alabama Historical Quarterly* 30, nos. 3 and 4 (Fall and Winter 1968): 181-202.

Grantham, Dewey. "The Southern Bourbons Revisited." *The Bobbs-Merrill Reprint Series in History*, Reprinted from *The South Atlantic Quarterly* 60, no. 3 (Summer 1961): 286-95.

Graves, Fannie Martin. "History of Elmore County through 1876." Master's thesis, Alabama Polytechnic Institute, 1937.

Green, Fletcher M. "Walter Lynwood Fleming: Historian of Reconstruction." *Journal of Southern History* 2 (November 1936): 497-521.

Gross, Jimmy Frank. "Alabama Politics and the Negro, 1874-1901." Master's thesis, University of Georgia, 1970.

Gutman, Herbert G. *The Black Family in Slavery and Freedom 1750-1925*. New York: Vintage Books, 1976.

Hardy, John. Selma: *Her Institutions and Her Men*. Selma: Time Book and Job Office, 1879.

Harris, William C. "Republican Factionalism and Mismanagement." In *Reconstruction and Redemption in the South*, edited by Otto H. Olsen, 78-112. Baton Rouge: Louisiana State University Press, 1980.

Hasson, Gail S. "The Health and Welfare of Freedmen in Reconstruction Alabama." *The Alabama Review* 35, no. 2 (April 1982): 94-110.

Hennessey, Melinda M. "Reconstruction Politics and the Military: The Eufaula Riot of 1874." *The Alabama Review* 38, no. 2 (Summer 1976): 112-25.

Hennessey, Melinda Meek. "Political Terrorism in the Black Belt: The Eutaw Riot." *The Alabama Review* 33, no. 1 (January 1980): 35-48.

Herbert, Hilary A., et al. *Why the Solid South? or Reconstruction and its Results*. Baltimore: R. H. Woodward and Company, 1890.

Hofstadter, Richard, ed. *Issues in American History: From Reconstruction to the Present Day, 1864-1969*. New York: Vintage Books, 1958.

Holt, Thomas. *Black Over White: Negro Political Leadership in South Carolina during Reconstruction*. Urbana: The University of Illinois, Press, 1977.

Hood, Janice Carol. "Brotherly Hate: A Quantitative Study of Southern Reconstruction Congressmen, 1867-1877." Ph.D. diss., Washington State University, 1974.

Hume, Richard L. "The 'Black and Tan' Conventions of 1867-1869 in Ten Former Confederate States: A study of Their Membership." Ph.D. diss., University of Washington, 1969.

_____. "The Freedmen's Bureau and the Freedmen's Vote in the Reconstruction of Southern Alabama: An Account by Agent Samuel S. Gardner." *The Alabama Historical Quarterly* 37, no. 3 (Fall 1975): 217-24.

Jay, John C. "General N. B. Forrest As A Railroad Builder in Alabama." *The Alabama Historical Quarterly* 24, no. 1 (Spring 1962): 16-31.

Jones, Allen W. "The Black Press in the 'New South:' Jesse C. Duke's Struggle for Justice and Equality." *Journal of Negro History* 64, no. 3 (Summer 1979): 215-28.

Kolchin, Peter. *First Freedom: The Response of Alabama Freedmen to Emancipation and Reconstruction.* Westport, Conn.: Greenwood Press, 1972.

Kramer, Edward Marven. "Alabama Negroes, 1861-1865." Master's thesis, Auburn University, 1965.

Lester, Richard Irwin. "Greensboro, Alabama, 1861-1874." Master's thesis, Auburn University, 1956.

Litwack, Leon. *Slaves Without Masters: The Free Negro in the Antebellum South.* New York: Vintage Books, 1974.

Logan, Rayford. *Betrayal of the Negro: From Rutherford B. Hayes to Woodrow Wilson.* New edition. New York: Collier Books, 1954.

McCrary, Peyton. "The Political Dynamics of Black Reconstruction." *Reviews in American History* 12, no. 1 (March 1984): 51-7.

McMillan, Malcolm Cook. *Constitutional Development in Alabama, 1798-1901: A Study in Politics, The Negro and Sectionalism.* The James Sprunt Studies in History and Political Science, no. 37. Chapel Hill: University of North Carolina Press, 1955.

Martin, Michael, and Leonard Gelber. *Dictionary of American History.* Totowa, N.J.: Littlefield, Adams and Co., 1978.

Meier, August. *Negro Thought in America, 1880-1915: Racial Ideologies in the Age of Booker T. Washington.* Ann Arbor: The University of Michigan Press, 1963.

_____. "Review Essay/Whither the Black Perspective in Afro-American Historiography?" *Journal of American History* 70, no. 1 (June 1983): 101-5.

Meier, August, and Elliot Rudwick. *From Plantation to Ghetto.* New York: Hill and Wang, 1966.

Memorial Record of Alabama: A Concise Account of the State's Political, Military, Professional, and Industrial Progress, Together with the Personal Memorial of its People, 1. Spartanburg: S.C.: The Reprint Company, 1976.

Mills, Joseph. "The Motives and Behaviors of the Northern Teachers in the South during Reconstruction." *Negro History Bulletin* 34 (March 1979): 7-9, 17.

Moore, A. B. "Railroad Building in Alabama during the Reconstruction Period." *Journal of Southern History* 1, no. 4 (November 1935): 421-41.

Myers, John B. "The Alabama Freedman and Economic Adjustments During Presidential Reconstruction, 1865-1867." *The Alabama Review* 26, no. 3 (October 1973): 252-66.

_____. "The Freedman and the Labor Supply: The Economic Adjustments in Post-Bellum Alabama, 1865-1867." *The Alabama Historical Quarterly* 32, nos. 3 and 4 (Fall and Winter 1970): 157-66.

_____. "The Freedman and the Law in Post-Bellum Alabama, 1865-1867." *The Alabama Review* 23, no. 1 (January 1970): 56-69.

_____. "Reaction and Readjustment: The Struggle of Alabama Freedmen in Post-Bellum Alabama, 1865-1867." *The Alabama Historical Quarterly* 32, nos. 1 and 2 (Spring and Summer 1970): 5-22.

The National Cyclopedia of American Biography, Being the History of the United States As Illustrated in the Lives of the Founders, Builders, and Defenders of the Republic, and of the Men and Women Who Are Doing the Work and Molding the Thought of the Present Time. Edited by Distinguished Biographers, Selected from Each State, Revised and Approved by the Most Eminent Historians, Scholars, and Statesmen of the Day. 61 vols. New York: J. T. White and Company, 1898.

Nieman, Donald G. "Andrew Johnson, the Freedmen's
    Bureau, and the Problem of Equal Rights, 1865-1866."
    Journal of Southern History 44, no. 3 (August 1978):
    399-420.

Norrell, R. J. "Perfect Quiet, Peace, and Harmony:
    Another Look At The Founding of Tuskegee Institute."
    The Alabama Review 36, no. 2 (April 1983): 110-29.

Olsen, Otto H. "An Incongruous Presence." In
    Reconstruction and Redemption in the South, edited by
    Otto H. Olsen, 156-201. Baton Rouge: Louisiana State
    University Press, 1980.

Owen, Thomas McAdory. *Alabama Official and Statistical
    Register*. Montgomery: Brown Printing Company, 1903.

_____. *History of Alabama and Dictionary of
    Alabama Biography*. 4 vols. Chicago: S. J. Clarke
    Publishing, 1921.

Owens, Harry Philpot. "History of Eufaula, 1832-1882."
    Master's thesis, Auburn University, 1963.

Perman, Michael. *The Road to Redemption: Southern
    Politics, 1869-1879*. Chapel Hill: The
    University of North Carolina Press, 1984.

Preston, E. Delorus Jr. "Thomas Walker and His Times."
    Journal of Negro History 21, no. 3 (July 1936):
    275-93.

Rabinowitz, Howard N. "From Reconstruction To Redemption in the Urban South." *Journal of Urban History* 2, no. 2 (February 1976): 169-93.

_____. "Holland Thompson and Black Political Participation in Montgomery, Alabama." In *Southern Black Leaders of the Reconstruction Era*, edited by Howard N. Rabinowitz, 249-80. Chicago: University of Chicago Press, 1982.

Reid, Robert. "Changing Interpretations of the Reconstruction Period in Alabama History." *The Alabama Review* 28, no. 4 (October 1974): 263-81.

Rhodes, Robert H. "The Registration of Voters and the Election of Delegates to the Reconstruction Convention in Alabama." *The Alabama Review* 8, no. 2 (April 1955): 124-25n.

Richardson, Clement, ed. *The Cyclopedia of the Colored Race*. Montgomery: National Publishing Co., Inc., 1919.

Richardson, Joe M. *Christian Reconstruction: The The American Missionary Association and Southern Blacks, 1861-1890*. Athens: The University of Georgia Press, 1986.

Ripley, C. Peter. *Slaves and Freedmen in Civil War Louisiana*. Baton Rouge: Louisiana State University Press, 1976.

Ritter, E. Jay. "Congressional Medal of Honor Winners."
Negro History Bulletin 26 (Jan 1963): 135-36.

Robinson, Armstead L. "Beyond the Realm of Social
Consensus: New Meanings of Reconstruction for
American History." *Journal of American History*
68, no. 2 (September 1981): 276-97.

Rogers, William Warren. *The One-Gallused Rebellion:
Agrarianism in Alabama, 1865-1896*. Baton Rouge:
Louisiana State University, Press, 1970.

Rogers, William Warren and David Ward. *August
Reckoning: Jack Turner and Post Racism in Post-Civil
War Alabama*. Baton Rouge: Louisiana State University,
1973.

_____ and _____. "Racial Inferiority and Modern
Medicine: A Note on the Colburg Affair." *The Alabama
Historical Quarterly* 44, nos. 3 and 4 (Fall and
Winter 1982): 203-12.

Rogers, William Warren, and Ruth Pruitt. *Stephen
Renfroe, Alabama's Outlaw Sheriff*. Tallahassee:
Sentry Press, 1972.

Roush, Gerald Lee. "Aftermath of Reconstruction: Race,
Violence, and Politics in Alabama, 1874-1884."
Master's thesis, Auburn University, 1973.

Russ, William A., Jr. "The Negro and White
Disfranchisement During Radical Reconstruction."

Journal of Negro History 19, no. 2 (April 1934): 171-92.

Russell, Mildred Brewer. *Lowndes County Courthouse: A Chronicle of Hayneville, An Alabama Black Belt Village, 1820-1900*. Montgomery: Paragon Press, 1951.

Sangster, Tom, and Dess Sangster. *Alabama's Covered Bridges*. Montgomery: Coffeetable Publications, 1980.

Sellers, James B. "Free Negroes of Tuscaloosa County Before the Thirteenth Amendment." *The Alabama Review* 23, no. 2 (April 1970): 110-27.

Schweninger, Loren. "Alabama Blacks and the Reconstruction Acts of 1867." *The Alabama Review* 31, no. 3 (July 1978): 182-98.

_____. "American Missionary Association and Northern Philanthropy." *The Alabama Historical Quarterly* 32, nos. 3 and 4 (Fall and Winter 1970): 129-56.

_____. "Black Citizenship and the Republican Party in Alabama." *The Alabama Review* 29, no. 2 (April 1976): 83-103.

_____. "James Rapier and the Negro Labor Movement, 1869-1872." *The Alabama Review* 28, no. 3 (July 1975): 185-201.

_____. *James Rapier and Reconstruction*. Chicago: The University of Chicago, 1978.

_____. "Thriving Within the Lowest Caste: The
Financial Activities of James P. Thomas In The
Nineteenth-Century South." *Journal of Negro History*
63, no. 4 (Fall 1978): 353-64.

Sherer, Robert G., Jr. "John William Beverly: Alabama's
First Negro Historian." *The Alabama Review* 26,
no. 3 (July 1973): 195-208.

Shofner, Jerrell H. "A Failure of Moderate
Republicanism." In *Reconstruction and Redemption
in the South*, edited by Otto H. Olsen, 13-46. Baton
Rouge: Louisiana State University Press, 1980.

Shugg, Ralph Wallace. "Negro Voting in the
Ante-Bellum South." *Journal of Negro History* 21,
no. 4 (October 1936): 357-64.

Sizemore, Margaret Davidson. "Frederick G. Bromberg
of Mobile: An Illustrious Character, 1837-1928."
The Alabama Review 29, no. 2 (April 1976):
104-12.

Sloan, John Z. "The Ku Klux Klan and the Alabama
Election of 1872." *The Alabama Review* 18, no. 2
(April 1965): 113-23.

Stampp, Kenneth M. *The Era of Reconstruction,
1865-1877*. New York: Vintage Books, 1965.

Steele, Robertha. "Some Aspects of Reconstruction in Mobile." Master's thesis, Auburn University, 1937.

Summers, Mark. *Railroads, Reconstruction, and the Gospel of Prosperity: Aid under the Radical Republicans, 1865-1877*. Princeton: Princeton University Press, 1984.

Swinney, Everette. "Suppressing the Ku Klux Klan: The Enforcement of the Reconstruction Amendments, 1870-1874." Ph.D. diss, University of Texas, 1966.

Taylor, Alrethus. A. "Historians of the Reconstruction." *Journal of Negro History* 23, no. 1 (January 1938): 16-34.

_____. "Negro Congressmen A Generation After." *Journal of Negro History* 7, no. 2 (April 1922): 127-71.

Taylor, Dudley. *The Sable Arms: Negro Troops in the Union Army, 1861-1865*. New York: W. W. Norton, 1966.

Taylor, James. "History of the Ku Klux Klan in Alabama." Master's thesis, Auburn University, 1957.

Taylor, Joe Gray. "Louisiana: An Impossible Task." In *Reconstruction and Redemption in the South*, edited by Otto H. Olsen, 202-35. Baton Rouge: Louisiana State University Press, 1980.

Thomas, James D. "The Alabama Constitutional
    Convention of 1867." Master's thesis, Auburn
    University, 1974.

Thompson, Mattie Thomas. *History of Barbour County,
    Alabama*. Eufaula, 1939.

Toppin, Edgar. *A Biographical History of Blacks
    in America Since 1528*. New York: David McKay, Inc.,
    1969.

Trelease, Allen W. *White Terror: The Ku Klux Klan
    Conspiracy and Southern Reconstruction*. New York:
    Harper and Row, 1971.

Turner, Maxine. "Naval Operations on the
    Apalachicola and Chattahoochee Rivers." *The Alabama
    Historical Quarterly* 36, nos. 3 and 4 (Fall and
    Winter 1974): 189-266.

Ullman, Victor. *Martin R. Delaney: The Beginning
    of Black Nationalism*. Boston: Beacon Press, 1971.

Vincent, Charles. *Black Legislators in Louisiana
    during Reconstruction*. Baton Rouge: Louisiana State
    University Press, 1976.

Wakelyn, Jon L. *Biographical Dictionary of the
    Confederacy*. Westport, Conn.: Greenwood Press, 1977.

Walker, Anne Kendrick. *Backtracking in Barbour County:
    A Narrative of the Last Alabama Frontier*. Richmond,
    Va.: The Deitz Press, 1941.

White, Kenneth B. "The Alabama Freedmen and Black Education: The Myth of Opportunity." *The Alabama Review* 24, no. 2 (April 1981): 107-24.

_____. "Black Lives, Red Tape: The Alabama Freedmen's Bureau." *The Alabama Historical Quarterly* 43 (Winter 1981): 242-47.

_____. Wager Swayne: Racist or Realist?" *The Alabama Review* 31 (April 1978): 92-109.

Wiggins, Sarah Woolfolk. "Democratic Bulldozing and Republican Folly." In *Reconstruction and Redemption in the South*, edited by Otto H. Olsen. Baton Rouge: Louisiana State University Press, 1980, 47-77.

_____. "The 'Pig Iron' Kelley Riot in Mobile, May 14, 1867." *The Alabama Review* 23, no. 1 (January 1970): 45-55.

_____. *The Scalawag in Alabama Politics, 1865-1881*. University, Ala.: The University of Alabama Press, 1977.

_____. "Unionist Efforts to Control Reconstruction Alabama." *The Alabama Historical Quarterly* 30, no. 1 (Spring 1968): 56-57.

Williams, Arthur. "The Participation of Negroes in the Government of Alabama, 1867-1874." Master's thesis, Atlanta University, 1946.

Williams, T. Harry. "An Analysis of Some Reconstruction Attitudes." *Journal of Negro History* 12, no. 4 (November 1946): 469-86.

Williamson, Edward. "The Alabama Election of 1874." *The Alabama Review* 17, no. 3 (July 1964): 210-18.

Woolfolk, Sarah Van. "Carpetbagger in Alabama: Tradition Versus Truth." *The Alabama Review* 15, no. 2 (April 1962): 133-44.

_____. "Five Men Called Scalawags." *The Alabama Review* 17 (January 1964): 45-55.

_____. "George E. Spencer: A Carpetbagger in Alabama: Tradition Versus Truth." *The Alabama Review* 15, no. 2 (April 1962): 133-44.

_____. "Five Men Called Scalawags." *The Alabama Review* 17 (January 1964): 45-55.

_____. "George E. Spencer: A Carpetbagger in Alabama." *The Alabama Review* 19, no. 1 (January 1966): 41-52.

Work, Monroe N. "Some Negro Members of Reconstruction Conventions And Legislatures of Congress." *Journal of Negro History* 5, no. 1 (Jan 1920): 63-118.

INDEX

465

INDEX